By Joe

Broadway Joe and His Super Jets

Joe Namath takes charge in the Super Bowl.

LARRY FOX

Broadway Joe
and His Super Jets

796.332
F

Coward-McCann, Inc.
New York

Library of Congress Catalog Card Number: 75–81011

PRINTED IN THE UNITED STATES OF AMERICA

To David and Jason,

the reasons for everything

Acknowledgments

A special note of appreciation to Bob Stewart, former sports editor of the New York *World-Telegram and Sun*. Bob was the first New York sports editor to realize that the American Football League was for real and should be covered. "Go up to the Concourse Plaza Hotel and talk to Sammy Baugh," was his assignment that started me on the road to the Super Bowl. Also thanks to Bill Shannon for his one-of-a-kind scrapbook that helped refresh memories of the early days. And appreciation to Jet-turned-broadcaster Sam DeLuca, Harold Rosenthal of the AFL, Don Weiss and Jim Heffernan of the NFL, Jim Trecker and Frank Ramos of the Jets, the Elias Sports Bureau, and, of course, for their patience in this and with other projects that helped form the background of the book, Weeb Ewbank and Joe Namath. Plus a final word to my good friend and colleague Murray Janoff of the *Long Island Press*. As John K. Free of the Jets recalls, in the beginning Murray and I formed the entire press corps. We lived many of the moments in this book together, and I have always appreciated his company and his counsel.

LARRY FOX

Contents

Introduction

Remember the golfer who tells his wife, "Sure, honey, I know it's our anniversary. Didn't we get married the same day I broke eighty for the first time?" Well, give or take a few days, I was married about a week before I played quarterback for the New York Jets.

This was in 1963, just after the Jets became Jets. They were still playing at the Polo Grounds, a historic ball park waiting around to become a housing project. I thought it would be a good stunt for the *Tonight Show* to work out with the team. Sonny Werblin, then president of the Jets, arranged it. In those days he was more famous for signing movie stars than quarterbacks.

"I want to be in the middle of the action," I told coach Weeb Ewbank, and he said he'd let me run some plays at quarterback.

"And I want to feel what it's like to be really hit by the pros," I added foolishly.

Ewbank was skeptical. "Well, the general idea is for our quarterbacks not to get hit, but we'll see what we can do," Weeb promised.

Weeb put in four special plays for me—a roll-out pass, a quarterback sneak, a drop-back pass with the defense blitzing and a straight hand-off. But a fifth play almost finished me before I had a chance to try the other four. It was called calisthenics. That's when I learned that genial, smiling Weeb Ewbank could give mean lessons to Vince Lombardi.

On the first pass play our director told the Jets to gag it up. "Try to look silly, bump into each other and fall down," he suggested nervously, wondering if these proud, highly trained professionals would be willing to go along with the stunt and look foolish. "Oh, you mean, just do like we did in games last year as the Titans," Don Maynard joked, and that's when I realized I wasn't the only ham in the ball park.

When it came time for the defense to blitz, I had a feeling Larry

Jet rooter Johnny Carson has a laugh on his *Tonight Show* with Jet end Bake Turner.

Grantham and the guys thought I was last year's paymaster showing up with a briefcase of those bouncing checks. But how could they have meant to hurt me when they were all laughing? After the pileup, the only guy who almost got killed was the director when he called from the sidelines, "That was fine, but let's try it once more." If Dick Guesman and several hundred pounds of his friends hadn't been sitting on me at the time, I'd have committed mayhem on the director myself.

After the filming, Coach Ewbank told the fellows to jog a lap around the field. I made it to second base a nose ahead of Sherman Plunkett and then decided I'd better quit before the 330-pound tackle stepped on me by accident.

Anyway, that's how far back I go with the Jets and why I can call Joe Namath a Joey-Come-Lately. Joe may have led the Jets to the world championship, but I was the man who really started them on the road to the Super Bowl. The Sunday after I worked out with them, the boys won their first victory ever as Jets for Ewbank. I'm sure watching me helped the confidence of the two regular quarterbacks, Dick Wood and Galen Hall. For the first time they realized they were better than somebody.

A couple of years later I helped entertain the Jets and their wives at a team Christmas party in the basement room of Toots Shor's restaurant. The late Al Kelly, a doubletalk expert, appeared, too. "I don't mind this guy's doubletalk, but I begin to worry when I think I understand him," I told the players. I think when those guys unloaded on me up at the Polo Grounds that time, I would have been right in Al Kelly's league.

Over the seasons I watched closely as Weeb Ewbank molded the Jets into champions. These were "my boys," and when some people used to claim the American Football League didn't hit, I knew better. No less than eight of them—Billy Baird, Larry Grantham, Winston Hill, Curley Johnson, Bill Mathis, Don Maynard, Mark Smolinski, and Bake Turner—were still with the club six years later when they won the AFL title.

I was thinking about them when I became the first nonreporter allowed into the Jet dressing room after they beat Oakland in the championship game before a screaming sellout crowd in chilly Shea Stadium. We had all come a long way from the Polo Grounds, and I didn't mind a bit when Gerry Philbin, the scrappy defensive end who tears up quarterbacks for a living, welcomed me with a champagne shower. I'm just glad he hadn't been around that day in the Polo Grounds. If he was, they might have been calling it the *Tonight Show,* starring Ed McMahon.

Later that night—much later—I helped the players celebrate the victory at their private party in Joe Namath's new bar, Bachelors III. It's a good thing they didn't have to play the Colts the next morning, but then there was probably a pretty good party going on in Baltimore, too, and they'd have had to call the game the Hangover Bowl. By the time we got down to Miami two weeks later, everybody felt fine, and of course we all had a super time.

Over the years, quite a few Jet players have appeared on my show. I've had Namath on several times; Johnny Sample, the talking man's cornerback, twice; and after the Jets clinched their division title, Joe Namath, Don Maynard, Jim Turner, and Bake Turner. Namath, Maynard, Turner, and Turner sounds like a law firm or a barbershop quartet, but Bake is the only one who sang. Did well enough to get called back for an encore, too—which made Ed McMahon jealous.

Namath tells me he'd like to make a career out of show business, although with those knees he'd better not plan any soft-shoe routines. I don't think he'll find the critics any tougher than the Baltimore Colts, and if I can help him get started, I will. After all, I helped clear his way with the Jets, didn't I? One look at me and they decided, "We've got to get a quarterback."

JOHNNY CARSON

Prologue

Joe Namath walked into his East Side restaurant, his eyes puffy, a paper container of coffee in hand. It was shortly after ten in the morning, but more than 100 reporters and cameramen jammed the small narrow night spot.

The date was June 6, 1969, twenty-fifth anniversary of the Allied invasion of France in World War II, D-Day. On this anniversary, less than five months after his own great triumph in the Super Bowl, Joe Namath said he was quitting football.

Pro commissioner Pete Rozelle months earlier had confronted Namath with evidence that gamblers had been frequenting his bar. The telephones had been used to make bets. There were hints that a police raid was imminent. Joe was absolved of any wrong-doing, but Rozelle finally gave Namath an ultimatum: Sell your interest in the bar or be suspended from football. The image of pro football, Rozelle insisted, must be above suspicion.

At first Namath was inclined to sell. He told Rozelle the day before the deadline that a sale was all set. But in the wee hours of the final morning Joe had second thoughts. He talked with teammates and friends. He did not talk with Sonny Werblin, who had been his mentor for so long; or with Phil Iselin, president of the Jets; or with Weeb Ewbank, his coach; or with Bear Bryant, his old coach at Alabama.

These were men of Rozelle's generation. They remembered D-Day. They would not say what Joe wanted to hear. Namath, just twenty-six, was one year old that day we landed in Normandy. He aligned himself again with his contemporaries. Rozelle was the college dean. Namath declined to accept his authority, as he had resisted others in the same position over the years.

"I'm not selling," Namath told reporters as tears choked his words. "I quit. They said I'm innocent, but I have to sell. I can't go along with that. It's principle. Last night I was going to sell my share of the club. We had the papers all set. But then I changed my mind. I realized I was doing something that wasn't right. It was logical, but it wasn't right, and I couldn't go through with it."

To Namath, the bar was a small thing financially. Quitting football would cost him many times over his share in the modest establishment. But to his partner and roommate, Ray Abruzzese, the restaurant represented years of savings. Without Namath, the place would be valueless. Abruzzese had been Namath's first friend when the lonely homesick freshman showed up at Alabama. Joe Namath would never forget.

There were others who felt that since the Super Bowl, Namath had been looking for an excuse, a reason to quit football, to end the pain. Although he tearfully insisted that "the last thing I want to do is quit football," the agony in his knees was still there, and months earlier he had talked openly about retiring. His doctors had told him then, medically speaking, "You should quit football."

Now Namath was preparing to retire after four seasons as one of the most exciting players in the history of the game. He still hoped that somehow the problem could be resolved, but he still proclaimed defiantly, "I will not change my mind." Such was their faith in Namath, their quarterback and leader, that several teammates said they'd quit with him. The Jets were thrown into an emotional turmoil. Would the veterans quit and destroy the team Weeb Ewbank had so carefully put together? Fans across the nation wondered, Was this the end of Broadway Joe as Sunday's hero?

Namath said it would have been "logical" to sell. But he never before had let logic interfere when he thought he was right. After all, it hadn't been very logical to "guarantee" a Super Bowl victory either.

Broadway Joe and His Super Jets

1

Namath Sounds Off

Joe Namath descended slowly from the airplane with the distinctive stiff-legged gait that will remain his souvenir of football long after he's put the last trophy on his shelf. Almost from the moment he emerged into the Fort Lauderdale evening, a constant platoon of reporters formed around him, many thrusting that latest tool of journalism, the tape recorder mike, into his face.

What about those statements after the Jets beat Oakland for the American Football League title last Sunday? Do you really think Daryle Lamonica is a better quarterback than Earl Morrall? Daryle Lamonica of Oakland better than Earl Morrall of the mighty Colts? Really, Joe. Come on now. Be serious.

Namath's shoulders never straightened from their permanent slouch, but his hooded eyes moved up to face yet another inquisitor.

"Yes, I said Lamonica is a better quarterback than Morrall. Why, there are three or four quarterbacks in our league who are better than he is . . . Lamonica . . . John Hadl of San Diego . . . Bob Griese of Miami . . . and myself," Joe said coolly. For good measure, he tabbed even his own sub, Babe Parilli, as a better passer than the man who had guided Baltimore to the championship of football's Establishment League.

The Super Bowl game between the Colts and Jets was ten days off, but Broadway Joe Namath had just fired the first shot for his team. He had put Baltimore on the defensive. The Colts were never to recover.

As the days passed, Namath never backed off on his quarterback appraisal. He kept pointing out that the AFL was the league of under-thirty quarterbacks. And he used this as a put-down for the vaunted Colt defense as well. "I study quarterbacks, all of them, and I know what they're doing," Joe declared, "and I'll tell you

Joe Namath:
"I guarantee it."

Vernon J. Biever

the Colts have never had to play *against* quarterbacks like we have in the AFL. Guys like Lamonica, Griese, and Hadl."

. . . *or Namath,* the listener thought. And the Colts bristled when their swinging, long-haired rival—so much the opposite of thirtyish, sober, crew-cut Earl Morrall—pointed out, "I've seen movies of the Colts and that one-eyed monster doesn't lie."

The Jets arrived in Fort Lauderdale to set up headquarters at the Galt Ocean Mile Hotel on a Thursday night, January 2, only four days after their final AFL victory and two full days ahead of the Colts. Critics of coach Weeb Ewbank—and at this stage he still had some—argued that he was bringing the boys down south too early. They forgot Ewbank had been this route before. He had his reasons.

Mainly he wanted to get the team away from New York's numbing cold. The Jets had clinched the AFL's Eastern Division championship by Thanskgiving Day, coasted through the rest of the schedule, and then enjoyed an extra week off while Oakland was routing Kansas City in a play-off for the Western title. Although they had beaten the Raiders in the AFL final, Ewbank knew another two-week layoff would be dangerous. His players needed to regain their sharpness. They had to sweat and bump heads; and nobody was perspiring in wintry New York. So he hustled them south. "These first few days will be like training camp all over," he promised. But just to make sure the Jets didn't leave their game on the practice field, there would be no curfew until the week before the Super Bowl itself.

Ewbank, sixty-one years old and a grandfather, had been in championship games before, starting as an assistant to Paul Brown with the mighty Cleveland Browns. In 1958 and '59 he had won National Football League titles as head coach of the Baltimore Colts. There was no Super Bowl then, and the AFL was just a faint gleam in founder Lamar Hunt's eye. At that time, winning the NFL was the pinnacle, and winning it twice in a row was like scaling Everest, jumping off, and then doing it again . . . on your hands. But after the 1962 season, the Colts had fired him . . . for finishing with a .500 record.

These Colts of 1969 were a veteran team and many of Weeb's old players were still wearing Baltimore uniforms. When Ewbank gazed across the painted green grass of the Orange Bowl on January 12, he would see faces, not face masks; men who were once boys.

All through the week he would reminisce. "Lenny Lyles . . . we tried him on offense first. He could really run, but he couldn't catch the ball. We called him Boardhands, and later we put him on defense. Ordell Braase showed up as a skinny kid out of South Dakota . . . weighed only 215 pounds and the Korean War was on then . . . told him to get in his military service and when he came back he weighed 235 and was a pretty good football player. Dan Sullivan . . . just a reserve guard when I left . . . they wanted to taxi him another year and he wanted to play so he came up and worked out with the Jets one day . . . told me he had to go back first and he would let me know what he decided to do . . . we never heard from him again."

There were younger Colts, too, like Bob Vogel, John Mackey, and Willie Richardson. Ewbank had scouted, drafted, and signed all of them, and then he was fired before they even had a chance to become rookies. But he still claimed them as his players.

And then there was Johnny Unitas, the quarterback Weeb had rescued from the Pittsburgh sandlots. Together they had been a team for greatness. Now Weeb had another champion and Johnny U. was on the bench with a sore arm, and second-string to Morrall.

The Jets and Colts had exchanged several game films in the weeks before the Super Bowl. Unitas had played a half in one of them. "He threw like a man who's hurting," Ewbank said without emotion, but then, one day, talking about Namath, he referred to his own quarterback as "Johnny."

Ewbank's heart betrayed itself only once in public. Asked again about the old days one morning, the memories surged in unchecked. "Unitas . . . Raymond Berry . . . Jim Parker . . . Alan Ameche . . . Marchetti, Donovan, Big Daddy—they were so great, it almost makes you choke up," he said as his voice, indeed, faltered.

To add to the emotion of this game, Colt coach Don Shula also was one of Weeb's boys. They went back even further than Baltimore. Shula had been a defensive halfback at John Carroll University in Cleveland when Ewbank was an assistant coach with the Browns. One of Weeb's assignments was supervising the college draft, and on the ninth round before the 1951 season he picked Don Shula. The sharp-eyed cornerback lasted two seasons with Cleveland and then was hustled off to Baltimore as one of the extra bodies in a fifteen-man trade. When Ewbank became head coach of the Colts in 1954, Shula was there waiting for him.

They were together three years. "He was smart, the smartest," Ewbank recalled. But when the Colts were able to get a faster man, Milt Davis, Shula was let go. Ewbank diplomatically tried to give the impression that he had traded Shula to Washington, but the record shows Don had been put on waivers by the Colts and then was signed by the Redskins as a free agent. The following season, 1958, Shula went into coaching.

Ewbank's current players, though, had other things on their minds besides nostalgia as they held their first team meeting in Florida on Friday morning. There was grumbling as coaches waited outside for the private meeting to end—complaints about rooms, plane tickets, expenses for wives and families in Florida, commemorative rings or watches for winning the league title, and the size of their individual checks for winning the championship game.

"The *nouveau riche,*" one reporter muttered scornfully, and Ewbank snapped that Don Maynard, whom he tabbed as one of the complainers, was nothing but a "human crab."

Only in retrospect did the grumbling take on a meaning beyond the picky complaints. These Jet players, 18-point underdogs from the so-called "Mickey Mouse" league, did not feel they should be grateful for their invitation to take the same field as the mighty NFL champions. They felt they belonged, and they wanted what they believed to be all the rights and privileges of champions.

With Namath leading the way, they maintained to all who would listen how much they belonged.

"This is the best championship team I've played on, stronger in every way than the Colts of 1958 and '59," veteran cornerback Johnny Sample rasped—and shocked NFL partisans waited for the earth to swallow him up for such heresy.

"Those odds are ridiculous," snorted Matt Snell, the sharp-tongued fullback who had been at Ohio State with two of the Colt stars, Tom Matte and Bob Vogel, and had been rated as fine a college player as either.

Snell felt the oddsmakers had been overly impressed with Baltimore's 34–0 romp over Cleveland in the NFL title game. "I saw those movies and you could tell the Browns weren't playing well. They'd shot their wad the week before in the division play-off against Dallas," Snell insisted, his angry voice rising.

And Namath, later in the week, stood up before the Miami Touchdown Club to receive an award and, in an air of euphoria and celebration, vowed: "We're going to win this game. I guarantee it."

Earlier in the week, Namath had made a more private prediction along these lines to Lou Michaels, tanklike defensive lineman and place-kicker for the Colts. The place was Fazio's, a swinging restaurant and bar up the road from the beach-front headquarters of both teams. It was the dinner hour Sunday night and there was scotch on the table (Johnny Walker Red, Namath insisted, when one gossipy columnist reported another brand) before and after the food.

Jim Hudson, Namath's roommate, was at the table when the heavy-bearded Michaels, younger brother of Jet assistant coach Walt Michaels, came along with Dan Sullivan, the old Jet-for-a-day. As Michaels recalled it later, the conversation went something like this:

Namath: We're going to kick the ———— out of your team.

Michaels: Haven't you ever heard of the word "modest," Joseph?

Namath: We're going to beat you and I'm going to pick you apart.

Michaels: If you do, Joseph, I believe you are the man to do it. But it's kind of hard throwing out of a well [surrounded by charging defensive linemen] and finding receivers.

Namath: Don't worry about that. My blockers will give me time.

Michaels: I never heard of John Unitas or Bobby Layne talking that way.

Namath: I believe that.

Michaels: If things [sic] get in trouble, then we'll send in the Master [Unitas].

Namath: I hope you do, because then the game will be too far gone.

Michaels: Our defensive linemen will be out to get your ribs, but I've told them not to touch your teeth—I want them.

As the brink neared, Michaels decided not to wait until the following Sunday to claim Namath's teeth. "Come on out to the parking lot and I'll knock your head off right now," he yelled at the Jet quarterback.

At this, Namath rose slowly, turned to his left, and walked to the men's room, leaving Sullivan to soothe his hot-blooded Colt teammate.

Later, as happens when the Johnny Walker flows, Michaels and Namath found themselves bosom buddies. Before long, Michaels was ready to "take back" everything he'd said about Namath, who, like himself, had after all fought his way out of one of Pennsylvania's many tough low-rent districts. "Underneath this guy there's a lot of good," Michaels conceded and he allowed as how Joe showed himself a real "gentleman" when he peeled off a hundred-dollar bill and paid the tab for all.

Everybody was kind of amused by the incident, including Namath. "Just good, clean fun," he said. Lou's brother Walt, a friendly bear of a guy, said, "I can see how it happened. They're both aggressive, cocky guys."

"Yeah, Joe must have been the eight hundred and thirty-seventh guy Lou has threatened to deck since I've known him," Don Shula joked, "and if he had gone ahead and hit him, he'd only have been about the thirty-seventh Lou has actually decked. Now all the guys are kidding Lou. They say he let Namath buy him off by picking up the check."

Shula was less tolerant about Namath's rating of his quarterback. Earl Morrall, the former Giant, had led the NFL in just about every department and had been named the league's Player of the Year for leading the Colts through a magnificent season in which they'd lost only one game. Now Namath, whose team had been beaten three times during the season, was putting him down.

"Who is he to rap my quarterback?" Shula asked angrily one day, but then he dismissed Namath contemptuously with, "Aaah, he can say whatever the hell he wants."

And Namath did. "I don't know much about betting," he told a television announcer seriously before adding with a twinkle, "but I'd say eighteen points is a pretty big price."

Namath did much of what he wanted, too. On Monday, both teams had scheduled a picture day. When the Jet bus left for their practice field at 9 A.M., the starting backfield—quarterback Joe Namath, halfback Emerson Boozer, and fullback Matt Snell—was in bed asleep. Roommates Boozer and Snell simply ignored their wake-up call. Hudson tried to rouse Namath, his roomie, but went on alone when he failed. "I've never seen such a guy for getting his twelve hours' sleep," shrugged the dark-haired defensive back from Texas, leaving a newspaperman to point out that Joe's trouble was he usually waited too long to start the twelve hours. (When Namath complained about getting up too late to buy a paper before they were all sold out, Babe Parilli cracked, "By the time you get up, tomorrow's papers are on sale.")

All three Jets were fined $50 for missing the "meeting," and Namath, as usual, tossed it off. "I always sleep in the morning. That's the thing to do. You've got to get your rest," he said with a smile.

But eventually, even Joe began to feel the pressure of the approaching game. Called to a mass press conference one noon, he sent down word he wasn't coming. "There's been too much bullshit written already. I'm only talking to reporters I know," he told Frank Ramos, the embarrassed press secretary. But he didn't carry through with the threat. The audience was too good.

Ewbank put the Jets on curfew the night after Namath's sleep-in, a day earlier than he had anticipated. The next day, Tuesday, the players were given their Super Bowl game plan, some 40 pages of plays, diagrams, and scouting reports in a midnight blue folder. As they filed into their dressing room at Fort Lauderdale's Yankee Stadium, spring training home of the baseball Yankees, each player handed his book to equipment manager Bill Hampton. After practice it was returned. Fine for losing the book: $200. Fine for missing curfew: $5,000, or one hundred times more than usual, a self-imposed discipline the players had instituted only once before that season, on the week-long trip to the West Coast.

The Wednesday and Thursday workouts were the best. Like all pro teams, the Jets avoid all-out scrimmaging once the season begins. But up front the linemen are encouraged to make those shoulder pads pop. Ewbank finally had to call off the workout. The players were hitting too hard. He was afraid somebody would get hurt.

Ewbank already had problems in this department. Don Maynard, the moody Texan who'd broken Raymond Berry's career record for receiving yardage that season, had a pulled hamstring. Ewbank had been minimizing the injury to his thirty-one-year-old flanker for several weeks. And it hadn't appeared to bother Maynard in the championship game when he caught two touchdown passes. But now Maynard wasn't going to work out until the day before the big game. Despite the veteran's assurance that he would be ready, Ewbank toyed with the idea of starting Bake Turner in his place.

Snell, the versatile fullback, had his problems too. He'd hurt his knee slightly in a late-season game while throwing a pass, of all things. On Thursday before the Super Bowl the knee was aspirated. That evening Snell walked around the hotel in shorts, a huge bandage decorating his knee. The next day he was furious to learn reporters had written about his knee being drained and he couldn't understand how they found out. He feared the Colts would try to finish the job now that they knew he was hurting.

As for Namath, the condition of his knees was normal—bad. His knee had been drained on Thursday, too, when he also received a pain-killing shot. But he'd long since learned to live with needles. Sunday, as he climbed into the bus that would take the Jets to the Super Bowl, he walked as stiffly as he had ten days earlier getting off the airplane. But he knew, and his teammates did, too, that there are no stairs on the football field.

2

The Game Plan

The Jets' hotel and the Colts' headquarters at the Statler Hilton were half a mile apart in Fort Lauderdale. A six-bus police-escorted caravan was arranged to take both teams and their official parties through the Sunday after-church traffic to Miami and the Orange Bowl. It was about a 25-mile trip.

The Jets were in the front buses, and as they pulled out into traffic, the driver announced to his passengers: "Gentlemen, the Baltimore Colts are behind us. Let's keep them there for the rest of the afternoon."

The American Leaguers were tense and nervous, as before any major game. But they were not paralyzed with awe as the Kansas City Chiefs admittedly had been before the first Super Bowl. The Jets were confident. The Jets were prepared. Namath's public pronouncements and Weeb Ewbank's private assurances had done their job.

The Jets had been given their first look at Colt movies on Friday morning after their arrival in Florida, although some had sneaked a peak earlier. Johnny Sample, the cornerback, for instance, had been studying Colt movies at home since the previous Monday, less than 24 hours after the AFL title victory over Oakland. An old friend from the NFL, Green Bay's Herb Adderley, had lent him the movies. The team as a group also watched the films on Saturday and Sunday, then again the following Wednesday, Thursday, and Friday. Through every film session, Ewbank followed a well-conceived strategy of comparing each member of the Colts to a player the Jets had faced in the AFL.

"Look at that Bubba Smith [the Colts defensive left end who'd played tackle the year before, his first as a pro]. He's quite a stud and he'll be great some day," Weeb would say, "but he's really only a rookie at his position. He's no better than Mays or Lassiter, and he certainly doesn't have the know-how of McDole.* We handled all of them, didn't we?"

* Jerry Mays of Kansas City, Ike Lassiter of Oakland, and Ron McDole of Buffalo.

Malcolm W. Emmons

The Jets' new-look offensive line was a key factor in Weeb Ewbank's game plan. Providing near-perfect protection for Joe Namath against the Colts are (from left) Winston Hill, Bob Talamini, John Schmitt, Randy Rasmussen and Dave Herman.

Ewbank went down the rest of the Colt roster. "Watch Billy Ray Smith [defensive left tackle]—he jumps up and down like Jim Hunt of Boston." And when he was done he knew "we weren't as afraid of them as the newspapermen kept telling us. We respected them, but we got the point across that we had beaten people just as good in our league."

This was Phase I of the Jets' psychological pregame preparation.

Phase II was presented to the Jets with their formal game plan on Tuesday. Ewbank stood up before his players and delivered one of the most important lectures of his coaching life: "Our whole thought for this game will be not to get fancy," he began. "Let's do the things we can do best and do them well. Other AFL teams got licked in this game because they lost their poise. That happened to us once during the season [at Oakland] and we can't let it happen again.

"Number one, we will be in the best physical condition for this game," he continued. "Number two, we will study for this game so that we won't make any errors. We won't miss assignments and we won't miss coverages, which is what beat Oakland last year. And, number three, we will have execution. The first two points actually boil down to poise. *Poise* and *execution*—those will be our secrets."

Ironically, for all of Namath's rapping, the Jets got one of their big boosts from a Colt statement. Jerry Logan, the veteran Baltimore safety, had been quoted in Florida about the way the Colt defense set out to intimidate opponents.

"So they say their defense is predicated on the idea of intimidating people," Ewbank snorted in the privacy of the Jets' guarded locker room. "Well, we're not going to be intimidated. We're not going to absorb blows, we are going to take the battle to them, and from the beginning, too. If we have to hit harder, we will; if they get a touchdown, we'll get two. Whatever it takes to win, we will win."

A pro football game plan is generally not so much a 60-minute blueprint as a starting point. The coaches tell their players: This is how we'll attack and defend in certain situations based on what the opposition has done in the past. It is based on our strengths and weaknesses as well as theirs. If the other team makes changes, the game plan must be adjusted. However, the Jets were confident that Baltimore, like themselves, would go with what they did best, the things that had brought them to the Super Bowl in the first place.

An important factor in any game plan is "keys"—not to be confused with the way it was said former Giant linebacker Sam Huff used to key on Cleveland fullback Jimmy Brown, following him on every play. Keys are the little giveaways of what a football team intends to do on offense and defense. In order to pull off a safety blitz, for instance, the safetyman must line up differently than usual. He could be faking, but in that case the cornerback might not be dropping off two steps to cover up for him. Those are keys. Which way the weakside guard pulls out can be an offensive key. That's why coaches and quarterbacks spend hours at the movies. The Jets had done their homework. And so had the Colts.

The Jet plan on offense was simple. As far as the ground game was concerned, they would start out running to the left, from both their strong left and strong right formations, the strong side being determined by the situation of the tight end. If he's on the right, that makes it strong right because of his presence as an extra blocker. For the pass, the Jets would try to establish a home run threat early, but then stick with the short game against Baltimore's feared zone defense.

The Jets knew Baltimore blitzed a lot, sending not only linebackers but also safetymen rushing in on the passer. When a safety blitz was on, Joe Namath would not always spot it in time to call a new play at the line of scrimmage. However, Namath and his receivers, George Sauer on the left and Don Maynard on the right, would all see the blitz developing at the same time. Whichever side the blitz came from, that receiver would know to break inside toward the vacated area over the middle no matter what pass pattern had been called in the huddle. Namath would then automatically throw to that spot, counting on his receiver to read the blitz, too, and be there.

Since Bob Boyd, the Colts' left cornerback, was the slowest man in the secondary—the Colts, in fact, played so much zone defense just to protect him—the Jets noted that Baltimore rotated its defense toward him. They figured that should give Sauer an edge against the stronger right cornerback, Lenny Lyles, and they would go in that direction at the start. Sauer also learned from the movies that at the right time he should also be able to beat Lyles outside as well as over the middle. That intelligence was filed for the right moment by Namath and Ewbank.

The blitz can be effective against a rookie or against a veteran who is slow to set up and release the ball. It is dangerous against good quarterbacks who can exploit the holes it leaves in the secondary. "We hope they blitz," Ewbank kept saying all week, and the National Leaguers looked at him as if he were crazy. But Weeb knew Namath's quick release could destroy any blitz.

The decision to run left was based mostly on the Jets' personnel. Ewbank insists he did not know that right defensive end Ordell Braase had a back injury, as the Colts claimed later. He did figure Bubba Smith as a more imposing physical obstacle, but that wasn't the key reason they would run the other way. In the weeks before the championship game, the Jets had made a major change in their offensive line. Rookie Sam Walton had played right tackle all year and was getting progressively worse. He'd suffered through several bad games at midseason and his confidence was shot, his techniques deteriorating. So, for the title game against Oakland, Ewbank made a move. With starters Bob Talamini and Dave Herman and sub Randy Rasmussen, he had three fine guards. He moved right guard Herman out to tackle and put second-year pro Rasmussen in at guard. Rasmussen responded with the game of his life against the Raiders, and Herman was able to handle Ike Lassiter, the big end who had helped ruin Walton during the regular season.

Ewbank determined to use this alignment again, especially since Bubba Smith and Lassiter were similar in size and style. If Herman could handle one, he could handle the other, Ewbank reasoned. However, Weeb still realized that Herman was playing out of position and that Rasmussen hadn't been playing that much through the year. He had two good, big, and strong veterans on the left, tackle Winston Hill and Talamini, so it stood to reason that the Jets would try to run behind them. (Late in the game they would go at Bubba for a couple of key first downs.)

On defense, the Jets looked for Baltimore to run quite a bit so they planned to stay with an "odd" defense, that is, placing a linebacker up on the line of scrimmage as a fifth lineman. On pass defense, they figured to mix coverages a bit more than they had during the season when they usually favored man-to-man over a zone. John Mackey, the Colts' All-Pro tight end, was the man they feared most. They planned to vary coverage on him, too; sometimes laying off the big guy, sometimes banging him at the line of scrimmage so he couldn't get out as easily for passes.

Earl Morrall was due to be the Colts' quarterback, although some observers felt Don Shula might go back to John Unitas. But Ewbank felt certain that Shula would not humiliate Morrall, the man who had won them the championship, by making a change. Besides, he had seen that movie of Unitas in action and he knew John's arm was still sore, no matter what Unitas was saying.

As for Morrall, the Jets knew he was no threat as a runner and he did not have a shotgun up his right sleeve. "He isn't like John in his prime and he can't whip the ball like, say, Lamonica, so we can play the receivers a little tighter," Ewbank explained. The Jets also planned to rush at Morrall with their hands up, to make him throw out of the same kind of well with which Lou Michaels had threatened Namath. Again, Morrall's lack of a strong arm would make that technique more effective.

By the time the two weeks of preparation were over, the Jets were ready. The game plan was solidified and Joe Namath had done his homework so well that Ewbank would send in only one play during the entire game—a play Namath wouldn't use. The Jets, in fact, were so thoroughly indoctrinated that tight end Pete Lammons begged Ewbank to stop showing them Baltimore movies. "You're making us overconfident," he complained.

3

The First Blow

The Jets Indian-filed through the passageway to their dressing room beneath the mammoth Orange Bowl and began their weekly pregame rituals as if this was just another Sunday in October.

There was only one laugh. Players quickly noted that the huge sign bearing commissioner Pete Rozelle's edict against gambling, as much a part of every pro dressing room as showers and adhesive tape, had been placed directly above Joe Namath's locker. "He's on to you," somebody yelled, and Namath smiled his little smile.

Weeb Ewbank and his assistants went out to check the playing field, and most of the players lounged around, half-dressed, reading the game programs. Their ankles had been taped back at the hotel after the pregame meal—choice of steak, hamburger, or waffles—but Namath entered the training room and stood on the rubbing table as Jeff Snedeker began the game-day rite of taping his knees.

With the table occupied, Paul Rochester, the beefy defensive tackle, lay face down on a bench in the dressing room to receive a long, leisurely back rub from a youngish but bald Texan unknown to most visitors in the room. The volunteer masseur was Jackie Copeland, the first trainer the Titans ever had. He left after two years when Sammy Baugh was fired and now he was a stockbroker in Dallas.

As at Shea Stadium, the lockers were arranged by position, and most of the Jets talked quietly in small groups. Johnny Sample, the veteran cornerback, was alone. The shower area was dry now, before the game, and deserted. Sample knelt in solitary prayer.

Of all the Jets, Sample seemed to feel the emotion of this game most intensely. He had come out of Maryland State in 1958 and made the Baltimore Colts as a rookie that championship year. When Baltimore repeated in 1959, his two interceptions played a major role in the title victory over the Giants. But, in 1961, Sample was traded to Pittsburgh. All-Pro that season with the Steelers, he was shipped ou a year later to Washington in another deal. After three years with the Redskins, he was dealt to Chicago but never reported. Sample insisted that his dispute with the Bears was based strictly on money. At about that time, Chicago owner-coach George Halas was being accused by another player (Mike Ditka) of being so cheap, "he threw nickels around like they were manhole covers." Nothing in Sample's own experience changed that opinion.

There were, however, other whispers as Sample dropped into NFL limbo that summer of 1966. The raspy-voiced Philadelphian did not smoke or drink, but word was out that he wasn't the kind of guy you wanted on your team. Sample was a loudmouth. He popped off. He jabbered all game long at the receivers he was defending. He hit hard and he wasn't always careful to watch for the sideline or listen for the whistle. He'd hurt you. He figured that was the way you played the game.

Bill Mathis leads interference as Matt Snell batters the right side of the Colt defense.

Malcolm W. Emmons

When the Bears made no effort to meet his terms, Sample was confident he'd be picked up by another NFL club. He was still under thirty then; he could help somebody. But the phone never rang. After a while he realized this was no accident. The Word—that faceless monster who wields a potent veto power in all sports—had conspired to end his NFL career.

However, by this time the NFL wasn't the only wheel in pro football. Weeb Ewbank, Sample's first coach, was in his fourth season with the Jets and looking for defensive backs. He and Sample got together. Their first contract contained all kinds of behavior and conditioning clauses. While the Word on an athlete never changes, Ewbank was willing to see if the man could. The answer came after one year. His teammates elected Sample their defensive captain.

But Sample's bitterness didn't end there. "I hate the NFL, I despise them," he'd say. "All I live for is getting into the Super Bowl and beating them. They blackballed me and I'll never forget it."

But when the Jets drew the Colts as their Super Bowl opponent, some of the anger faded. "The Colts and their owner [Carroll Rosenbloom] always treated me nice. Some of my best friends in football are with the Colts. I'll have to keep telling myself it's the NFL we're playing, not the Colts. It's the NFL I hate," Sample said.

In his wallet Sample carried a faded clipping that quoted Green Bay coach Vince Lombardi after the Packers' first Super Bowl victory over Kansas City. The headline read: KC NOT IN CLASS WITH NFL'S BEST—LOMBARDI.

Sample, who'd been physically ill from tension the night before the game, remembered all this as he and Namath, the offensive captain, walked out to greet the Colts and the officials at midfield for the ceremonial coin toss.

The real toss, of course, had taken place earlier, under the stands. The Jets had won and they elected to receive. When he walked out on the field after the kickoff, Namath knew the first series of plays he planned to call, plays designed not only to hit probable weaknesses but to expose the Colts' defensive plan.

After two plays, the pattern of the game was set. Matt Snell, the Jet fullback, came into this game with a quota of bitterness, too. He'd been snubbed for AFL All-Star honors and he'd had it up to here with reading that the Jets had no running attack, especially as compared with the Colts. On the first play of the game, he smacked over left tackle for three yards and then, following tackle Winston Hill and guard Bob Talamini, as he was to do all afternoon, he crashed through the same area for a gain of nine. All his fury exploded at the tackle, and Rick Volk, the 195-pound safetyman, lay dazed on the ground and had to be helped off the field. The Jets had struck the first blow.

Although they failed to get another first down, the Jets did manage to control the ball more than four minutes at the start, a good sign, AFL rooters thought. As they left the field, Namath slapped a few guys on their hip pads. "Come on, come on," he encouraged, "today is our day."

After Curley Johnson's punt, the Colts went into business on their own 27. Now everybody would learn if that AFL-leading New York defense meant anything. At first it didn't look like it. On the first play, Earl Morrall threw a short screen pass to tight end John Mackey, who ran right over Jet safetyman Jim Hudson for a 19-yard gain. Then halfback Tom Matte swept right end for 10. Another first down. Fullback Jerry Hill, Matte, and then Hill again crashed for another first-and-ten. The Colts looked like supermen, the Jets were missing tackles all over the field.

But then Gerry Philbin, the Jets' All-Star defensive end, stuck his face mask into the Baltimore juggernaut. On Hill's first-down run of five yards, Gerry had gambled on his charge . . . and lost. But Philbin knew he was good, even if NFL fans wouldn't concede it. He came right back with the same daring rush . . . and threw Hill for a three-yard loss.

Stopped on the ground for the first time, the Colts abandoned their running attack for this series and went to the air. Their target was Randy Beverly, a free agent the Jets had promoted from the minor leagues two years before. Beverly was voted the weak link in the Jet secondary before the game, and he knew they'd be picking on him. "I just don't want to look like a clown," he had confided during the week.

The Colts sent veteran split end Jimmy Orr at Beverly, but Morrall's short pass was dropped. Then they put in their double tight end offense with six-foot-two, 235-pound Tom Mitchell, an AFL reject, of all things, in the lineup along with Mackey. Beverly, five feet eleven, 198, was physically overmatched when Mitchell came at him, grabbing a pass from Morrall for a 15-yard gain as Billy Baird, the free safety, made the tackle.

Mitchell's reception gave the Colts a first down at the Jet 19. Those goalposts were getting too close. The Jets had to start making those tackles they had been missing. Linebacker Larry Grantham, who

Vernon J. Biever

The Colts' blitzing Mike Curtis can't get there in time to stop Joe Namath completion to Bill Mathis.

called defensive signals, decided the Jets had to try to rush Morrall out of his game plan.

Then came one of those real breaks. Morrall had a receiver free when safetyman Jim Hudson fell down, but Willie Richardson dropped the ball. The Colts were feeling some pressure, too, it seemed. On the next play, Morrall overthrew Mitchell, and then, on third down, he was chased out of the pocket by ends Verlon Biggs and Philbin. Middle linebacker Al Atkinson smacked him down at the line of scrimmage. Ewbank had been right. Morrall was no threat as a scrambler.

With the scoreboard showing fourth down, Lou Michaels, Namath's new buddy, lumbered onto the field to try a field goal. Bobby Boyd, the bald cornerback who had been the quarterback when Jet assistant Clive Rush was working at Oklahoma, held. Boyd knelt at the 27 and Michaels sighted into the tricky winds blowing in from the open end of the stadium. His kick, from "can't-miss" distance, was wide right. On the sidelines, the Jets' own place-kicker, Jim Turner, watched closely. As golfers say when they watch another player putt before them to check the break of the green, Turner was "going to school" on Michaels' miss.

Now the Jets had the ball for the second time and Namath started to look for holes in the Baltimore zone. Under pressure, he threw short to Snell, who dropped the ball; hit tight end Pete Lammons for two yards; and then completed a swing pass to halfback Bill Mathis that went for 13. Now's the time, Namath thought. The Colts were "thinking short" along with him. It was the spot to unleash Don Maynard, go for broke.

Maynard headed off on the straight fly pattern down the right sideline. He left Bobby Boyd, the left cornerback who had short responsibility, as if the veteran defender was just another blade of Orange Bowl grass. Jerry Logan, the safety, picked him up deep, just as it says in the textbook, but soon Logan was steps behind and fading. Maynard was free and Namath lofted a perfect spiral toward his streaking flanker.

Only Maynard wasn't streaking at full speed. He had told coaches before the game his leg was fine. It wasn't. He was slower by inches and that's what the game is all about. Because Maynard had hardly practiced all week, Namath couldn't compensate. The ball fell just off his fingertips.

The statistics showed this as just another incompletion. A zero.

Actually, it was one of the most important plays of the game. The strength of zone defense as played by the Colts is against the long pass. In baseball vernacular, you can bunt on the zone and spray singles, but you can't hit home runs. On one play, Maynard destroyed that concept as thoroughly as Hitler destroyed France behind its Maginot Line. A great passing combination, thrower and receiver, can beat any defense. For the rest of the game, Baltimore had to play Maynard scared. And, as they saw the Colt defense lean toward Maynard, Namath and split end George Sauer knew they would be playing a lot of catch the rest of the afternoon.

"Poise," Ewbank had preached before the game, and soon that was all the Jets had standing between the Colts and their goal line as the first quarter drew to an end.

A 51-yard punt by David Lee had pinned the Jets back on their own four. The Colts overshifted their defense to protect the side the Jets had found so vulnerable, so Namath sent Matt Snell the other way, to his right, for gains of four and five yards. With third-and-one, Namath called Sauer on a short outside pattern to get the first down. The quick pass was on the money, and Sauer had his first down at the 17 when Lenny Lyles smacked him from behind and forced a fumble that was recovered by Baltimore sub linebacker Ron Porter at the Jet 12. Sauer was desolated as he trudged off the field with the offensive platoon, but Namath never flagged in offering encouragement.

This was the kind of blunder that had destroyed both Kansas City and Oakland in the previous Super Bowls. Give the NFL a break and they'll kill you, the experts maintained. It was time for the AFL's annual El Foldo Festival in Florida, but somebody forgot to tell the Jets.

On the first play after the recovery (and final play of the first quarter), Morrall sent fullback Jerry Hill crashing into the left side of the line, but Gerry Philbin, Al Atkinson, and Larry Grantham were crashing, too. They threw Hill for a one-yard loss.

Matte swept left end with a pitchout for seven, and with third-and-four at the six, Morrall decided to go for the score. He had both tight ends in the game, Mitchell and Mackey, and he sent the former Oakland Raider over the middle. Mitchell was open and Morrall drilled the ball as hard as he could; perhaps too hard, he felt later.

From pregame scouting, the Colts knew all about how well Jet linebackers helped out on pass defense. For this game, aware the Colts had no breakaway running backs, the linebackers concentrated

Joe Namath and Winston Hill walk grimly off the field as the ball changes hands.

even more on clogging the passing lanes. Morrall never saw Al Atkinson drifting back over the middle, and the Jet linebacker was able to tip the pass. Deflected just enough, the ball hit Mitchell on the shoulder and flew high in the air. Beverly went after it and made a diving, rolling interception in the end zone. "Is it good?" he screamed at the official and the signal told it all: *Jets' ball!*

After the touchback, the Jets took over on their 20 and it was Snell, Snell, Snell, Snell, four straight times for first downs out to the New York 46. Winston Hill moved his man, whether Braase or Michaels, virtually at will. Right linebacker Don Shinnick was no factor. Lenny Lyles, the cornerback, had to come up and make most of the tackles, head-on. Snell, a raging bull this day, weighs 220. Lyles and the right side of the Colt defense were taking a beating.

The Jets got a break when Shinnick failed to hold a sure interception, but Namath then read the safety blitz and hit Bill Mathis with a shortie for six. The Jets were in Baltimore territory for the first time, at the 48.

Namath, picking the Colt defense like a locksmith, then went back to Sauer for gains of 14 and 11 yards to the 23. On the latter play, Lyles gambled for an interception and Sauer would have been home free if Volk, back in the game, hadn't come up to make a saving tackle.

The Colts undershifted their defense here, so Namath sent halfback Emerson Boozer the other way, the right, for a two-yard gain to the 21. Then Joe called another pass. He saw left linebacker Mike Curtis drifting over to help Boyd against Maynard. That had to mean Snell was free short and, bang, a 12-yard completion to the nine.

Now it was Snell again, playing the greatest game of his life. He went right for five and then Namath sent him back wide against the shell-shocked defenders on the left. Winston Hill drove Lou Michaels out of the play. Boozer kept the crashing Volk from getting a hand on Snell, and the inspired fullback smashed through the late tackle of linebacker Dennis Gaubatz on the goal line. Turner kicked the extra point, and with 5:57 gone in the second quarter, the AFL was ahead for the first time in three Super Bowl games, 7–0.

That touchdown meant more than seven points, much more. The Jets not only had survived the mistake of Sauer's fumble, they had taken the ball back and rammed it under the Colts' chin straps on an 80-yard drive that took 12 plays. This is the way one football team demonstrates its superiority over another. Only one touchdown behind, the Colts and Morrall came back trying the bomb. That's when the Jets knew they might have 'em on the run.

After an exchange of missed field goals, the Colts again found themselves starting at their 20. Morrall was 0-for-three on passes to Richardson, but he tried his young flanker again. Richardson had been spending the afternoon listening to Sample's chatter, but this time he tuned him out for a six-yard gain. The Colts then sent Matte steaming around right end. Strong safety Jim Hudson missed him at the line of scrimmage. Sample blew the tackle a few yards down-field, and finally Billy Baird, the other safety, ran Matte down and forced him out of bounds after a 58-yard gain to the Jet 16. As Matte hit the ground, Sample came in late to join the tackle, knees first. When they unpiled, Matte had to be restrained from attacking the Jet cornerback.

The Colts had broken another big play. In easy range of a touch-down, there seemed no way they could be denied at least a field goal. Jerry Hill rammed left tackle for one and then Morrall looked for Richardson in the end zone. He had him, too, or so it seemed, but Sample had other ideas. For once, he shut his mouth and opened his arms, ducking under Richardson's shoulder for an interception at the two. As he caught the ball tumbling to the ground, Sample knew he could get up and run. But he didn't want to take any chances on a fumble, especially with the half running out. All he knew was that he had the ball and, as long as he kept it, the Colts couldn't score.

As the play was whistled dead, he rose to his feet in front of the still-stunned Richardson. "Here it is, here's what you're looking for," Sample told the Colt flanker . . . and he tapped him on the head with the ball. Richardson, who had been jabbering back at Sample up to this point, was silent and would remain so the rest of the game. "I wanted to break his head off," he confessed later.

The Jets, though, still couldn't get their first down to kill the clock. They had to punt from their own seven, and with 43 seconds left in the half, the Colts were back at the Jet 42.

This was a slightly different Jet lineup, though. During the first quarter, middle linebacker Al Atkinson had suffered a painful shoul-der injury, but stoically played on. Two plays before the half, the doctor escorted him to the dressing room to steal a few minutes so the pain-killing injection could take full effect. The shoulder taped, Al finished out the game. Most of his teammates didn't even know he'd been hurt. For these final plays of the half, Larry Grantham

Johnny Sample breaks up a second-period Earl Morrall pass to Willie Richardson.

moved into the middle from right linebacker and slender Paul Crane took Grantham's place. The Colts seemed to notice the change at once and ran their first play at the new boy. But the 205-pound Alabaman stopped Hill for a gain of a yard.

Only 25 seconds remained. Morrall took the snap and spun for the handoff to Matte running wide right. Bill Baird, the free safety, committed himself from the left side of the field to stop what he thought was an end run or to help out if it was an option pass. But, suddenly, Matte stopped and passed the ball back to Morrall. It was the flea flicker, a play from prehistoric football, but one that still works, somewhere in pro football, two or three times a year.

It was working now. Randy Beverly was covering split end Jimmy Orr short, but Baird was supposed to pick him up long, and Baird, though hurrying to get back, wasn't there. The veteran Colt receiver was all alone inside the 10, waving his arms to attract Morrall's attention. It was a sure touchdown. The Colts had pulled the same play against Atlanta during the regular season and Morrall had thrown to Orr for an easy six-pointer.

Orr was still the primary receiver, but this time Morrall wasn't even looking toward the nifty redhead near the left sideline. He seemed almost hypnotized by fullback Jerry Hill over the middle. For a moment, Hill was open and Morrall unloaded the pass in his direction. But the ball had 30 yards to go and Jim Hudson, the Jet safetyman who plays with fire in his eyes, was closer than that. He cut in front of Hill to intercept Morrall's pass at the 12 as the half ended.

(Later, Morrall was to explain that Matte's return lateral had forced him to turn away from Orr's direction to catch the ball. "I saw no movement there," Morrall said, referring to the corner where Orr was open. But Orr was indignant when told of Morrall's excuse. "What do you think this·is?" he asked, waving his arms over his head. "We worked this play once before for a touchdown. I was where I was supposed to be and Earl knew where I was supposed to be."

(As a further irony, this was the last play the Jets had worked against on their last day of practice. Ewbank had Babe Parilli pull it without warning against the first-string defense. It worked then, too.)

Most coaches hate a one-touchdown lead at halftime. It's better than being behind, but it's almost worse than no lead at all. It's just enough to make the players think they're doing well. Ewbank was worried as he took his team into the dressing room.

He knew the Jets would have to kick off to start the second half. That gave the Colts the ball, and if they could drive for a tying touchdown, they'd also have that most prized commodity in all football— momentum. Weeb also knew, and so did everyone within sight and sound of this game, that relentless NFL pressure had forced American League teams to collapse in the second half of both previous Super Bowls. It might have helped Weeb to know that his players were worried, too.

4

"I'm a Poor Winner"

Baltimore coach Don Shula had his own worries as he brought his team out for the second half. Earl Morrall, his starting quarterback, had accomplished nothing in the first 30 minutes. He had completed only five of fifteen passes and thrown three interceptions. Worse, he had been given no less than five scoring opportunities and failed to get even a field goal out of them.

Shula still had Johnny Unitas on his bench. Perhaps Unitas had no arm, but Johnny U. seemed to believe he was okay and, more important, the players would believe in him.

Should he switch to Unitas or stick with Morrall? Shula finally decided he owed Morrall one more chance. After all, it was Morrall who had got them there in the first place. Morrall deserved it. It was more than just a sentimental decision. For one thing, Morrall had come through in the clutch for Shula before this season. For another, humiliating Morrall at this point would irrevocably destroy his future value to the team.

Shula decided to give Morrall one more opportunity to move the ball club. But that one chance became two, and more precious minutes were lost.

After Curley Johnson's kickoff, the Colts set up at their 25 and Morrall sent Tom Matte cracking over right tackle. But Verlon Biggs, the moody, almost sullen defensive end, forced a fumble with his tackle and linebacker Ralph Baker recovered for the Jets at the Colt 33. That precious momentum had passed from the Colts' hands along with the football. On the sidelines, Shula silently conceded that the fumble hadn't been Morrall's fault. He would give Earl another series of downs to move the club.

The Jets managed to advance down to Baltimore's 11, but then the Colt defense, which had shut out four NFL opponents this year, got stubborn. Lyles crashed through to drop Boozer for a five-yard loss on a sweep, and then Namath heard those dreaded words from his right tackle, Dave Herman: "Look out, Joe!" It meant only one thing. Bubba Smith had broken through Herman's block and for the first time he was able to throw Namath for a loss. On third down from the 25, Logan almost intercepted Namath's pass to Lammons, but it dropped incomplete and that left it up to Jim Turner, who this season had kicked footballs for more field goals and more points than any man in pro history.

Babe Parilli knelt at the 32-yard line, took the center snap, and in one motion spun the ball so the laces faced away from the kicker. Turner dug his square-toed shoe into the ball and the Jets had a 10–0 lead.

Ewbank sighed with relief. Ten points, he said, was a "helluva lot different" from seven. It cut a whole dimension from the Colts' offense. They would have to do a lot more scoring to win.

As the Colts moved on the offense, Morrall was at quarterback, but a hum of anticipation stirred the huge crowd of 75,377 fans. Johnny Unitas, his famous No. 19 jersey unmarked by combat or perspiration, was warming up behind the Colt bench.

Morrall's "last shot" turned out to be a blank. He overthrew Mackey; hit Hill with a dinky flare pass that gained zero yardage; and then found himself chased out of the pocket by Biggs and dropped by sub tackle Carl McAdams for a two-yard loss when he tried to scramble.

Ironically, as Unitas was getting ready to come in, Namath had to leave the game. It was second-and-nine at the Colt 23. Namath sent Maynard winging toward the end zone and again the wiry Texan had a step on Jerry Logan. But Colt defensive tackle Fred Miller was putting on a hard rush. His pressure forced Namath to throw long, and the tackle sent Joe off the field shaking his right hand.

Namath had been troubled by a recurrent jammed thumb off and on for two seasons now. "No, it's not that again, it just got weak all of a sudden," Namath told Ewbank and Dr. James A. Nicholas. "I can work it out."

Parilli, meanwhile, anxiously entered the game. He threw short to Sauer when rushed by Baltimore's third-down safety blitz and then changed from thrower to holder as he knelt at the 30 for Turner's second field goal.

The Jets now led by 13–0. As Johnny Unitas stopped for a final word from Shula, Namath was playing catch behind the Jet bench to

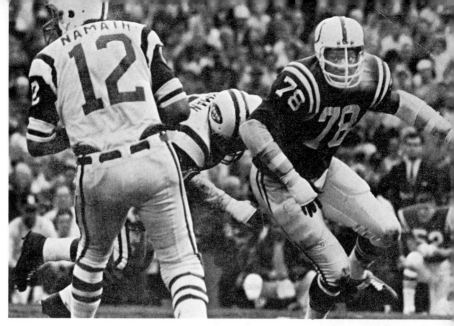

Vernon J. Biever

Bubba Smith gets past Dave Herman and has his eye on Joe Namath.

Babe Parilli holds as Jim Turner kicks one of his field goals against the Colts.

Vernon J. Biever

see if he could shake off the sore hand. Harvey Nairn, a rookie on the taxi squad, was on the sidelines in street clothes. He dropped Namath's first pass, and Lou Sahadi, a magazine editor who was on the bench gathering material, stepped in to relieve the embarrassed rookie. Sahadi didn't miss a one.

There was a roar of recognition as Unitas started toward the huddle. "Okay, see if you can get something going," Shula told him. "Good luck, John," added Morrall. There was nothing else he could say.

Every man on the Jets took a hard swallow when Unitas came in. "I was scared to death," Ewbank admitted later, and his players made the same confession. They weren't embarrassed to be frightened, either. This was the Master, the cool and daring quarterback genius who'd pulled out so many big games after all hope was gone. What miracle did he have waiting this time? Maybe he only had a sore arm up his sleeve, but the Unitas mystique sent a chill through the entire stadium. Sore arm? This guy could beat you from an iron lung.

Johnny U.'s first series showed little, three plays and a punt . . . and Namath came back into the game for the Jets.

The white-shirted New Yorkers started at their 37, and in four plays they had a first down at the Baltimore 10 as Sauer again victimized Lyles with catches for 11 and 39 yards. The Jets were amazed that Lyles was playing Sauer so loose. But the defense tightens up as it nears the goal line, and the Jets knew pride would stiffen the Colts even more. They also knew Baltimore would be gambling for the ball. "Be sure to get those three points," Ewbank yelled as his quarterback passed him at the sidelines, and Namath nodded impatiently. Joe wasn't a rookie anymore. He knew this was no time for razzle-dazzle, no time for interceptions, fumbles, long losses. Namath just sent Snell and Mathis straight into the line, and when the Colts held at the two, Turner kicked his third field goal from the nine.

With 1:34 gone in the last quarter, the Jets had a 16–0 lead. The Colts now had to score two touchdowns, plus a field goal, to win. Would they have enough time? With a sound arm, Unitas would *make* time, but now the Colts weren't so sure. Shinnick and Braase had been benched, and for the first time, the National League champions began to lose their poise.

After two short gainers, Unitas passed to Richardson for five at the sideline and Sample ran his man out of bounds right at the Colt

bench, a tactical error. Sample found himself surrounded by un-
friendly blue jerseys and Tom Mitchell was banging him on the head
with his helmet. Fortunately, Sample was still wearing his own hard
hat. The official not only didn't throw Mitchell out of the game, he
told Sample to stop fighting.

Unitas kept the Colts moving after this interruption and now he
was at the Jet 25 zeroing in on Jimmy Orr in the end zone. Orr was
an eleven-year veteran; not much speed anymore but a million moves
and he knew when to use them. He'd wait half a game to set up his
man and now he thought he had Beverly. But Beverly was nobody's
clown today. He drove in on the red-haired split end and took the
underthrown pass away from him in the end zone. His second interception of the day. As he looked off to the side, there was a yellow
marker on the field. A penalty signal? No, a potato chip wrapper. The
interception was good.

Frustration exploded within the Colts. There was Matte, the eight-
year veteran, screaming at Sample from 20 yards away. "You're a
dirty player," Matte yelled in conclusion to other selected remarks,
referring to his contention that Sample had kneed him in the back
after the whistle on his earlier long run.

Sample just smirked. "Yeah, well you're a bush leaguer," he
sneered. "Anybody who got as far ahead as you did that time should
have scored easy."

Something snapped in Matte. He charged Sample as if they were
playing bullfight and Sample was the red cape. The Jet veteran stood
his ground, eyes on the charging halfback. At the last minute, he
simply threw a rolling block at Matte, ducking under the Ohio Stater
and sending him flying. Then he laughed.

"Don't worry, Weeb," Sample said as he left the field. "I ain't get-
tin' thrown out."

The Jets had 11:06 to kill, but they only wiped out a small piece
of the clock. Turner missed a 42-yard field goal attempt, and the
Colts regained possession at their 20 with 6:34 to go. There was no
more time to spare for the Colts and Unitas now. They had to get
on the board, and many of their most loyal fans were wondering not
if their super team would lose but whether it would be shut out.

Three times Unitas dropped back to pass and three times he threw
incomplete. Fourth-and-ten on his own 20, the years, as if by magic,
suddenly peeled away. Johnny U., the Master, hit Jimmy Orr for 17
when he had to and gained the possession first down. He threw two

Randy Beverly pulls off his second interception in the end zone against Jimmy Orr as Jim Hudson stands by to assist.

Jets' Al Atkinson restrains the Colts' enraged Tom Matte.

more incompletes and then went to Mackey for 11 and another first down. John Elliott of the Jets was called for a personal foul on the play, so add another 15 yards, Mr. Referee, and now the Colts were at the Jet 37. Matte ran for one, the old change of pace, and then Unitas passed to Richardson for 21 yards to the Jet 15.

It was 1958 against the Giants again—and all the great games. Unitas picking a defense apart and working the sideline like an artist, making the clock almost an ally rather than an opponent; it was Fred Astaire young again on the *Late Show*.

Unitas overthrew Matte from the 15, but then he hit Orr for 11 to the four and the Jets were penalized half the distance to the two when Atkinson joined in late on the tackle.

With first down at the two, Unitas called Matte over left guard where he was stacked up by Paul Rochester for no gain. But again a flag flew. The Jets were offside. Half the distance again; to the one. Here Unitas sneaked up the middle, but Biggs was waiting for him. No gain. Matte hit right guard and Atkinson piled him up. No gain. Finally, on third down, Unitas sent Hill over left tackle with Matte in front to help drive Biggs out of the play. After 56 minutes and 41 seconds of the Super Bowl, the Colts had finally scored to make it 16–7. Some Mickey Mouse defense!

To score, the Colts required a fourth-down pass completion, three Jet penalties, and three shots from the one. They had also used more than three minutes, not long under ordinary conditions but too long at this point. The Colts needed a home run at this stage of the game and there wasn't a home run arm on the roster.

Everybody in the ball park knew the Colts would try an onsides kick. They were adept at the technique. Michaels kicked left-footed and that gave the ball an unusual spin. His teammates seemed to know where every crazy bounce would take it.

The Jets, like every other team, have a special unit for fielding onside kicks if they know one is coming. Backs and ends man the front line instead of tackles and guards. Michaels nubbed the ball and it spun upfield past two Jet pass receivers, George Sauer and Bake Turner, to be buried under a pile of flailing bodies. When the struggling players were peeled away, the Colts had the ball and safetyman Rick Volk was lying unconscious. His teammates dragged him off the field to save a time out and later that night he went into convulsions and was hospitalized briefly for a concussion.

The recovery, credited to Tom Mitchell, gave Baltimore possession at the Jet 48 with 3:14 to go, and Unitas quickly drove the Colts to the 19. Now it was fourth down and Shula faced a tactical decision. He could take the certain field goal, gamble on another onside kick, and then try for the winning touchdown. After all, two and a half minutes remained to play. However, Shula also knew that even if he got the field goal, he still needed a touchdown to win and he might never get better field position than he had now. If he got the touchdown now, then he only needed to make it within field goal range for a chance to win. He left Unitas in the game to go for six. The Master dropped back, looked for Orr, and fired. But Grantham, the linebacker, tipped the ball and it flew over Orr's head. The gun hadn't sounded, but the game was over.

"Bubba Smith? Piss, piss, piss. Bubba Smith? Piss, piss, piss," Dave Herman chanted as he charged down the runway from the field. The vulgarism was a cry of victory, for himself and for his team over highly rated opponents.

The Jets' victory dressing room, of course, was chaos; sweating, weary players, officials, coaches, and friends, plus newsmen jockeying for position between television cameras and coiling cable.

"I feel purged," Sample rasped. "All the poison went out of me in this game."

"This was a victory for the American Football League. We overcame our critics!" Namath proclaimed as he and Sample announced the game ball would go to the AFL office.

Ewbank, dripping from his second clothes-on shower in as many games, called it "the start of a new era."

But there was bitterness, too, and not just because pro commissioner Pete Rozelle, ever mindful of football's TV image, had barred champagne from the winning dressing room.

"I'm only talking to New York writers," Namath shouted angrily over the din. "They were the only ones who believed in us." It took club president Phil Iselin and Ewbank to persuade Namath to relent. "You know me," he finally apologized. "I'm a poor winner."

Later it was announced that Namath had won the *Sport Magazine* automobile prize as the outstanding player in the game. It was just another blow to Matt Snell, who had played the greatest game of his life, scored his team's only touchdown, and broken Super Bowl rushing records with 121 yards on 30 carries.

"I didn't even get a vote for the AFL All-Star team," he repeated to newsmen in his clipped, bitter voice. "Don't talk to us now, go

Joe's dad (right) joins the celebration with Weeb Ewbank.

talk to them. You guys spent all week telling us how great they were—Matte and Hill—now go talk to them!"

Later, though, Snell had time for a little joke. "They said the Colts were the greatest, so I guess that makes us against the law," he said with a hearty laugh.

Joe Foss, first commissioner of the AFL, came in to congratulate the winners and so did Rozelle, still considered by the players as an NFL man. Earlier in the week, Atlanta coach Norm Van Brocklin had said Namath would be playing "his first pro game" when he went against the older league in the Super Bowl. "Hey, Pete," Bake Turner yelled as Rozelle entered the room. "Welcome to the AFL!" Rozelle did not smile.

During the excitement, a small, swarthy man of sixty-one pushed through the crowd. He was wearing an incongruous straw hat, souvenir of the Orange Bowl. "I told you what was going to happen," John Namath said to his son as they embraced.

"Yeah," Joe answered with a fond chuckle, "but you didn't have to play."

5

"Congratulations!"

If the National Football League had been a little more cordial to the sons of two millionaire Texas oilmen, there might never have been an AFL and a Super Bowl.

The new league was conceived by diffident but determined Lamar Hunt, a former third-string end at Southern Methodist University and son of the fabulously wealthy H. L. Hunt. Young Lamar is probably the only soft-spoken oil millionaire in Texas, but his quiet manner hid a determination to achieve a place in this world on his own. Hunt was twenty-six when he decided that place would be in professional football and he attempted to buy the NFL Cardinals, then in Chicago, and move them to Dallas. However the Bidwell brothers, who eventually moved their club to St. Louis, were interested only in selling minority shares. They turned him down. Next Hunt inquired about possible NFL expansion into Dallas. Recalling a previous failure in that city—with a team that was to become the Baltimore Colts—commissioner Bert Bell held out little hope. So in January of 1959, Hunt resolved to form his own league. It would start play in 1960.

No matter how rich he is, no man can own a whole league, so Hunt began his search for partners. The first man he contacted was K. S. (Bud) Adams of Houston, another oil-rich young man who had played some football at Kansas. Hunt and Adams had never met, but Lamar knew Adams also had once tried to buy the Cardinals. Like Hunt, Adams was not interested in a silent partnership. Quite the contrary, Adams is almost a caricature of the rich Texan, loud and flamboyant. He quickly agreed to join Hunt in the risky enterprise.

With Dallas and Houston set, the new league found its next backers in Denver, Minneapolis, and Los Angeles. Then Lamar Hunt turned to New York.

The first man Hunt contacted was Bill Shea, a lawyer with strong pro football and political contacts. Shea was energetically working

Sammy Baugh (left) and Harry Wismer shared high hopes.

to bring National League baseball back to New York after the departure of the Giants and Dodgers. Part of the project involved getting the city to build a new stadium, one that eventually was to bear Shea's name. Too busy to get involved in pro football himself, Shea steered Hunt to Harry Wismer . . . and that's how the Titans of New York, their official designation, were born. (Buffalo and Boston subsequently filled out the eight-team league and Oakland was called in to replace defecting Minneapolis.)

Harry Wismer, then forty-nine years old, had come a long way from Port Huron, Michigan, where he was a high school halfback, and he did it on his own with the aid of energy, ambition, cunning, a limitless ego, and the loudest mouth east or west of the Mississippi. He never got over his resentment of the "rich men's sons" who were his partners in the AFL, especially when he saw the franchise, which he knew could make him their equal, slipping away.

Wismer went to Florida to play college football, transferred to

Michigan State, and then suffered an injury that turned him to broadcasting. As an announcer, he became one of the best-known voices in sports. In 1946 he and then Congressman John F. Kennedy were on the same list of America's outstanding young men as compiled by the Junior Chamber of Commerce.

Wismer was famous for two inventions as a broadcaster—the 55-yard line and the phony audience. Once, carried away by an exciting run, he described it: "And there he goes! He's at the 35, the 40, the 45, the 50, the 55-yard line!!!!" He also dressed up his broadcasts by mentioning the many celebrities in the crowd who were dropping by the radio booth to say hello to their good friend, Harry Wismer. It would surprise no regular listener to hear that Albert Schweitzer and Charles de Gaulle were attending a Redskin football game.

Wismer made his first move out of mere broadcasting when he married a niece of Henry Ford in 1941. The marriage, eventually terminated in divorce, opened many doors for the brash, handsome young man. Wismer got into pro football as a stockholder in the Detroit Lions, which he later parlayed into a substantial share of the Washington Redskins. He also built up nonsports interests. By 1960, the AFL's inaugural year, he was successful, well known, and, by most standards, quite well off. Compared to his partners in the AFL, however, he was in on a shoestring. He had some pro football expertise, but he did not have the financial or temperamental resources for the long haul. His ego refused to allow him to bring in partners who would demand a say in running the ball club in return for their investment.

Wismer actually counted on the magic of his name to sell the Titans to the public. Subway advertising cards called them "Harry Wismer's Titans of New York." His picture, of course, was prominent. When Los Angeles wrote for some team pictures to help publicize a Titan appearance, he sent them 100 head shots of himself. Wismer saw the football team as an extension of his own ego and he did succeed in identifying the two. The trouble was, nobody liked Harry Wismer and the more they saw and heard of him the less they liked his team, too. It was a shame.

Wismer loved to greet everyone he met with a hearty "Congratulations!" He figured that everyone has done something he feels he should be congratulated for, even if it was just getting out of bed with his head on after a night on the town. His idea of a joke was to get on a crowded elevator and say, in a loud voice, "Well, they've just shot Castro." Sometimes he made it Khrushchev.

In the mornings, Wismer was an astute promoter, capable of charming the world, from Senators to bill collectors. Everybody in the AFL acknowledges a debt to Wismer for obtaining a television contract from the American Broadcasting Company that assured survival for the shaky league. After a two- or three-hour lunch, however, his employees learned to avoid him as he turned bitter and vindictive and saw demons and NFL plots behind every chair and unfavorable newspaper clipping. His 3 A.M. calls to newspapers, wire services, and radio stations reporting bogus "scoops," some of them quite macabre, were notorious. So were his raving threats of lawsuits to newspapermen, the same reporters his ever-changing army of publicity men had spent all day cultivating.

Wismer's Titan operation should have been the league's showcase. Instead, it turned out to be its horrible example. The team office for two years was Harry's Park Avenue apartment. His desk and secretary took over the living room, the ticket department was in a bedroom, the coaches used the kitchen, and press agents were in the pantry blocking the bathroom. The apartment entrance was almost impossible to find. New Yorkers might have been willing to knock down the door to buy tickets, but they couldn't find it.

Wismer's first long-term press agent—he lasted a whole season—was Ted Emery, a likable fellow who had done sports publicity for Dartmouth. Emery soon found the Titans were quite different from the Ivy League.

If he wanted to send out a press release, Emery could get no writing paper in the offices of the Titans of New York. Wismer instructed him on those occasions to make a tour of office supply firms, imply that he was prepared to make a big order for the team, and then ask for some samples. By the end of the year, Emery was running out of stationery stores. Wismer gave Emery no expense account for entertaining visiting newsmen, so they would take Emery out and buy his dinner. During one week, all game preparations ground to a halt; the team's one movie projector broke down.

The ticket department was chaos. A visiting press agent, Bob Burdick of the Chargers, wandered into the apartment one evening to find thousands of dollars' worth of tickets strewn carelessly on a big double bed. The two ticket men were arguing over who should go to dinner first and they ended up going together, leaving the tickets entirely unguarded. The Titans weren't worried about anybody stealing the tickets, they gave thousands away, but they would have been liable to the government for the taxes if they had been lost. While the ticket men were gone, a man came in to buy a pair. Burdick simply handed them over and left the man's ten-dollar bill on the bed.

Wismer was an erratic man given to flashes of brilliance. His football team exactly reflected the man.

The players soon found out what Emery and their coaches had learned early. League rules required that a visiting team be in the city where a game was to be played 24 hours before the kickoff. Wismer bent the rule beyond recognition. Most team flights that first year departed after 8 P.M. the night before a game. Why? So Wismer wouldn't have to give the players dinner money.

When linebacker Larry Grantham signed his contract, he thought he was getting a $1,500 bonus. Only after he received his first few paychecks did he realize the "bonus" was considered an advance against salary.

The big disillusionment came during the 1960 exhibition season. After starting their workouts at the University of New Hampshire, the Titans broke camp and headed west for a long exhibition tour. The first three games were played at Los Angeles, Sacramento, California, and Abilene, Texas. Game No. 4 was scheduled against Houston in Mobile, Alabama. Wismer learned it would be cheaper to make the 900-mile overnight trip from Abilene to Mobile by train rather than by plane since, presumably, he would save a hotel bill. Steve Sebo, the general manager, was delegated to break the news of the unorthodox travel arrangements to head coach Sammy Baugh. Sebo is a genial and smiling fellow. "We'll be in air-conditioned cars all the way, get great meals on the train, and have a fine relaxing time, much better than bouncing around from airport to airport and rushing for hotels," he told Baugh as enthusiastically as he could.

"Look, Steve," Baugh replied in his most biting and sarcastic drawl, "you can shit the players all you want—and I may even help you—but please don't try to bullshit me."

The trip, of course, was a nightmare. There was no air conditioning, no good meals, no good sleep, and Texas in late summer is a hellish oven. There were no showers, of course, and no hot water for shaving. Coming to the end of a long road trip, the players were just about out of clean clothes. When the bedraggled team arrived in Mobile, they learned a parade had been scheduled to welcome them at the station.

"Everybody in ties," Sebo ordered. So flanker Don Maynard, always the nonconformist, defiantly knotted his necktie without bothering to put on a shirt over his dirty T-shirt.

Bill Mathis, a rookie halfback, had just been obtained in a trade with the Oilers, and he met the Titans at the train station. "He looked like the greatest thing we'd ever seen, a real All-American," one old Titan recalled years later. "He was clean!"

Sebo, the man in the middle on this trip and other disasters, was the first person Wismer had hired after getting the New York franchise. They had been classmates at Michigan State, and Sebo had gone into college coaching. The last few years he had been head coach at Penn. His contract was about to expire and the alumni committed themselves to firing him. As a going-away gift, he presented them with the embarrassment of an Ivy League championship. The firing was more a reflection on Penn alumni than on Sebo. He was a thoroughly likable and able man. Wismer hired him as general manager one week after he was let go at Penn. Unfortunately, Wismer never let Sebo, or anyone else, do his job.

Wismer's next task was to find a head coach. The only prerequisite was that the man have a big name. He ended up with one of the biggest—all-time pro passing great Sammy Baugh, who had set a book of records with the Redskins. The lean and leathery Texan received a three-year contract at $28,000 a season. His coaching record before and after the Titans was nothing distinguished, but he was just the man for this ragtag team. The players loved him, he refused to be bullied by Wismer and he finished at 7–7 two straight years.

The AFL had conducted a college player draft based on pooled scouting reports by John Breen, one of their most capable early employees, who still works for the Houston club. The Titans had some fine names on their list. It was an omen of things to come that they signed only two—Blanche Martin, a halfback from Michigan State who never made it, and Larry Grantham, a linebacker from Mississippi.

Grantham also had been drafted by the Baltimore Colts, and Weeb Ewbank saw this lean, quick-moving Southerner as a good all-around athlete for his special teams. But the Colts had just won their second straight title and Grantham knew few rookies would make the squad. Besides, he weighed only 195 pounds, quite small by NFL

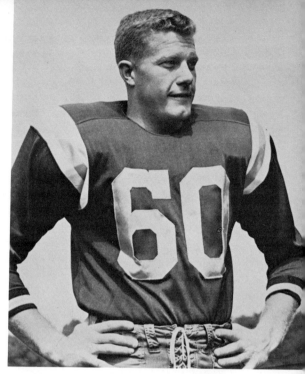

Larry Grantham chose the Titans.

New York Jets

standards. When both teams offered him the same money, Grantham signed with the Titans.

He not only made the team, but he became an All-Star and one of the club's individual leaders. Assistant coach Johnny Del Isola devised a special shifting defense to cover up Grantham's lack of size, but it wasn't until Ewbank took over that he became a complete linebacker. A dental examination proved the difference. Grantham's teeth were in terrible condition. The Jets had them repaired and, lo and behold, in one summer he put on 20 needed pounds. His career almost literally was saved by the skin of his teeth.

For the rest of their first roster, the Titans culled refugees from the Canadian leagues, NFL rejects, and recent retirees, like guard Bob Mischak, a handsome West Pointer who had quit the New York Giants the year before. Sebo and Baugh, using contacts built up in two lifetimes of football, put together a pretty good team for this stage of the AFL's development.

It took several weeks of training camp to line up a quarterback, but he was a goodie: experienced and flamboyant Al Dorow. Dorow, a former Michigan Stater with NFL experience, had been playing in Canada. The Chargers wanted him, too, but the Titans got Dorow, not by offering him more money, naturally, but because they had put him on their negotiation list first.

Dorow, an outspoken and stubborn veteran who was to have arguments with his teammates, with Wismer, and with Baugh, needed receivers, of course. He got two dandies in Art Powell and Don Maynard. Powell, a self-centered athlete of immense talent—he was tough and physically all you could want in a receiver—had been a rover. He played a year of junior college ball and then one year at San Jose State, where he led the nation in pass receiving. Ineligible to be signed by an NFL team, he quit school and played in Canada. When his class graduated two years later, he signed with the Philadelphia Eagles, who used him as a regular defensive back. He wanted to play offense, though, and quit the Eagles and the NFL to sign with the Titans. Two years later he was to play out his option with the Titans and jump to Oakland.

The other receiver was Don Maynard, a lithe former track star who could run like a West Texas rabbit. Maynard had sealed his doom as a rookie running back with the Giants in 1958 when he showed up in cowboy boots and then-anathema sideburns. The Giants used him to return kicks and he dropped a couple. The next season, Allie Sherman, then a Giant assistant, told Maynard he didn't like the long stride he took running end sweeps. "I can run faster my way than any of your other backs," Maynard replied angrily, and that was the end of his NFL career.

He went up to Canada in '59, made sure there was no option clause in his contract, and the next year was available for the new league when Sammy Baugh came calling. Baugh had known Maynard in college. "The Giants used him out of position," he insisted, and history proved him right.

Dorow was a free-lance quarterback. He liked to run and scramble. Pass patterns? Who needed 'em? The Titans didn't even have a play book. But with his crew of veterans Baugh felt he didn't really need one. Football plays are all alike; only the nomenclature differs from team to team. A veteran like Dick Christy could report on a Tuesday, as he did after a 1961 trade, walk through the offense once, and play halfback on Sunday. Baugh kept his offense simple and didn't let Wismer send in any plays. "Besides," he snorted, recalling publicist Emery's scrounging trips, "before you can have a playbook you've got to have paper."

Baugh and Wismer weren't getting along. Wismer wanted his coach to be a social companion, too, someone he could show off to friends. Baugh would have no part of it. Since Sam would not follow in Wismer's shadow, Harry eventually forbade his coach to make any public speaking appearances. He wanted the limelight himself.

But Baugh and the players got along famously, and they won three of their first four before the team suffered a shocking tragedy in Houston. Howard Glenn was a twenty-five-year-old second-string guard out of Linfield College. He had twice tried to make the Giants, and the Titans picked him up in mid-September.

During an October 2 game in Dallas he had been knocked out and took, it was noted in retrospect, "a long time reviving." But kayos—getting your bell rung, as players joke—is part of pro football and he seemed fine the following week in Houston. The temperature was in the nineties that afternoon, and Glenn soon had to leave the game. He complained he "felt tired" and they sent him into the clubhouse for a drink and some salt pills. Suddenly he became hysterical and then lapsed into a coma. Although he never regained consciousness, he wasn't taken to a hospital until after the game and he died 40 minutes after arrival.

At first it was thought he had died of heat prostration, but an autopsy revealed a broken neck. He obviously had been hurt in the Houston game, but the suspicion remained that he had only aggravated a previous undetected injury. A stunned Titan ball club returned to New York, chin straps dragging. This was the kind of year it was going to be, and playing in the decrepit, ghostly Polo Grounds before phantom crowds was no help either.

But there was hope for the future as the Titans won three of their last four games to finish second in the Eastern Division. Bob Mischak made the All-Star team at guard and five others were named to the second team. Their offense had been the most exciting in the league, and plans were being completed for a new ball park to rise in Flushing Meadow.

Most important, the league and the team had survived. With a little help the Titans could be contenders for a title in 1961. But when Steve Sebo sat down to draft college players for the Titans' second season, his scouting material consisted of one of those football magazines you can buy on the newsstands in September for 50 cents. He probably had to lay out the four bits himself.

6

Feudin' and Fussin'

Even with his unsophisticated scouting aids, Steve Sebo put together quite a draft list. Included in his early choices for 1961 were Herb Adderley, who went on to fame with the Packers; Tom Matte, who went on to fame with the Colts; and Bill Brown, who went on to fame with the Vikings. Nobody went on to fame with the Titans, because nobody signed with the AFL club.

All the Titans could show for the 1961 draft were their twenty-first and twenty-seventh-round picks, both busts. The failure was even more striking because this was the AFL's greatest year in the draft. The NFL still didn't take the new league seriously and let go almost by default dozens of college graduates who would be stars for years. Only after such top ten picks as E. J. Holub, Larry Eisenhauer, Jim Tyrer, Jerry Mays, Fred Arbanas, Billy Shaw, Earl Faison, and Keith Lincoln signed with the AFL did the older circuit realize it was involved in a real war.

Wismer had blown a great opportunity. His veterans were still good enough to break even under Baugh in 1961, but from then on they would fall steadily behind.

When Baugh reported back to New York from his Texas ranch, he learned how few rookies had been signed and he was furious. Wismer tried to minimize the failure. "A lot of teams are overloaded at different positions. When they have to cut at that spot, we'll be able to pick up some pretty good men," he had a reluctant Sebo explain "Anyway, the draft is overrated. How many top choices ever really make it?"

Baugh, however, would not go along with the party line. "There' no way you can win games by using people who aren't good enoug to make the teams you're trying to beat," he snorted between chew on his familiar cheekful of tobacco. (When indoors and in relativ

privacy, Baugh would do his spitting into a water glass, quite discon-
certing for a first-time interviewer.)

The Titans did make some improvement, however. Their best
rookie turned out to be a free agent named Dainard Paulson, a highly
religious young man who never let his beliefs stop him from com-
mitting legal mayhem on the football field. A product of Oregon
State, he had delayed his pro career one season because he felt he
wasn't big enough. But the blond safetyman soon became the best
defensive back on the team and lasted into the Jet regime.

A fine deal with Oakland turned up the late Dick Christy, a halfback. Tricky Dick, a hard-nosed, cocky pro, had some NFL experience. But Oakland coach Eddie Erdelatz, who'd come out of the
college ranks at Navy, wanted Boy Scout types. He should have kept
more Dick Christys. After losing his first two games of 1961 by a
combined score of 99–0, Erdelatz was fired. Christy wasn't fast and
he wasn't big, but he was tough in the open field. He still holds some
AFL punt return records.

Curley Johnson—Curley was his real name—proved another fine
pickup. He was cut early in the season by Dallas, and although not
classified as a true "original," he survived right up to the Super
Bowl. Curley had once been a flashy running back with the U. of
Houston. Now he was heavier and, on the field, at least, less flashy
than steady. He could fill in at tight end, halfback, and fullback; kick
off; punt a football into the clouds; and loosen up any tense situation
with a ribald remark. He was still doing all these things as the Jets
moved toward their confrontation with the Colts.

A hard-living linebacker named Hubert Bobo—a hero to lady fans
from coast to coast—showed up on another cut list. He played middle
linebacker and could knock the shoulder pads off any runner he could
reach. He couldn't reach too many, though. Bad knees. A slick safetyman named Lee Riley moved across the river when cut by the Giants,
and Bill Mathis, matured from 205 to 220 pounds, was virtually a
new man, too.

Mathis, a drawling Georgian out of Clemson, had his finest year
in 1961. He carried the ball more times than anybody in the league
and he gained more yardage than anybody except Houston superstar
Billy Cannon. He made the All-Star team, too. The players called
him Cymbals because he had bad hands and couldn't catch the ball.
But after a knee operation took away his speed, he transformed himself into an outstanding receiver and improved to become one of the

finest blockers in football. "That Mathis don't make no mistakes," was the appraisal.

A bachelor, he never got Joe Namath's publicity with the chicks, but there always seemed to be a Miss America candidate to meet him in every city. And a city boy he had become, settling down in New York as a stockbroker in the off-season. The kid from Manchester, Georgia, traveled a long road to the Super Bowl.

The Titans changed their training camp in 1961, from the U. of New Hampshire to the Bear Mountain Inn, a picturesque hour's drive from New York City. Nothing else changed. Instead of a nightmare train ride to Mobile, their exhibition fiasco was a bus trip to Boston on which the driver got lost. As usual, with Wismer on the scene, events off the field obscured the team's respectable 7–7 record and third-place divisional finish.

Baugh continued to criticize Wismer and events reached farce level by the second game of the season. The Titans had beaten Boston in their opener, 21–20, but then lost in Buffalo, 41–31, as the Bills' front line gave New York quarterback Al Dorow a terrific going-over. Late in the game, Dorow tried to scramble and was tackled at the sideline by Richie McCabe, a Buffalo defensive back. Dorow thought he had been tackled out of bounds, and in frustration as much as anything, he threw the football at McCabe. That's when the fight began. For an experienced player, Dorow had made a near-fatal mistake. He started the fight right in front of Buffalo's bench. Even Custer had better odds at Little Big Horn, and the Bills' burly coach, Buster Ramsey, was seen throwing a punch, too.

After the game, Baugh didn't exactly rush to Dorow's defense. How about the fight? "You've got to be stupid to start a fight near the other team's bench." How about the beating Dorow had taken from the Bills' pass rush? Had the blocking broken down? "It was Dorow's own fault," Baugh charged. "There are a lot of plays he could have called to keep the other team from rushing him like that. He should have called more running plays, too."

Later Baugh denied this was "second-guessing" his quarterback, but it sure sounded like it to a lot of people. (On occasion, Dorow would freely criticize his blockers, and once Baugh accused his quarterback of being more interested in protecting his record consecutive-game streak of touchdown passes than in winning games. It was not a happy relationship.)

The Bills were scheduled to visit New York on Thanksgiving Day, and the rematch would have been a natural attraction. In a typical Wismer ploy, the imaginative team president wired New York's police commissioner, demanding adequate protection at the Polo Grounds so his quarterback would not be attacked again. Buffalo owner Ralph Wilson then wired the commissioner: THE BUFFALO BILLS WELCOME NEW YORK'S FINEST ON THE FIELD AT THE GAME WITH THE TITANS THANKSGIVING MORNING AS LONG AS NONE OF THEM BLOCK, TACKLE OR CATCH PASSES.

It was hokum, but what the heck?

Wismer had a self-destructive streak, however. Just when the ballyhoo should have reached its peak, Wismer blew the game right off the sports pages. Word leaked out (from the NFL, of course) that the AFL had conducted a "secret" college draft to get a jump on the rival league. Wismer was called for confirmation. It was a good time to remain silent, but there was no way anybody could keep Harry Wismer from talking at 2 o'clock in the morning, which was when Lester Bromberg of the New York *World-Telegram and Sun* called him up. Wismer, recklessly, not only confirmed the draft but named his top six choices, headed by the late Ernie Davis, an outstanding Syracuse halfback.

If Wismer had kept his mouth shut, everything would have been all right. Now that the secret draft was no longer secret, AFL commissioner Joe Foss had to take action. Foss knew the AFL depended on colleges, not only for material but for access to scout that material. If AFL scouts were barred from campus and stadium, they would be at a fatal disadvantage. The former South Dakota governor and World War II Marine flying ace and Medal of Honor winner was the AFL's first commissioner. Maybe he didn't fathom all the fine print of a waiver rule, but he had assistants to take care of that. His job was to lend respectability to the shaky league, and he did just that. Now that fragile image—and his own, as well—was threatened. The colleges were screaming in protest. They feared, and with justification as it turned out, that pro teams would secretly sign players before the college season ended. Foss had to act. He voided the draft.

Wismer blew his top. He accused Foss of trying to wreck the league, of being an NFL agent. As "proof," Wismer pointed out that Foss had been proposed as commissioner by the Minneapolis group that had defected to the NFL before the new league's first season. He noted that Foss still had business connections with those men. He blamed him for the league's lower TV revenue in 1961, saying that Foss had almost been fired that summer, and should have been. He insisted he would go ahead and sign the players on his premature draft list.

On Thanksgiving Day morning, an announced crowd of only 12,023 showed up at the Polo Grounds to see the "grudge" match. The Titans won the game, 21–14, but the best show was in the press box, where Joe Foss, the commissioner everyone called by his first name, showed up to answer his critic at halftime. Of all the accusations, the one questioning his integrity hurt Foss the most. There were tears in his eyes as he answered Wismer's charges.

"For the good of the league, it would be a smart thing to get rid of Wismer," Foss said emotionally. "He's more interested in publicity, any kind of publicity, than in running a good operation. With the remarks he made blasting me the last day or so it is obvious he's out to get my pelt."

Foss said he had a year to go on his contract as commissioner and that he had to beat down Wismer's revolt or resign—"And I don't intend to resign."

(Despite Wismer's threats to get the commissioner's job, it was pretty obvious when the league held its winter meeting that Foss had the votes. "There's been some discussion about whether I'm doing a good job. Does anyone have anything to say?" Foss asked his owners. Nobody said a word. Even Wismer was silent, the upset of the year. When the meeting was over, Wismer posed for pictures lighting the commissioner's cigar. Harry only worried about tomorrow's press clippings.)

When the AFL went into its regular draft on December 2 in Dallas, Buffalo, picking ahead of the Titans, chose Ernie Davis. Wismer instructed general manager Steve Sebo to draft Davis, too. Poor Sebo had to go through this embarrassing charade for 45 minutes before changing to his No. 2 choice, Minnesota quarterback Sandy Stephens.

Wismer later said he planned to deal for the rights to Davis. "I doubt whether Buffalo can pay Davis what I offered him," Wismer said. That had to be the joke of the year, the cruelest irony being, of course, that Davis, who signed with Cleveland of the NFL, already was ill with leukemia and never played a minute of pro ball before his premature death.

Baugh exploded at all of Wismer's talk about Davis. He said Harry

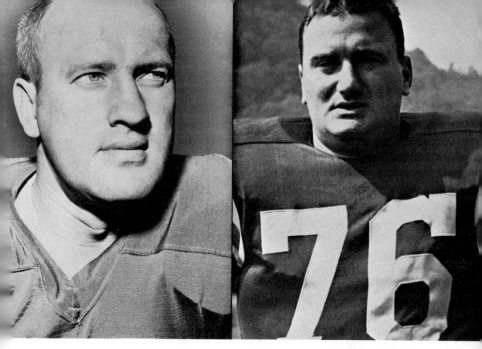

Al Dorow (left) and Sid Youngelman were Harry's men.

should concentrate on signing the players he had drafted instead of blowing smoke about a man who belonged to somebody else, especially when that somebody else, Buffalo owner Ralph Wilson, was a millionaire who could buy and sell Wismer as well as any dozen top college players. And Baugh revealed that Wismer, while proclaiming he had given Sebo a "blank check" to sign college players, would not let his general manager out of town to cash it.

By now, Wismer had determined to fire Baugh, but he needed an excuse. To provide justification, he called in three players who spilled their guts to a newspaper columnist. The three were quarterback Al Dorow and defensive tackles Tom Saidock and Sid Youngelman. All three were promised off-season jobs by Wismer, and he came through for Dorow and Youngelman. Saidock was lucky he didn't get the job. The other two ended up complaining Wismer didn't pay them what he'd promised, and all three ended up in Buffalo by way of trades before the next season.

The three players talked about the lack of organization on the club, the lack of a playbook, the fact that one of the assistant coaches, a particular friend of Baugh's, had fallen asleep during a film session.

The Titans then left town to close the 1961 season in Dallas. The team had no taxi squad—at one time, Dorow was the only healthy quarterback—and only 19 men on a squad of 33 were physically able to play.

Baugh's players were enraged at the three men they considered stool pigeons. Nobody spoke to any of them on the entire trip. There was nothing the others could do to the two tackles, but they decided to "open the gates" on quarterback Dorow and refuse to block for him. However, Baugh got word of this and called the team together. "I've heard what you're planning to do, and I'm asking you not to," Baugh said quietly. "The best thing you can do for me is go out and play the best game you can."

And so they did before losing by 35–24 to a tough Dallas team that would win the league championship the next year. The Titans were always to remember Baugh with affection. And they didn't forget Dorow, either.

7

Good-bye, Harry

A new cast of characters surrounded Harry Wismer as the Titans entered their third season in 1962. Steve Sebo, the general manager, had escaped to the relative serenity of the University of Virginia as director of athletics, and Wismer announced that Clyde (Bulldog) Turner, a former star center with the Chicago Bears, would be his new head coach.

Turner, coincidentally, had attended the same Texas high school as Baugh. At forty-two, he was a couple of years younger, and their careers at Sweetwater High had overlapped for only a season or two. They also had played against each other for years in the pros, and Turner certainly matched his predecessor as a football name. He had been an outstanding player at Hardin-Simmons College in Texas and then gone on to make pro football's Hall of Fame during the glory days of the Chicago Bears. Old-timers still talked with awe of Bulldog's feats of strength.

Big and beefy, Turner was as effusive as the lean Baugh was laconic, as malleable as Baugh was stubborn, and he loved company over a beer as much as Baugh shunned it. Turner had spent 13 seasons with the Bears as a player before joining their coaching staff. At that time it was thought he might eventually succeed venerable George Halas, who also owned the team, as head coach. But when Wismer found him, Turner was out of football.

Wismer announced that Turner would be given a two-year contract at $28,000 a year, the same salary as Baugh, and also would handle the duties of general manager. Baugh, who had a year to go on his contract, would be retained as a "consultant." Later, capable and refreshing George Sauer was named backfield coach. Bones Taylor and John Del Isola of Baugh's staff were kept on because they, too, had been operating under three-year contracts.

Everybody took Wismer's announcements at face value, a dan-

Clyde (Bulldog) Turner

gerous thing to do, until the Titans reported to training camp at East Stroudsberg (Pennsylvania) State College. It was their third training base in as many years. Apparently—an old Depression joke—it was cheaper to move than to pay rent. Needless to add, Wismer also had changed press agents, hiring Murray Goodman, one of the best in New York, as "assistant to the president."

The Titans hadn't even completely unpacked in training camp when Goodman and the other newcomers realized what they had let themselves in for. For guess who showed up at East Stroudsberg ready to go to work? Sammy Baugh. Wismer had never officially notified him that he had been fired!

Baugh's contract specified that he was to serve as head coach, so this consultant business was a fraud, too. Wismer apparently had hoped that Baugh would not show up in July so he could accuse Sammy of breaching his contract. That way he might avoid paying him off. But Baugh was on to his old boss. He refused to be slickered out of his third year's salary and he was man enough to swallow some pride to get it. Wismer had refused Baugh's phone calls all winter and spring, and he refused to meet him now. Baugh vowed publicly that he would be on the field every day—as head coach—until the matter was settled. A really sticky situation was avoided only because Sam and Bulldog had been friends for more than twenty years. It took several days, all of Goodman's persuasion, and intervention by commissioner Foss before Wismer finally settled Baugh's contract.

In the months before camp opened, Wismer also had realized that Turner would have trouble enough just being a coach without the added responsibilities of general manager. So he gave the title to Sauer, a college football Hall of Famer out of Nebraska and later a respected coach at Kansas, Baylor, and Navy. This meant that Sauer, who worked under Turner as backfield coach, was on the other hand over Turner as general manager. As it was, the arrangement made more sense than a lot of things that year.

Al Dorow, the quarterback who'd turned on Baugh, was still with the club when camp opened. But he was feuding with Wismer over his off-season wages, walked out of training camp briefly, and soon was sent off to join Saidock and Youngelman in a trade with Buffalo. Wismer, incidentally, almost queered the deal by announcing it prematurely. Harry loved to announce big trades. It was a weakness of his. Some of the deals he made up for the press were better than real ones.

Once again the Titans closed out their exhibition schedule and opened the regular season with a West Coast trip. In their final preseason game, they lost to San Diego, 14–9, for a 0–4 practice record. Wismer was furious. Since he considered the team an extension of himself, the Titans could never lose because they (meaning he) were inadequate. Their losses could only be explained as the result of plots to betray him. He accused his players of lying down against the Chargers and refused to pay them the $50 for an exhibition appearance stipulated by league rules.

The veteran players, who often had been forced to wait for paychecks in the past, saw an ominously familiar pattern developing. They wanted to make an issue of the payment right then. But Sauer counseled patience. Besides, what could the players do, stranded more than 2,000 miles from home?

The next week the Titans were to open their season in Oakland and the Raiders were as feeble as the Titans. Prospects were good for a victory that would appease Wismer and they became even brighter with the arrival of a groovy, long-haired quarterback named Lee Grosscup.

Lee Grosscup

Grosscup, handsome, glib, and literate, had been stamped and sealed for greatness off one college game in his junior year. He was the quarterback when the University of Utah came to West Point to play Army. Even though his team lost, Grosscup had a great day, filling the autumn air with footballs thrown long and accurately. It was a perfect spot for a showcase. Army always draws national coverage, especially at home, and dozens of big-city newspapermen from nearby New York wrote glowing accounts of Grosscup's passing. Also in the stands was Allie Sherman, then a Giant assistant. Sherman, later to become head coach, saw in Grosscup the once-in-a-decade passer who can make good teams into champions. Although Lee played little as a senior at Utah—he was hurt and a new coach changed the offense—Sherman's scouting report was remembered. Grosscup became the Giants' No. 1 draft choice for the 1959 season.

Lee's Giant experience was a nightmare of unfulfillment. A magazine article he wrote appeared in print just as his first training camp opened and antagonized all the veterans. None of them would so much as talk to him. And Sherman grew increasingly disenchanted with Grosscup's glib ways, so different from his own intensity. Lee refused to conform and spent three nonplaying years on the Giant squad. However, he remained a hero to many New York fans, probably because he was never given any opportunity to disillusion them. Early in the 1962 training camp, the Giants dealt him off to Minnesota, and just before their opener, the Vikings cut him, too.

The Titans had to surrender a draft choice to Denver for the rights to Grosscup and then they went after him. At least Sauer and Goodman did. At this point, Wismer was refusing to talk to his two aides. He would speak only to Turner, and Bulldog was afraid to call him. Grosscup also had offers from Canadian teams, and precious hours passed before the Titans received transcontinental approval to sign Grosscup. (By this time, Wismer's apartment building had been torn down. He moved to a suite in the Hotel Chatham and continued to operate his ball club from the living room.)

Signing Grosscup was a great coup, and Goodman introduced his new property with a gala press conference in San Francisco. Lee joined the Titans on a Friday and determined to play in Sunday's opener. Given a cram course in Turner's rudimentary offense, Grosscup came off the bench and threw touchdown passes the first two times he handled the ball, one an 80-yarder to Art Powell. Later he completed another TD pass of 64 yards to Powell in the 28–17 victory. It was a stunning introduction and that week everybody got paid.

The next week, however, was another nightmare as the Titans moved on to San Diego to practice for Sunday's game with the Chargers. The midweek highlight came when a local bus company, stiffed by Wismer the previous year, left the players stranded at their practice field. They had to hitchhike back to the motel. That Sunday they were crushed by the Chargers, 40–14.

Pro football rules require that players be paid within 24 hours after a game. Most teams hand out paychecks in the dressing room after the final gun, but Wismer always took every minute of his 24 hours. And since players always got Monday off, the actual payday for the Titans was Tuesday.

However, when the Titans returned to New York after a wild boozy flight from the San Diego debacle, the players were anxious for their checks. They were home now and needed the money to move their families to New York and rent apartments. Several optimists showed up at Wismer's suite on Monday only to be told, "The checks aren't quite ready." On Tuesday, Wismer ordered a heavy workout, watched the boys practice on the New York University campus, and then departed. He left no paychecks behind, only cursing, muttering ball-players.

"Don't worry, they're coming," Sauer told Larry Grantham, the defensive captain and player representative. "Yeah, so's Christmas," snapped the star linebacker, who happened to work in a bank during the off-season.

After practice, Bob Mischak, the All-Star guard, called a players' meeting. They voted to complain to the league office and gave Wismer a deadline of noon Wednesday to come up with their money. "Regardless of whether we win or lose, we're still supposed to get paid," Mischak, captain of the offensive platoon, told Turner, who seemed to shrink physically with every new crisis.

A picture day had been scheduled on Wednesday and the players agreed to pose for press photographers while waiting for high noon. The deadline passed but no checks arrived. They did show up an hour later, but by this time the players had dressed and it was too late to practice.

To make the situation worse, this was a "short" week. The Titans were scheduled in Buffalo on Saturday night instead of the usual Sunday afternoon. Wismer then took the incredible mess and turned it into near-disaster. If the players wouldn't practice, his coaches wouldn't coach. He wired all staff members not to participate in Thursday's workout on threat of being fired. George Sauer, retained by the Jets as director of player personnel and now general manager of the Patriots, still has that unbelievable telegram.

When the players reported on Thursday, Turner read them the telegram and disappeared. However, Sauer appealed to the players' pride as professionals in a short pep talk. "Go out on the field and have the best practice you ever had," he told them—and they did.

Devising their own game plan under the leadership of Mischak and Grantham—two players who with Sauer, Goodman, Bones Taylor, and John Del Isola kept the foundering franchise afloat—the Titans went up to Buffalo and won the game, 17–6! Overlooked in that excitement was a footnote to the previous season. Early in the second quarter, the Titans staged an all-out pass rush against their old friend, Al Dorow. Dorow got the pass away for a completion but then was buried by the onrushing line. When they unpiled, Dorow's throwing arm was seriously and painfully injured. His career was ended.

The season was an artistic as well as financial failure. The only highlights were Grosscup's debut, the strike victory at Buffalo, a shocking 23–3 upset over San Diego, and a wild 46–45 Thanksgiving Day victory at Denver. With Bill Mathis hurt most of the season, the Titans were last in team rushing and next to last in scoring even though in Powell, Maynard, and Christy they had the top three pass receivers in their division. Their record was 5–9 and they were last in the Eastern Division.

Turner was in over his head, and following the popular Baugh didn't make it any easier for him. He pleaded with players to suggest plays and he wanted only to be liked. The 1962 season produced some interesting characters though, such as Alex Kroll, Hayseed Stephens, Ed Sprinkle, and Jim Tiller, the latter billed optimistically as Tiller the Thriller. Kroll was an All-American center out of nearby Rutgers, the highest draft choice the Titans ever signed. They picked him No. 2 and signed him because he wanted an advertising career and this was the closest team to Madison Avenue interested in his services. He actually sought out the Titans, instead of the other way around.

Hayseed Stephens was a rookie quarterback out of Hardin-Simmons, Turner's alma mater. He had been playing for a minor league team when the Titans picked him up at midseason. Only five feet eleven, or less, he was too short for his position, although he could scramble a bit. He did make one notable contribution, however, during a game in Dallas. A fight broke out between Titan linebacker Jerry Fields and Texan halfback Abner Haynes, and soon a dozen players from both sides were flailing away. After the melee, officials searched for somebody to throw out of the game. The Titans had no spare linebackers, making Fields unexpendable, so quick-thinking Hubert Bobo fingered innocent Hayseed as the culprit. The nonplussed third-stringer was ejected and the Titans were able to continue playing eleven men on defense.

Sprinkle was a former teammate of Turner's with the Chicago Bears, a defensive lineman rated as the meanest hatchet man in the NFL. He just showed up one day, drinking beer on a road trip with Turner. Later it was learned he had been coaching in the minors, had lost his job, and was now a Titan assistant. Keeping Turner company appeared to be his major responsibility.

And then there was Tiller the Thriller, a 165-pound rookie halfback from Purdue. Tiller was fast and Tiller was shifty, but he never seemed to realize the object of the game was to run *toward* the opponent's goal. He would scramble from sideline to sideline, thrilling the crowd

. . . and then get thrown for a 20-yard loss. He couldn't block and he couldn't catch the ball. As a football player, he was a total loss.

But Tiller the Thriller had one great fan where it counted, the second Mrs. Wismer. (Harry had been "secretly" married that summer to the widow of racketeer Longie Zwillman; the best man, of all people, being commissioner Joe Foss.) Mrs. Wismer thought the Thriller was sensational and insisted the Titans put him back on the roster after he had been cut early in the season. One day the Wismers attended practice and Harry asked Turner to see if he could break Tiller loose on a long run for the benefit of his bride. So Bulldog gave the defense a wink and everybody fell down. The players were surprised that it still didn't take Tiller two plays to score.

Wismer's financial problems deepened as his team hit bottom on the field. The Titans had drawn more than 100,000 fans each of their first two seasons, but in 1962 they managed only a total of 36,161 for all seven home games. The stock market break of 1962 not only had diminished Wismer's stockholdings but also strapped any friends to whom he might have gone for backing. He was in a corner, living for his guarantee checks from road games until the Internal Revenue Service started grabbing them for back taxes. Even the ploy of naming the wealthy Mrs. Wismer as president of the club after eight games failed to improve the Titans' financial picture.

The situation came to a head after the ninth game. Wismer had ignored a lot of bills and juggled a lot of checks, but now he had a payroll to meet and no money. He issued payroll checks anyway and they bounced and now the whole matter became public knowledge. The league had to step in, make the checks good, and then take over financial responsibility for the team for the rest of the season.

Wismer was given three weeks to sell the team, but he proved a lot more dangerous on an open field than Tiller the Thriller. He produced phantom purchasers by the platoon, threatened countersuits by the dozen, and changed lawyers more often than he had changed press agents. Each maneuver gained him more time and made the league more desperate for a resolution. The season had ended and Wismer still owned the team. It was time to draw up schedules for 1963, including the all-important television programming. The status of the New York franchise had to be settled.

Wismer finally was produced in federal bankruptcy court in downtown New York's Foley Square. The hearing was impeccably choreographed. An army of creditors stood in turn and recited what the

Titans owed them. An open secret then was revealed. Commissioner Joe Foss had been working behind the scenes to find a buyer. He had succeeded. There was an offer of $1,000,000 to buy the franchise but it would expire within hours. Would the creditors accept the offer even though it wouldn't pay them off 100 cents on the dollar? The favorable vote was unanimous.

Wismer, however, went down fighting. He reluctantly agreed to the sale, if some securities he had used as collateral for loans would be returned to him. The bank, anxious as anyone to get the mess over with, agreed.

The new owners were announced as a five-man syndicate headed by David A. (Sonny) Werblin, leading Wismer to sneer, "How old do you have to be before people stop calling you Sonny?" It was Harry's last living headline. His health and spirit broken, Wismer would show up at an occasional Jet game over the next several years. He died December 4, 1967, of injuries incurred when he fell down a flight of steps at four in the morning. He was fifty-six.

8

Sonny

When Sonny Werblin took over New York's hollow-shell AFL franchise, most sports fans responded with a drowsy, "Who?" But in the world of entertainment, Werblin's arena, he was one of the backstage giants. In this world, a titan like Frank Sinatra chooses his friends and his enemies. But one day, in a bull session about show business personalities, Sinatra's name came up and Werblin snapped, "I don't speak to him," leaving no doubt as to who had stopped talking to whom over an old business dispute.

It was show business that actually brought Werblin and the AFL together. The likable, well-groomed executive was president of the Music Corporation of America's television arm. MCA, a vast entertainment complex, served as the AFL's original agent in negotiating the first television package. Through this connection, Werblin grew to know pro football and to become aware of its tremendous growth potential. And AFL commissioner Joe Foss became aware of the dynamic Werblin. When the Titans collapsed, Foss approached Werblin about buying the club.

Werblin saw pro football as *the* growing sport. He was convinced New York could support two teams. With a strong New York entry, the future of the AFL would be assured and television revenues would boom. He was hooked.

As Werblin began rounding up partners for the venture, other groups were also approached by Foss, while some in turn approached the commissioner. Although Mrs. Charles Shipman Payson, owner of the baseball Mets, personally was "appalled" at suggestions she get into pro football, her financial advisers were not so overwhelmed. They knew Shea Stadium would need a football house team. The Mets would be the prime tenants when the stadium opened, but they realized the success of any new facility depended on getting people in the habit of going there for entertainment in season and out. M. Donald Grant,

David A. (Sonny) Werblin

Met board chairman and keeper of Mrs. Payson's share of the Whitney millions, held conversations with Foss about the Titans. Although the Met group later backed off, they probably still would have taken the team as a last resort.

Other groups also talked of rescuing the franchise if certain conditions could be met, the most frequently mentioned being the hiring of Green Bay miracle worker and majordomo, Vince Lombardi, to run the operation.

Werblin, however, brooked no if-money in his little group, which was made up of old friends who also were associates at Monmouth Park, a New Jersey racetrack. In addition to Werblin, the syndicate consisted of Leon Hess, a shy millionaire who spent most of his time scurrying around the world to build his Hess Oil Company into a giant; Townsend B. Martin, banker, horse breeder, and convivial member of an old and monied family; and Philip H. Iselin, white-haired, blue-eyed, and deceptively self-effacing garment industry tycoon.

Later, Donald C. Lillis, a stockbroker and self-made millionaire who had been involved in the Met group that had been seeking the Titans, asked to be invited in. Lillis also had horse racing connections as president of Bowie Race Course in Maryland. Werblin, Hess and Martin each owned 23½ percent of the team, Lillis 19½ percent, and Iselin 10 percent.

It was agreed from the beginning that Werblin would be president and operating head of the team. His partners couldn't have picked a better man to handle their money. Financial success had been Werblin's trademark from his college days at Rutgers. Born on St. Patrick's Day, March 17, 1910, Werblin, who is Jewish, adopted Irish green as his color scheme. Green, of course, is also the color of money, a coincidence not lost on anyone.

Werblin was center on the undefeated 1927 football team at Brooklyn's James Madison High and later played freshman ball at Rutgers until a broken shoulder ended his career. (Later, as an interested alumnus and university trustee, Werblin was to advise Rutgers' All-American Alex Kroll to sign with the Titans.)

The broken shoulder didn't stop Werblin's off-field activities, though. He became a campus correspondent for nine New York and New Jersey metropolitan newspapers and soon was operating a small syndicate of his own, farming out some of the lesser assignments to other students. He also found time to form a statewide high school debating league, which still exists. That brought in spending money, too.

When Werblin left Rutgers in 1931 in the teeth of the Depression, he literally had to take a cut in salary, and the school, incidentally, decreed that henceforth no student would be allowed to monopolize the campus correspondence jobs.

Werblin first went to work for the New York *Times* as a copyboy. After a short time he was given a small raise, quite an achievement in an era of layoffs and salary slashes. Werblin actually might have ended up a newspaperman writing about teams like the Jets, but one day he happened to learn the salary of the managing editor of the *Times*. When he realized how little that awesome figure actually got paid for his lofty position, that was the end of Sonny Werblin, Cub Reporter. He quit the *Times* and joined a struggling new company called Music Corporation of America as a $21-a-week office boy. There is a story, probably apocryphal, that soon after joining the company, Werblin went into the president and asked if a few dollars a week could be deducted from his meager salary toward stock purchases in MCA

It was a page right out of *How to Succeed in Business Without Really Trying* but nobody ever accused the strong-willed Werblin of not trying. He brought dedication and outstanding ability to MCA, and both he and the company prospered. He soon was promoted to "band boy" on the road with Guy Lombardo, which meant he guarded the instruments, set up the music, and went out for the coffee. He began booking acts for MCA in 1934 and became the greatest agent in show business history. He's the pioneer credited with making a maligned profession respectable. He took the 10 percenters out of flashy racetrack clothes and dressed them in banker's gray. When Werblin retired from MCA-TV in 1965 to devote full time to the Jets, *Variety,* the show business trade paper, called him the broadcasting industry's "greatest promoter and salesman."

He was also a shrewd, hard businessman. The NFL might have been warned of its new adversary by checking Madison Avenue gossips for the story of one of Werblin's major TV coups. *Wagon Train,* a Western series, had been one of the National Broadcasting Company's most successful programs for years. It was an MCA package, and Werblin was the only man who noted the small print in the contract which specified that NBC soon had to exercise its option to renew the show. The deadline was fast approaching. NBC apparently considered the whole matter a technicality until its executives woke up one morning and discovered Werblin had sold *Wagon Train* to the rival American Broadcasting Company for substantially more money. Werblin then went back to NBC and sold the network a new show, *The Virginian,* to replace the one he had lifted.

When the AFL-NFL war reached the alley-fighting stage, Werblin knew all about "playing out options."

A perfectionist, Werblin was to supervise every aspect of Jet operations. "I'm my own general manager," he would confide, referring to his role in signing players. He was also his own publicity man and, especially after Joe Namath came on the scene, a father figure for selected favorite players. If the complex electronic message board at Shea Stadium flashed a typographical error, within seconds he was on the private phone in his box raging at his aides to find out what had happened.

And behind the big bonuses for players and splashy press parties, he ran one of the financially tightest ships in the league. One year he refused to spring for a press guide until threatened by a league fine. And in the early days, while sportswriters were being taken out to dinner at the posh 21 Club, employees in one back-room department had to spread their lunch period out over several hours. There were three of them—and only two desks. If somebody was always out to lunch, they could get their work done.

Critics—and he had 'em—called Werblin "a Harry Wismer with money." Other critics tempered their evaluation. He was Harry Wismer "with class."

Class he had, and he endowed his football team and the whole league with big helpings of that precious commodity. The purchase of the bankrupt franchise was announced to the press on March 15, 1963, two days before St. Patrick's Day, Werblin's fifty-third birthday. Naturally, the new colors were green.

9

Weeb's Underground Railroad

When Sonny Werblin took over actual direction of the newly christened Jets in late March of 1963, he realized his first task would be to build an image. Then he could build his football team. Despite their new ownership and new name, the Jets would have trouble signing players and even finding a training camp in those early days. People who had been burned by those rubber checks remembered the odor.

So the first edict issued by the new president was to ban any reference to the old Titans. As far as Werblin was concerned, the Jets were starting fresh. Werblin's second step was to hire a publicity director to help mold that new image. The man he chose was Joe Cahill, highly regarded sports information director at West Point. To Werblin, there was nothing incongruous about putting the headline before the horses. And, of course, one did require a press agent to announce the hiring of a new coach. (The second year of Turner's contract was immediately bought up.)

It took only a few weeks for Werblin to get his man. Talking one night to noted sports columnist Jimmy Cannon, Werblin was reminded that Weeb Ewbank was available. Weeb had recently been fired by the Baltimore Colts and would be just sitting around to collect on the rest of his contract for the next two years. Cannon thought Ewbank would rather be coaching.

Werblin dropped all the other names on his list and sat down with Baltimore owner Carroll Rosenbloom to work out a settlement on Weeb's contract. When Weeb insisted on being general manager as well as head coach, Werblin gave him the dual title. The big stumbling block was Ewbank's charming wife, Lucy. She just didn't want to move to the big, bad city of New York. But Werblin and his wife, Leah Ray, turned on their own charm and showed Mrs. Ewbank some of the New York area's suburban greenery. That did the trick. Weeb,

Weeb Ewbank

who had built the Colts into champions from similarly unprepossessing beginnings, signed a three-year contract for $100,000.

After looking over the Jet roster and realizing that every worthwhile draft choice had been lost, all Ewbank could tell the press was, "I've seen sicker cows get well."

Ewbank was a lot more complex person than his easy smile and ready supply of down-home homilies would lead New Yorkers to believe. He had been a standout athlete at Miami of Ohio, that incubator of top football coaches, and played some professional baseball on the side. A quarterback in college, he played just ahead of Paul Brown, the man who brought him into pro coaching with the Cleveland Browns. Weeb always had a great feeling for quarterbacks and would protect his field leader to the end, even if it meant criticizing other players to do it. Fundamentals and organization, two Paul Brown trademarks, were Ewbank's strength, discipline and motivation his weakness. Today's sophisticated players did not always respond to his grade-school-primer approach. He was a better coach with "yes-sir, no-sir" rookies than with veterans. Inability to handle the veterans was given as the reason the Colts let him go.

Basically, Weeb was still a Hoosier schoolteacher from Richmond, Indiana. If he had one unvoiced regret, it was that his choice of profession required him to leave the Midwest and seek success in the big cities of the East. Behind his amiable façade were those other intrinsic traits of the small-town Midwest character—a belief in the basic virtues and shrewdness, suspicion, caution, respect for a dollar, and a desire to be liked.

If you checked the background of Ewbank's associates, there usually would be a thread leading back to some common experience. (When Ewbank signed an unknown new director of player personnel after the Super Bowl, it turned out the man had coached against Weeb in high schools thirty years before.) Ewbank had the same feeling for players. A youngster he had drafted out of college, no matter how far removed, always kept a special place in his affection. It was no accident that he waited until his first season was almost over to claim another AFL player on waivers and that in his first seven years as Jet coach he made only one really major shake-the-roster trade. His early camps were cluttered with players Ewbank remembered from the NFL and the Colts.

Ewbank would cautiously construct his fireplace one brick at a time. There were no shortcuts for Weeb, but once built, it would draw well and it would last. It was no accident that his imprint remained so clear on the Super Bowl Colts six years after he left them.

George Sauer was retained as Jet talent scout, and Ewbank then put together one of the youngest and brightest coaching staffs in pro football. All in their early thirties, they were Clive Rush, Walt Michaels, J. D. Donaldson, and Chuck Knox. Only Michaels, a longtime all-pro linebacker with the Cleveland Browns, had extensive professional playing experience. (Rush had played a year at Green Bay before going into coaching. His roommate with the Packers was Babe Parilli.) And Michaels, who had just been let go after one season as an assistant at Oakland, was the only man with a pro coaching background. He and Sauer, who spent most of his time scouting colleges, were the only two with firsthand knowledge of the AFL.

The Jets were so short of talent that Ewbank scheduled a public tryout camp at Van Cortlandt Park in the Bronx and even took several players from that group to the Peekskill Military Academy training site for a second look. The AFL also held an "equalization draft" to enable the Jets and Oakland to pick up a couple of rookie players each from the other clubs.

(Oakland was in even worse shape than New York. The Raiders had won only one game the year before and were in danger of losing their franchise. The same year Weeb was hired by the Jets, Oakland named young Al Davis as head coach and general manager. Davis, a slicker from New York City, was different from Weeb in every way. He took all the shortcuts Ewbank spurned, including the signing of Titan end Art Powell, who had just played out his option. Davis picked up every AFL reject he thought could help his "Foreign Legion" and made the Super Bowl a year ahead of Weeb. Future years will tell which man built more soundly.)

During Ewbank's first summer, he made two player transactions that would reveal the path he planned to take. Bob Mischak, a three-time All-League guard, was traded to Oakland for Dan Ficca, a second-year pro who hadn't even been a regular when the Raiders won only one game in fourteen the year before. The trade stunned everyone close to the team. It appeared Ewbank just wanted to get rid of an older Titan who was also one of the clubhouse leaders. Ficca lasted long enough to get his pension as a journeyman regular. Mischak gave Oakland three good years before returning to West Point as an assistant coach.

After unloading Mischak, Ewbank made a deal with San Diego fo

Dick Wood (left) and Sherman Plunkett, two of Weeb's old boys.

tackle Sherman Plunkett, first of many "old boys" brought in that summer. Plunkett, obtained for a draft choice, was an awesome physical specimen. He stood six feet two and weighed upwards of 300 pounds. Yet he could move like a giant cat and he was almost impassable on pass blocking. Plunkett had been drafted out of Maryland State by the Browns in 1956 and then moved on to Baltimore in 1958, where he was a swing tackle on Ewbank's championship teams. He joined the Chargers in 1961, but San Diego coach Sid Gillman soon tired of telling Plunkett to lose weight.

"I've always told Sherman that if he got down to two eighty-five he'd be an All-League tackle. I still think so," Ewbank said optimistically. Plunkett, the beef rippling down the back of his neck, was a good-humored fat man and a pretty fair football player. But he never got even a distant glimpse of that 285 pounds Weeb was always talking about.

At first, the Jets had no scale that would register over 300 pounds, and Ewbank would joke he checked Plunkett's weight by how hard the arrow hit the upper register. Later they did find a freight scale and Plunkett showed up the summer of 1967 weighing 343 pounds. By this time he was thirty-three years old. His legs had been carrying too much weight too long, and they gave out in the middle of the '67 season. Defensive ends were blowing by him on their pass rush, something that never happened before. In addition to his physical stature, Plunkett was one of the leaders of the Jets' Negro players. When he reported still overweight for 1968, Ewbank publicly fined him, drummed him off the starting team, and then summarily cut him. Plunkett had been fat a long time. His mistake was still being fat when there was a rookie in camp (Sam Walton) ready to replace him.

The Jets went into that first camp with only two quarterbacks, John Green and Lee Grosscup, the 1962 incumbents, coming back from knee injuries.

The quarterback story that season had a full measure of human interest. Green had gutted out the last part of 1962 with two bad knees and was what you'd picture a pro football player to be—tough, lean, and taciturn. As for Grosscup, well, he at least was lean and he had that powerful arm. He'd hurt his knee several games after that spectacular 1962 debut in Oakland and kept trying to play off and on with little success. He might have been the star to save Wismer's franchise, but he couldn't do it on one leg.

Now, up at Peekskill, an old community nestled on the Hudson River some 50 miles north of New York City, he was trying again. But this time the arm wasn't there. Grosscup claimed it wasn't sore, but he wasn't throwing the ball with the zip of past days, either.

There was good reason for him to conceal any injury: he desperately needed to stay with the Jets. He had just written a book on his 1962 travels and travails—from Giants to Vikings to Titans—and sales and a possible postfootball career would hinge on how well he did with the new Jets. The book, entitled *Fourth and One,* was scheduled to come out with the opening of the football season. Grosscup didn't even last until publication date.

In his third-floor dormitory room he discussed his future with a reporter after learning he'd been cut. He could go here, he could go there, he'd never really had a chance to find out if he was a football player. Lee was pursuing a rainbow. It would be years before he would recognize it, in the bush leagues of football, his life a shambles. Interviews for those "cut" stories are always painful, and as the reporter turned to leave, Grosscup called out, "By the way, review copies of my book were sent out this week. Did you get yours yet?"

Green, the other quarterback, survived a little bit longer, and then

Ewbank reached into the past for another "old boy." His name was Dick Wood, a spindly six feet five with a powerful throwing arm and five knee operations. Wood hadn't even been a regular in college, but he taxied with the Colts for two years under Ewbank and then drifted around the AFL for a couple of seasons. He'd be promoted off the taxi squad in places like San Diego and Denver only when the regulars were injured. With his taped and braced knees, Wood physically resembled a stork, and a San Diego reporter once wrote, "Every time he runs, he scares me to death."

But when Weeb learned he could get Wood as a free agent, he grabbed him. For one thing—as an intelligent schoolteacher with a master's degree in education—he knew Weeb's system thoroughly from his days in Baltimore, and the Jet opener was less than a week off. For another, Wood could throw a long pass and Ewbank would just build his offense around Wood's undeniable, if limited, talent.

Wood was a fine young man. He was called on for more than he was physically able to produce in the New York spotlight. But he bore the burden and the boos for two seasons with dignity. Where the Jets would have been without him is distressing to contemplate.

Weeb's attitude toward Wood reveals another of the coach's strong points. Whatever Weeb has—that's the greatest. Publicly, and even privately, Weeb would rave about Wood's skills, starting with that acknowledged "strongest arm in football." When the rigid-thinking quarterback was unable to communicate with free-lancing Don Maynard, it was Maynard whom Weeb criticized and threatened to send away in a deal. Weeb's quarterback was, and is, always right. Only after he traded him did Weeb admit, "Wood isn't the kind of quarterback you win championships with."

Ewbank also wanted a new quarterback to play behind Wood, and he got one to replace Green a week after the season opened. The new QB's name was Galen Hall, and he was a short, dumpy, balding twenty-three-year-old out of Penn State who had just been cut after two seasons with Washington.

Weeb brought Hall into camp under utmost secrecy. For some reason he thought somebody would want to beat him out. He refused even to reveal his name until he'd signed him to a contract. But reporters have ways of ferreting things out, so one writer printed a story fully detailing Hall's background, including his date of birth, dimensions, and 1962 statistics. He just didn't mention his name.

Hall was five feet ten and weighed 216 pounds. He was a nervous eater. What he worried about, mostly, was having to play, because he knew he wasn't in shape. The more he worried about not being in condition, the more compulsively he ate and the worse shape he got in, which, of course, made him worry . . . and eat . . . all the more. "Whatever you do, don't get hurt," he would plead with Wood during the season.

When the inevitable happened, three games from the end of the season, Hall had to play. Exposed, as he feared he would be, he retired after the final game. With the scoreboard still flashing a 48–0 defeat in freezing 9-degree weather in Kansas City, he admitted, "I'm just not good enough." Galen Hall may not have been a heroic figure, but he was smart enough . . . and man enough . . . to turn his back on the rainbow.

Former Colts kept streaming into Peekskill right up until the opening game kickoff. Most were duds, some survived for a year as stopgaps, but a few turned out to be gems. Two of them, defensive back Bill Baird and tackle Winston Hill, were starters in the Super Bowl, and two others, end Bake Turner and fullback Mark Smolinski, were valuable and versatile subs who played key roles as regulars during Weeb's building years.

Baird, a little fellow out of San Francisco State, had laid out a season after finishing college and had gone into teaching. The season of 1962 Ewbank had brought his Baltimore team out to play San Francisco and Baird worked out with the Colts one day. When Weeb saw the little tiger sticking with the likes of All-Pro Raymond Berry, he invited Baird to camp the next season.

By the time Baird arrived at Baltimore, however, Ewbank was gone. But Don Shula still gave him a good long look, keeping him until the final cut. The man who beat Baird out was Jerry Logan, a fourth-round draft choice that season who was bigger and deemed more ready for NFL competition. Baird, with no bitterness, moved up the Eastern Seaboard to New York to join his original discoverer, Weeb Ewbank. He arrived two days before the opener and became a regular about halfway through the game.

Hill, a six-foot-four, 253-pound former tennis captain out of Texas Southern, had been drafted in the eleventh round by Ewbank and the Colts. He was doing well in training camp, real well, and after one rough scrimmage, all his teammates congratulated him. "Man, you've made the team," they told him, and they were glad because Winston Hill is a very likable guy.

The next day coach Don Shula called Hill into his office. Winston expected the best; he heard the worst. The Colts' No. 1 draft choice, Bob Vogel, had just joined the club from the College All-Star squad. Vogel also played tackle. The Colts couldn't keep both. They were committed to Vogel and they had seen enough of Hill to know he was at least a year away. The Colts were very nice, but Hill's release was final, and the next day he, too, booked passage on Ewbank's Underground Railroad from Baltimore.

Hill wasn't exactly an instant success with the Jets. In fact, they eventually cut him, too, and wanted to send him home to Texas. Hill just refused to go. He pleaded with Ewbank to let him stick around on the taxi squad for no pay in hopes he could learn enough to make it next year. Impressed by the big youngster's tenacity, Ewbank relented. A couple of games into the season, line coach Chuck Knox thought Hill was at least ready to play on special teams. Winston proved a destroyer on the so-called suicide squads, and when Jack Klotz, a holdover Titan, was hurt, Hill moved into the starting lineup. He never left it.

Away from the Peekskill training camp, Werblin was as busy as Weeb. He bought advertising space all over town and he ordered a radio campaign to promote the new Jets. The punchline for these commercials featured a nasal New Yorker named "Jet-Set Janie" asking, "What kind of name is Weeb?" The Jets needed all the promotion they could get. Their players were unknowns and they would be stuck for another season in Harry Wismer's graveyard, the decaying Polo Grounds. Shea Stadium wouldn't be ready for another year.

Werblin realized his players' morale needed a lift, too. "You'd tell people your name and they wouldn't know you. Then you'd say you played for the Titans and they'd laugh," linebacker Larry Grantham was to recall.

One day at Peekskill, Werblin saw the equipment manager, Nick Torman, patching up a pair of shoulder pads with adhesive tape. "What are you doing?" Werblin bellowed so all the players could hear. "Throw them out. Nobody on the Jets uses secondhand equipment!"

This later became one of Werblin's favorite stories.

Sonny also would make all road trips with the team, another way of letting them know they had an owner who cared. This was just before jet plane charters became available. Some of those piston flights were backbreakers—the team might spend eight hours from New York to Denver with a stopover for fuel in Omaha.

The Jets lost their opening game in Boston, 38–14, but nobody was too disheartened. Ewbank had made 23 personnel changes the week before the game, including the unretirement of his defensive line coach, Walt Michaels. A couple of linebackers were hurt and some newcomers weren't ready yet, so Michaels played the whole game against the Patriots. Michaels was thirty-four and hadn't played since the 1961 season, but he didn't do badly. Still, he didn't press his luck. He retired for good after that one game.

Wood, who'd been with the team for only two practice sessions before the opener, threw four interceptions but came back to spark a three-game winning streak that propelled the surprising Jets right into the Eastern Division title race. (Although they were to win only two more games after that spurt, the Jets were never far off the pace, thanks to the early cushion and the fact that this was a bad year for the Eastern Division. Boston and Buffalo played off for first place with 7-6-1 records.)

The highlight of the streak was the first victory, achieved at home by a 24–17 score over Houston. This was the first time a New York team had ever beaten the Oilers. The big play was the 97-yard return of a short Houston field goal attempt by Marshall Starks. Starks, from the U. of Illinois, had been drafted by the NFL Cardinals the year before. They cut him, however, because of his nonchalant attitude. He rode a bus to New York from his job in a Rockford, Illinois, YMCA to make the Van Cortlandt Park tryout. According to Ewbank, that 97-yard touchdown run was the worst thing ever to happen to Starks. Suddenly he was a hero again, and the rest of the season was a carefree anticlimax. The next year he broke his leg and then sloughed off the therapy program that might have saved his career. He could have been an exciting pro.

The Jets, who were to have trouble winning on the road until their championship season, then carried their three-game winning streak to the West Coast for their annual two-game series in California. They lost the opener in San Diego, 24–20, after leading, 10–3, at the half, and that night Werblin decided to take all his coaches and a couple of writers across the nearby Mexican border to wide-open Tijuana for a little fun. The group made the usual tourist round until Ewbank got tired of being stopped at every alley and cabstand b shifty-eyed little men offering to take him to view the best in "feelms, feelthy feelms."

"Good God, man!" the little coach exploded. "Don't you realize I look at movies forty hours a week?"

Ewbank thought the key to the Jets' defeat in San Diego was a missed 13-yard field goal by Dick Guesman, the defensive tackle who doubled as place kicker. Earlier in the season, Guesman had missed a 12-yarder at Boston. However, the big guy had shown he could kick some long ones, too, and Ewbank determined to spend the week in California curing Guesman's erratic toe.

Ewbank prided himself on his ability with kickers. He recalled how Lou Groza, whom he'd known at Cleveland, always kicked with the same motion, like a golfer with a grooved swing. When practicing, Groza would wear a deep rut in the practice field turf. Steve Myhra, his kicker for several years at Baltimore, was quite different. To discover what made him so unpredictable, Weeb once marked off a rectangular patch of plain dirt for Myhra to kick in. Ewbank wanted to be able to check Myrha's footprints. Instead of Groza's precise groove, Myhra left a trail of "chicken tracks." The players joked that Myhra was "digging his own grave" in that little plot of ground, but at least Ewbank knew why Myhra was undependable as a kicker. He approached the ball differently every time.

Ewbank used movies to analyze Guesman, and slow-motion films revealed the big tackle was pigeon-toed. His foot actually made contact with the ball at an angle. So Ewbank designed a shoe with an angled toe to compensate, but it didn't arrive in time to save the Jets from a 49–26 beating at Oakland. Just to confound his coach, Guesman kicked a club-record 51-yard field goal against the Raiders in his old shoes.

The week before that game, Ewbank had taken his team from San Diego to Santa Rosa, California, a small city 60 miles north of Oakland. There were hot sulphur baths near Santa Rosa, which nestled at the entrance to Jack London's Valley of the Moon, and Ewbank figured that was just the thing to soothe those San Diego bumps and bruises. George Halas, whose Bears were also out on the coast for a week to play the Rams and 49ers, thought so, too. That Tuesday, players from both teams mingled in the hot sulphur pool in pro football's first informal merger. It was quite a sight.

The Jets didn't much dig the baths until they learned there were several wineries on the route back with free tasting rooms for visitors.

Watching the grape stompers at work, guard Pete Perrault turned to 300-pound Sherman Plunkett and declared, "Sherm, in that league you'd be all-pro."

Ewbank, of course, had another reason for bringing the Jets to Santa Rosa. He wanted to take his squad of virile young men away from temptation. It didn't work. The camp followers, who flock about every sports team, appeared as if by magic and there were enough bachelors on the squad to encourage them. No wonder it's such a chore for AFL teams to win that second game on the West Coast. It wasn't much consolation to Ewbank, heading home after a one-sided loss to Oakland, that the Bears, en route to the NFL championship, lost their only game of the season the same day in an even bigger upset to San Francisco, 20–14. The Bears had been out there for a week, too. Neither coach blamed the sulphur baths.

Back home, the Jets' fortunes didn't improve. They were tied by Denver, 35–35, and then humiliated by San Diego, 53–7. The final moments of both games were demoralizing. Bill Mathis, the Jets' regular halfback, was injured for the Denver game and Dick Christy took his place before a Saturday night crowd of more than 20,000. Christy had been a little-used substitute all season, but this time he had to play the entire game in addition to his kick return duties. Late in the third period, he hurt his knee but played on. His fumble in the final minutes set up Denver's tying touchdown, and, as the gutty veteran hobbled down the Polo Grounds steps on his crutches, he heard Ewbank blaming him for blowing the victory.

Against San Diego the following week, the Jets fell behind, 45–0, before scoring their only touchdown with 56 seconds left to play. When they got the ball back, the Chargers, instead of killing the clock, tried to score again. As the final gun sounded, the Jets were called for pass interference on their eight. Since a game can't end on a penalty, the Chargers were allotted one more play. Scorning a merciful line plunge, John Hadl passed the eight yards to Jerry Robinson for a touchdown. And, to rub a little extra brine into the Jets' wound, Hadl then passed to Dave Kocourek for a two-point conversion. The Chargers had scored more points after the game than the Jets had managed in the regulation 60 minutes.

Sonny Werblin was red with rage and embarrassment, and he never really forgave Charger coach Sid Gillman for that humiliation before a Jet home crowd. "They talk about the milk of human kindness—

the only thing that flows in Sid Gillman's veins is yogurt," Werblin said bitterly.

Three weeks later, however, the Jets scored their most impressive victory under Ewbank, a 17–0 upset of Kansas City, the first time the Chiefs had ever been shut out. A major contributor to that triumph at Shea Stadium was Paul Rochester, a husky, beer-drinking defensive tackle whom Ewbank had claimed on waivers from Kansas City the week before the game. Rochester was the first AFL player Weeb had ever picked up, and he was to prove an experienced anchor during the years Ewbank built his Super Bowl defensive line.

Rochester had become available because of a personality clash with Kansas City coach Hank Stram, who cut Rocky with the explanation, "He's pretty good, but the league is outgrowing him." Six years later, at the Super Bowl victory party, Rochester would recall Stram's write-off and laugh.

The Jets completed their first season with three straight losses and their final home crowd was a Wismerish 5,826 against Buffalo. Obscured by all the image talk and roster changes was another last-place Eastern Division finish and a 5-8-1 record that was only half a game better than Bulldog Turner had managed.

Still, this was a much-improved team whose record had suffered because the rest of the league was getting stronger at an ever-increasing pace. But Weeb now knew what he needed for the long haul, and Werblin, encouraged that the Jets were moving into new Shea Stadium the next season, set out to get it for him.

10

Snell Snubs the Giants

Even before the last punt had been blocked and the last tackle missed in 1963, Sonny Werblin and the Jets already were hard at work on the future.

Werblin actually was busy on two fronts, talent and television. The AFL's TV contract with the American Broadcasting Company still had a year to run, but Werblin, commissioner Joe Foss, and the other owners realized it would be best to start dickering for a new agreement as soon as possible. That way they wouldn't be victimized if 1964 should turn out to be a dud. Besides, the NFL was bargaining for its own new contract, and competition for that package would stimulate interest in all pro football. On January 29, 1964, it was announced that the AFL and the National Broadcasting Company had agreed to a five-year contract paying the league $36,000,000, or $900,000 per club per year, starting in 1965. This was more than four times what they had realized in any season with ABC.

The new TV contract guaranteed the AFL's survival. It came about only because the New York franchise was now a solid member of the family. Werblin's influence in establishing the league thus was felt long before anyone knew there would be a Namath in his future.

As the Jets began to survey the college field, they first took a look at "futures" they'd inherited from the final Titan draft list. Futures were five-year collegians, boys whose college class had graduated but who still had a year of eligibility remaining. The practice of drafting and signing futures has since been discontinued, but at that time it was a very important part of every team's drafting strategy. (And one of the keys to Green Bay's long success under Vince Lombardi, too.)

The old Titans had selected five futures in 1963. The Jets, who retained rights to them, went after three and signed every one despite NFL competition. Truly this was a new era. The three were Pet

The Pro: Dave Herman.

Liske of Penn State and Mike Taliaferro of Illinois, quarterbacks, and guard Dave Herman of Michigan State. Liske had also been drafted by the Philadelphia Eagles, while the Taliaferro and Herman signings were all the sweeter because both were taken away from the rival New York Giants. (The Jets also signed Bert Wilder, who would become a four-year defensive line sub, as a future from the Titans' 1962 list. His eligibility at North Carolina State had been further extended by a service hitch. Wilder, incidentally, passed up his fifth and pension-qualifying year with the Jets to enter religious youth work.)

Herman would become the best of all of these Titan legacies. A fierce and wild competitor, he played the game with reckless abandon. Line coach Chuck Knox liked to tell his players, "Look 'em in the eye and hit 'em in the numbers." He didn't have to tell Herman twice. This was the only way this nearsighted and color-blind Ohioan knew how to play the game.

Football didn't come easy for him at first. Herman had set his mind on Michigan State early in high school and then virtually forced the Spartans to award him a scholarship. Since football tryouts were illegal, the school would invite prospects to the campus and then suggest other informal games, like water polo, to test their competitive zeal. Herman could barely swim, but that didn't matter. He half-drowned most of his competition to win that scholarship.

Herman started out on special teams with the Jets, but worked his way determinedly onto the regular lineup and put together a long-term consecutive-game starting streak once he won that job. Off the field, the model of a cool and calculating young athlete-businessman, he would work himself into a near-manic fury before every game. Hours before the kickoff he would stare unseeing through old friends. Teammates soon learned to stay away from Herman on the sidelines for fear he'd turn on them, too. In his early days as a pro, his claim to fame was the number of helmets he broke—yes, broke—lunging headlong into enemy players.

Liske, who lacked a very strong arm, lingered with the Jets for one season. Likable and Ivy-Leagueish, he was traded to Buffalo and then drifted to Canada, where he enjoyed a successful career because of his dual abilities as quarterback and defensive halfback.

Taliaferro (pronounced Tolliver) remained to play a bitter counterpoint to the glittering Joe Namath story. He'd been a late bloomer at Illinois, and he didn't really excite pro scouts until the last game of his college career when he led the Illini to a 17–7 victory over Washington in the 1964 Rose Bowl. The Giants were quite interested in him, too, but he chose the Jets because he thought they'd provide him a better chance to play.

Nobody ever guessed more wrongly, and knowledge of this mistake changed Taliaferro into a bitter, moody young man. When Mike was ready to make his pro decision, the Jets had nobody but Dick Wood and his wired knees to play quarterback. The Giants, on the other hand, had one of the all-time best in veteran Y. A. Tittle and a promising younger man in Glynn Griffing. However, after Taliaferro made his decision to go with the Jets, the Giants in training camp summarily cut Griffing despite his long-term contract. And at mid-season of what would be his last campaign, Tittle was injured. Taliaferro, generally acknowledged as far superior to the Giants' rookie sub, Gary Wood, assuredly would have been given the opportunity to replace Tittle. With that chance, he would have been master of his own future.

With the Jets, though, he watched from the bench while Wood started every game until the final weeks of the season. And the next year Joe Namath arrived on the scene. In his disappointment, Taliaferro in later years may have forgotten that he actually started the

1965 season ahead of Namath. All he had to do was win. But he kept trying to prove he could throw the ball farther than any quarterback in the world, and that's why he lost—lost games and his job. Eventually he asked to be traded and he proved less than spectacular when given a full shot at the starting job in Boston.

When the Jets went into their championship game against Oakland without him, Taliaferro sent his old teammates a good-luck telegram. He was a good kid with a lousy sense of timing.

"I kept telling him he was better off and would enjoy a long and well-paid career as our number two quarterback, but he insisted he wanted to play," Ewbank would recall sadly.

As they prepared for the regular draft, owner Werblin and coach Ewbank differed strongly on their lead-off choice. Werblin, then, as always, star-conscious, wanted the Jets to go for George Mira, an exciting quarterback from the U. of Miami. Mira was of Puerto Rican ancestry, which would have drawn fans from New York's large Latin population. He was a natural, except for one thing. Ewbank didn't like him as a quarterback. Weeb thought Mira was too short (five feet eleven) for his position, and he was a scrambler, anathema to the little fundamentalist. Ewbank, a brilliant judge of quarterbacks, didn't think Mira (a) would be able to beat out Wood as a rookie and (b) would develop into a winning pro regular anytime soon. He was right on both acounts, as Mira's subsequent career with the NFL 49ers proved.

Newspapermen, who had heard Werblin rave about Mira, were ready to write down the little quarterback's name in their notebooks when the Jets called out their first draft choice—Matt Snell of Ohio State.

Matt who? Onlookers were stunned. Who in hell was Matt Snell?

About the only people in New York who'd heard of Snell were neighbors at Carle Place, Long Island, and followers of Long Island high school sports. Snell had been an all-everything at Carle Place and then dropped into oblivion at Ohio State. The reason was obvious to those who cared to look deeply, which is what pro scouts get paid to do. Snell had been the Buckeyes' best athlete. He could play any position and so was able to build an All-Star reputation at none. During his varsity career, he played fullback, defensive end, linebacker, and tight end. Ewbank could see him as a professional star at any of those positions . . . and the Jets needed help at all of them. However, Woody Hayes, the Ohio State coach, pleaded with Ewbank to give the kid a shot at carrying the ball. He said Ohio State's basic offense never gave Snell a chance to really display his talents at fullback. Matt could run and catch passes, too, Hayes insisted.

Still, no outsiders were really convinced of Snell's worth until the National League conducted its draft a week later and the Giants picked him third. The NFL was still the public's criterion of excellence, and as Werblin conceded later, it was the Giants who made Snell a name.

Drafting Snell was one thing, signing him another; but the Jets had prepared well for this battle. A week before the draft, Werblin had invited the parents of several New York-area college prospects to a Jet game as his guests. He even sent limousines to bring them to the Polo Grounds. It was a bitterly cold day, and Werblin, who sat in the stands with his wife for all games, saw a hot chocolate vendor pass by the Snells' seats. He called the vendor over and told him to deliver some hot chocolate to the freezing couple. "Thanks for taking care of my folks," Snell said when he finally met Werblin.

Soon after the draft, the Jets sent Clive Rush, one of their top assistants, to Ohio State. Rush had been an assistant coach at OSU when Snell first enrolled. He knew Matt—and, more important, Matt knew and trusted Rush. Clive laid the groundwork.

When the time came for actual negotiations, the Giants dispatched young Tim Mara, son of one of their owners, to deal with Snell. Matt, a proud youngster, was insulted that the Giants hadn't sent a top management man or even a coach to see him. Who represented the Jets? David A. (Sonny) Werblin, that's who. And he was accompanied by a tax lawyer to advise Snell how best to accept his $30,000 bonus and $20,000 first-year salary. That was pretty good money then, and Snell signed immediately. The Giants had been roundly defeated.

The Jets also signed their third choice, Gerry Philbin, and their sixth, Ralph Baker. They lost their second, fourth, and fifth picks. Bonuses hadn't reached dizzying heights yet, but the war for college talent was already being fiercely waged.

For instance, the Jets nailed Philbin by keeping the U. of Buffalo defensive end occupied in an airport while his plane for Detroit and contract talks with the Lions was leaving. Philbin, though, didn't really have his heart set on making that plane. The Lions had just finished telling him in most condescending fashion how lucky he was, a small guy (242 pounds) from a small school, to be drafted by such a great

Barton Silverman

Class of '64: Matt Snell takes a handoff from Mike Taliaferro.

team. Five years later he was to show the Lions how small he was by crunching their quarterback's ribs in an exhibition game.

On the other hand, the Jets lost their fifth choice, Ben McGee, a defensive end from Jackson State, to the Steelers, when his college coach snatched a ready-to-sign contract out of his hand. Jet assistant Walt Michaels was handing him the pen when this happened. "Did you try everything you could?" Ewbank asked when informed of the distressing news.

"Everything but violence," replied Michaels, convinced the college coach had been on the Steelers' payroll.

Snell, Philbin, and Baker were to become instant regulars with the Jets, and all three played major roles on the Super Bowl eleven. Down near the bottom of the draft list was the name of a future for 1965, quarterback Jerry Rhome of Tulsa. Although he was never to play a single minute in Werblin green, he would soon figure most importantly in the Jet future.

After the draft, Jet coaches scattered to survey the leftovers, the free agents. In addition to their regular draftees, they brought to camp that summer a green center from Long Island's little Hofstra University, John Schmitt, and a place-kicker from Utah State named Jim Turner, who had been dropped by the Redskins in training camp the year before. Schmitt, as the regular center, and Turner, with three field goals, would be Superheroes, too.

For a total of $140,000 in bonuses spread over all the signees, good and bad, Werblin, Ewbank, and scout George Sauer were to produce a rookie class that graduated five regulars (Herman, Snell, Philbin, Baker, and Schmitt), a sub (free agent Bill Rademacher of Northern Michigan), and a record-breaking place-kicker (Turner) into the Super Bowl. The 1964 draft marked the real beginning of the Jets' championship team.

Ewbank, however, didn't stop with rookies, and during the summer he completed two major deals. He bought veteran guard Sam DeLuca from San Diego and he made a nine-player trade with Denver.

DeLuca, a native of Brooklyn, was a class pro with seven years NFL, AFL, and Canadian experience. He had "retired" from the Chargers for one year in 1962 and now was threatening to quit again unless traded back east. San Diego general manager and coach Sid Gillman obliged. Although his knee gave out before the 1967 season and he watched the Super Bowl victory as a Jet broadcaster, DeLuca had a big role in their success. He knew how to win, and many young Jets who went on to beat Baltimore had learned from him.

The big trade sent five men to Denver, including Dick Guesman, the pigeon-toed place-kicker, and Ed Cooke, a tough-as-rusty-nails defensive end sometimes known as Clothesline Cooke after a favorite pro technique of stiffening pass receivers and ball carriers. In return, the Jets received defensive back Bob Zeman, end Gene Prebola, defensive tackle Gordy Holz, and middle linebacker Wahoo McDaniel.

The key, Ewbank proclaimed, was McDaniel. Zeman and Prebola were cut in training camp, Holz after one season. McDaniel lasted only two years but he carved an unforgettable place in Jet memories. Wahoo may have been the original wild Indian. His given name was Ed, but he signed all his autographs as "Chief Wahoo," the name he used as a professional wrestler. "The name McDaniel hasn't made a nickel for me yet," the part-Choctaw from Oklahoma explained.

McDaniel had been drafted out of Oklahoma U. by the Chargers in 1960, but signed instead with the NFL Dallas Cowboys. They cut him in training camp and he moved on to the AFL Houston Oilers as plain Ed McDaniel, a guard. The next season he turned up in Denver as Wahoo McDaniel, linebacker. The Jet deal for McDaniel was completed soon after the Giants had traded away their own great and colorful middle linebacker, Sam Huff. "A good thing," McDaniel sneered. "This town isn't big enough for Huff and me."

For all his brags and escapades, McDaniel wasn't a bad football player. He wasn't great, of course, but at this stage, greatness wasn't required to make the Jet team. Wahoo's biggest game with the Jets was his first. It was a balmy Saturday night in September and the Jets were unveiling their new team and their new linebacker in brand-new Shea Stadium. Denver was the opponent, a scheduling coup on two counts. Not only would McDaniel be able to wreak mayhem on the team that had scorned him, an old wrestling ploy, but Denver was one opponent the Jets figured to be able to beat.

Most observers thought the Jets would be lucky to attract 30,000 for their opener, but the final count was an AFL record 44,497. This was more than the Titans had drawn in all of 1962 and double any 1963 Jet crowd in the Polo Grounds.

The whooping fans saw quite a show as the Jets romped to a 30–6 victory. The defense, led by McDaniel, stopped the Broncos without a touchdown.

McDaniel attacked Bronco ball carriers as if they were dressed in

New York Jets

Chief Wahoo McDaniel

Seventh Cavalry blue. The public address announcer began by simply intoning, "Tackle by McDaniel." Then he switched to, "Tackle by Wahoo." Finally he would call out, "Tackle by guess who?" and the crowd would roar back, "Wahoo!" Of course, it got ridiculous. McDaniel was being credited with every tackle and every pass deflection for both sides, it seemed. But Werblin and the Jet fans didn't care. At last they had a hero.

The next week, the McDANIEL on the back of the linebacker's jersey was replaced, with league permission, with a simple WAHOO. McDaniel's wrestling price escalated, too.

Almost overlooked in McDaniel's debut was the performance of Matt Snell, the rookie fullback who had joined the team late from the camp of the Chicago All-Stars. Snell ran 22 times for 82 yards and caught three passes.

After a week off, the Jets went up to Boston and lost on a windy day, 26–10. Dick Wood threw five interceptions, but Ewbank blamed the receivers, especially Don Maynard, for running poor patterns. But the next week, Maynard and Wood got their signals straight for a 69-yard last-quarter scoring pass to tie San Diego, 17–17, before another record crowd.

The tie was followed by home victories over Oakland and Houston. The 24–17 defeat of the Oilers included a touching note. Matt Snell set a club rushing record, and more than 32,000 fans thoroughly enjoyed the victory in this brand-new ball park. Snell and Shea, symbols of the future. On the Oiler bench sat Sammy Baugh, now Houston's coach. In the stands was a sickly Harry Wismer. Wismer had asked Sammy to let him ride out to the stadium in the Oiler team bus and Baugh had obliged. Wismer and Baugh, totems of the past.

By beating Boston in their seventh game, 35–14, as Dick Wood threw four touchdown passes, the Jets compiled a 4-2-1 record for the first half of the season. But from then on they were to win only one more game. Injuries were the main reason, and when a fellow like Philbin went out for the season with a dislocated shoulder, the Jets just had no replacements. Regardless of the reason, this is when the mystique of the Jets' second-half collapses was born. It was to haunt Ewbank all the way to the championship and almost cost him his job.

As they staggered down the stretch, the Jets were taking physical beatings from their opponents, too. In a 20–16 loss at Denver, both Jet quarterbacks were kayoed. Ed Cooke, the ex-Jet, flattened Taliaferro and dealt out injuries to linemen Gene Heeter and Mike Hudock. Earlier another player had coldcocked Wood, who recovered just in time to replace the woozy Taliaferro. (Turner, the place-kicker, would have been the third quarterback.)

Three weeks later, the Jets moved on to San Diego and Hudock, whose back had been hurt, still wasn't ready. So the Jets put through a rush call to John Schmitt, the big and eager rookie from Hofstra who had been on their taxi squad all year. Schmitt had been scheduled to make the trip to the coast, but somebody forgot to tell him. So he was picking up a few extra bucks delivering packages during the pre-Christmas rush. They almost literally hauled him off his truck late Saturday, but he managed to be in uniform to make the opening center snap across the continent on Sunday.

The first snap was almost his last. Ernie Ladd was playing defensive tackle for the Chargers then, and he was a sight to make any rookie quaver. The veterans didn't have to look at him. They knew enough to be nervous any time they got within 50 miles of Balboa Stadium. Ladd was six feet nine, a well-proportioned 313 pounds, and he had a mean streak as wide as his shoulder pads. Opposing players said the powerful tackle had only one real weakness besides a disinclination to go all out on every play. He concentrated so much on physically punishing the blocker opposite him that he sometimes forgot the object of the game is to stop the ball carrier.

To make sure Schmitt knew he was there, Ladd lined up nose to nose against the rookie center and on the first play almost tore his knee apart.

John, a gritty type whose determination is masked by a pleasant smile, endured for a few more plays. But that one shot was the beginning and end of his season. He went back to New York for surgery and there was doubt that he would ever play again. But John is a dedicated guy. He attacked the rehabilitation program as if more than just his football life depended on it, and he spent another full season plugging away on the taxi squad. When expansion finally opened up a regular job, he clenched his fist around it and never let go. He was to more than hold his own in future meetings with Ernie Ladd and against the best in the NFL, too.

Although his team slid at the end to another 5-8-1 record, the Jets moved up a notch to third in the Eastern Division, ahead of Houston, and Ewbank could look ahead to better days. His rookies had made their mistakes and survived. Matt Snell had enjoyed a brilliant first campaign and was named the AFL's Rookie of the Year. He was a close second to Cookie Gilchrist of Buffalo in the ground-gaining statistics and he also made the top ten in pass receiving. This was the first of many times he was to complete such a double. His blocking was good and getting better. "A complete fullback," Ewbank said as he counted at least one position set for many years. There were others in the same category, although their arrival wasn't as readily noted by press and public as Snell's. "We're green and growing," Ewbank kept insisting. And he was right, even though the won-loss record didn't show it.

Meanwhile, Werblin basked in a season's top crowd of 60,300 against Buffalo, bigger than anything the baseball Mets had drawn in their ultrasuccessful Shea Stadium debut. The season total of almost 300,000 for seven home games was best in the league. The NFL was marshaling a regiment of "baby-sitters" to hide out college prospects from the young league during the 1965 college draft, but Werblin and the Jets were ready for them. Their battle plan was set. Like General Grant, they were moving south.

11

$400,000

It was only a junior high school basketball game between teams from Ellwood City and Beaver Falls, two small communities only eight miles apart in Pennsylvania's Beaver Valley west of Pittsburgh. The coach of the Ellwood City team was from that area, too, from Sewickley, Pennsylvania. His name: Chuck Knox. As the game progressed, his attention focused on a lithe, dark-haired member of the Beaver Falls team who seemed smoother, more advanced, and better coordinated than any of his fourteen-year-old teammates. "I could see then," Chuck Knox would say years later in his capacity as an assistant coach with the New York Jets, "that Joe Namath was going to be a really good athlete."

This was the first of many scouting reports the Jets were to study through the autumn of 1964. This was to be the season they went after a quarterback in the college draft. It was a good year for quarterbacks. John Huarte was winning a Heisman Trophy with Notre Dame. Out on the West Coast, Craig Morton was knocking 'em dead for California. Archie Roberts was breaking all the Ivy League records at Columbia. And Steve Tensi was winning raves for Florida State in the Deep South.

But as George Sauer, director of personnel, sifted his reports, one name kept jumping out from all the rest. Despite the hobbles of a midseason knee injury, Joe Namath of Alabama looked like the best of all.

Bear Bryant, Namath's coach, called the sleepy-eyed quarterback "the best athlete I've ever coached." Namath had a quick delivery, a strong arm, and, just as important, the mystique of victory. He had not suffered through a losing season since his sophomore year in high school. The Jets knew Namath would require knee surgery before he ever played as a pro, but they had confidence in the skillful hands of their team physician, Dr. James A. Nicholas. Besides, knee operations no longer held the terror of past years.

As the high command prepared to make its drafting decisions, Sauer sat down to type out his final report to Ewbank and Werblin. Sauer, a former coach, uses a five-point scale to rate players in all categories, ranging from one down to five.

On Namath's sheet, the skill ratings read: quickness—1; agility—1; strength—2; reaction time—1; coordination—1; size potential—1; durability—2; speed for position—2; intelligence—1; character—2; aggressiveness—1; pride—1.

Will be everybody's number one draft choice, Sauer typed, underlining the words for emphasis himself.

Sauer then gave Namath an overall rating. If a player deserves no better than a 5, Sauer just tears up his report. A 1 means potential to be a professional star. Namath earned a 1-plus—superstar!

After deciding on Namath, the Jets had to set about getting him. In a secret draft, plans were laid by AFL owners so New York would be able to claim the best college quarterback in the nation. Commissioner Foss, of course, was not invited, and the league later was to deny that this was really a draft. They just called it a meeting at which they discussed mutual needs and estimates of their ability to sign different players in competition with the NFL.

Namath, even in college a freewheeling "swinger," had let it be known that he wanted to play professionally in a big city. New York was his kind of town. That suited Werblin just fine.

As the season drew to a close, it was obvious that Denver would have the worst record in the AFL, then Houston, and then New York. The tactics of arranging the draft were important. The other teams could not face their fans if they just gave away the nation's best quarterback prospect.

Denver was no obstacle because the Broncos had already traded away their first draft choice to Houston for quarterback Jacky Lee. That left the Oilers with two first-round choices, which provided some maneuvering room. Jerry Rhome, the quarterback from Tulsa whom New York had drafted as a future the season before, was the key.

Rhome was also one of the big quarterbacks of 1964 and broke all sorts of national collegiate passing records that season. One Monday his coach brought him to New York for an All-American publicity appearance before the Football Writers Association. The visit also marked a command appearance before Werblin, who took the boy to dinner.

As it turned out, the two didn't hit it off. Rhome was introverted, where Werblin was looking for somebody who gave off sparks. Fortunately for front office harmony, Ewbank didn't like Rhome, either, as a quarterback. He felt Rhome was too short at six feet even, and his arm wasn't as strong as his list of records might indicate. Tulsa, he decided, had dedicated its season to building up Rhome's statistics.

Later, when Werblin finally met Namath, they hit it off brilliantly. In Joe Namath, football and show biz were wedded in perfect harmony.

The Oilers knew they'd have little chance of signing Namath, so owner Bud Adams unselfishly traded that lead-off draft choice to the Jets for the rights to Rhome, who had an understandably very big name in the Southwest. So it was no giveaway by Houston, even though Rhome signed with the NFL after the Oilers declined to meet his continuing contract demands.

As with Snell the year before, the Jets didn't wait until the day of the draft to open their campaign for Namath's signature. In laying the groundwork, Chuck Knox played an important role. As an assistant at the University of Kentucky, Knox had tried to recruit Namath out of Beaver Falls High. Their real friendship dated from that experience.

Knox and Namath had continued to be aware of each other's existence because Kentucky and Alabama play in the same conference. A couple of summers after Knox had moved on to the pros, the Jets were in Tampa, Florida, to play Buffalo in an exhibition game. Ray Abruzzese, an Alabama teammate of Namath's, was with the Bills, and Joe had come down to see his buddy play. As Knox was in the end zone putting his linemen through some pregame warm-ups, he heard a drawling voice call out, "Hey, Coach Knox." It was Namath, already a college star and ready to start his senior season. You better believe Chuck Knox remembered him and greeted him warmly. He introduced Namath around. He told him he'd keep in touch.

When the Jets were getting ready to go into the draft, Knox called Namath at Tuscaloosa, Alabama. They talked as friends. Knox told him what it could mean to a kid from western Pennsylvania to play in New York. About all the little extras, the fringe benefits, the endorsement money. Knox was somebody from back home. Namath listened and he assured Knox that he had no predisposition toward the National Football League.

"We have as good a shot at getting him as anybody," Knox told his bosses.

The plot was thickening over in the NFL, too. Y. A. Tittle was retiring, an open secret, and the Giants were in dire need of a quarterback. With their 2-10-2 record, they would bat leadoff in the NFL draft, which was taking place on the same day. Surely they would draft Namath, too.

The Jets, as expected, went for the Alabama quarterback, but across town, the Giants pulled a stunning surprise. They drafted, and almost immediately announced the signing of, Tucker Frederickson, a good but not generally well-known running back from Auburn. Several picks later, the St. Louis Cardinals made Namath their first-round choice.

Soon after the draft, Alabama accepted a bid to play Texas in the Orange Bowl on New Year's night. The Tuesday after Alabama's final regular season game, Namath's coach, Bear Bryant, called both pro teams. Joe would be under terrific pressure to decide his professional future. Bryant would like the whole thing settled immediately so his quarterback could prepare for the bowl game with a clear mind.

About this time rumors began to circulate that the Cardinals actually were acting as agents for the Giants, who feared the embarrassment of another Snell-type defeat by those cross-river upstarts. This was never proved, but negotiations gave the Jets some basis for suspicion.

The meetings took place in Birmingham, Alabama. Mike Bite, Namath's young lawyer, shuttled back and forth between Werblin and Billy Bidwell, vice-president of the Cardinals. Bite quickly became suspicious that the Cardinals might be negotiating for another team because at every escalation of the bargaining, Bidwell would say he had to call his older brother, Stormy, for instructions. Bite finally insisted on talking to the senior Bidwell direct. "This is what we want," he demanded. "Give me a yes or no right now." Bidwell said he'd have to call Bite back, and the little Alabama lawyer nodded to himself.

As the Jets and Namath drew closer, the Cardinals finally handed Bite a standard NFL contract. The name of the team was left blank. Namath could fill in whatever city he wished. But it was their last gasp. They dropped out of negotiations, telling the press they had quit when bidding reached the outrageous sum of $389,000.

Since the Jets presumably were offering more, that's how the magic figure of $400,000 was born. As the Giants had done on a smaller scale with Snell the year before, the Cardinals had succeeded 400-fold in making Namath a national figure.

Years later, it was reported that the contract actually amounted to a $427,000 package.

The contract itself was for three years, but with the standard option clause it was guaranteed for four. Namath's actual salary over this period: $25,000. A low figure, but one Ewbank insisted upon to maintain squad morale. However, on top of this $100,000, Namath received a $200,000 bonus, payment to be spread out over five years but deferred until after his playing career; and three-year "scouting" jobs for his three brothers and brother-in-law at $10,000 each per year. That would be another $120,000. Add the Jet-green Lincoln Continental convertible and the $427,000 total sounds about right.

When Namath was talking to the two pro teams, Bryant ordered him to decline as much as a soft drink from either side. The coach wanted no taint on his star quarterback's amateur standing before the Orange Bowl game. However, before Werblin left Birmingham, he had Namath's handshake. *Famous last words,* Werblin thought as he headed north, but Bryant reassured him: "Don't worry. If Namath gave you his word, that's all there is to it."

Just to make sure, though, the Jets sent Chuck Knox to keep an eye on things when the Crimson Tide squad moved to Miami for final Orange Bowl preparations the week before the game. Four days before the game that would wind up Namath's college career and launch him into the pros, Knox and the Jets got a bigger scare from Namath than anything the NFL could provide. Joe had first hurt his right knee in Alabama's fourth game of the season. The leg just collapsed on him. The same thing happened three games later. But both times he was able to come back the following Saturday and resume his collegiate career. He actually missed only one full game all season. In a Monday practice before the Friday night Orange Bowl, Namath's knee went out on him again. It looked doubtful that he'd be able even to dress for the big game, but as the lights blinked on in the huge stadium, there was Namath in uniform, wearing sneakers instead of football shoes to ease some of the pain.

Namath didn't start the game, but when Alabama fell two touchdowns behind, Bryant turned to his ailing senior. As Namath prepared to come in, the huge throng of more than 72,000 stirred with anticipa-

University of Alabama

No. 12 at Alabama, Joe Namath started as a runner, too, but after his injury he finished his college career as an off-balance passer, shown here throwing off the wrong foot.

tion. This was the electricity Werblin had been seeking, and damned if Namath, damaged knee and all, didn't almost pull it out.

Down the field he drove the Crimson Tide, completing 18 of 37 passes for 255 yards and two touchdowns. There was glory even in his last-down try at the winning touchdown. In the closing minutes, Alabama was stalled at the Texas one. Bad leg and all, Namath tried to wedge it in on a quarterback sneak. He lost, 21–17, but he was a heroic figure.

The Orange Bowl game was played at night for the first time that year. There was no competition on national television from any of the day's other bowl games. Millions watched Namath's electrifying and gritty performance. It was known the Jets were going to sign Namath the next day, and a friend told Werblin, "You've just got the benefit of the greatest pilot film in TV history."

(That game also produced several other future Jets: linebacker Paul Crane from Alabama and Longhorn stars Jim Hudson, George Sauer, Jr., Pete Lammons, and John Elliott. Hudson, then a quarterback, threw a 69-yard scoring pass to Sauer, and Lammons intercepted two Namath passes.)

The Jet entourage enveloped Namath after the game now that he would no longer be under the protection of Bryant and Alabama. Weeb Ewbank actually met Namath on the field and escorted him to the dressing room. The contract was signed that night and Werblin made the announcement at a Miami press conference the next morning.

What manner of young man—a slouchy, six-foot-one, 195-pounder with a gimpy leg—had inspired such a lavish contract, largest by far in the history of pro football?

At twenty-one, his financial future was secure, but when Joe Willie Namath was born on May 31, 1943, the youngest of three sons and a daughter of John and Rose Namath, that kind of future seemed as far away as his father's native Hungary. His parents were divorced when Joe was in grammar school, and both remarried. Joe was brought up by an indulgent mother, whom he adores, and he's quick to admit, "I wasn't the easiest kid in the world to raise."

Beaver Falls, Pennsylvania, population 30,000, is a steel town 30 miles west of Pittsburgh on the Beaver River, near its junction with the Ohio. Most of the town is on the wrong side of the tracks. Namath grew up in one of the worst of the bad sections. Anything for a buck. He'd steal golf balls, used soda bottles for the deposit, and scrap metal for junk. Sometimes he'd sneak into the junkyard, steal some stuff, and then sell it back. He used to laugh when friends warned him against the con men and hustlers in New York. "I pulled all the hustles. Don't you know you can't con a con man?" he'd assure them.

All he wanted to do was get out of Beaver Falls. The less he knew about the mills the better. He didn't even want to know what his father did there. If it wasn't football, he'd join the Air Force. Anything to get out.

Namath may have attracted Knox's eye in junior high, but he didn't really make it in football until his sophomore year in high school. They'd been playing him at safety as a freshman and he hated it. Almost quit the team, too. But a new coach, Larry Bruno, gave him the ball one day and made a quarterback out of him. Bruno didn't tame him, though. Nobody did, although maybe Bear Bryant came close. A steel town is a tough town, and Namath didn't get his kicks playing tennis at the country club.

Nobody puts on a pair of cleats and shoulder pads in western Pennsylvania without some college scout seeing him and before he was through, this wildcat in the ducktail haircut and leather jacket had a lot of them watching. There were 52 offers of college scholarships, plus half a dozen baseball offers including $50,000 from the Cubs to play the outfield. But persuasive Tom Nugent finally corraled Namath for the University of Maryland. Namath was virtually enrolled when somebody remembered to check his grades. Nugent couldn't get Namath in school!

However, he didn't just drop Namath back in Beaver Falls. It would be pretty tough for the kid to get another scholarship at this late date, and besides, if he did get a scholarship, it might be from one of Maryland's opponents. So Nugent placed a call to Tuscaloosa. Bear Bryant not only was a friend of his but a friend he wouldn't be playing for a few years. Bryant had no trouble getting Namath enrolled.

(One of the most touching vignettes of Super Bowl week involved Nugent, out of football and now a Miami television sportscaster, interviewing Namath before the game. "I bet if you'd got him into school at Maryland you'd still be coaching," someone called out. Nugent smiled, thinly.)

Namath's career at Alabama provided almost an exact preview of his early years with the Jets. At first, none of the other players took to this Yankee with the strange ways, strange accent, strange long haircut, and unbelievable ability. But Ray Abruzzese, a Philadelphian who had gone through the same ordeal when he'd enrolled at Alabama a couple of years before, became his friend. Even now, with Abruzzese out of football, they share a New York apartment and are business partners.

Namath led the Crimson Tide to a 10–1 record as a sophomore, including a 17–0 victory over Oklahoma in the Orange Bowl. In his junior year, Alabama was 9–2 and beat Mississippi, 12–7, in the Sugar Bowl, but Namath was suspended from the squad before the last game of the season for breaking training. ("I deserved it," he would say bluntly in later years. Bryant, the coach who had suspended him, and Werblin were about the only older men to whom he would show real deference.) In his senior year, Alabama won 10 straight before losing to Texas in the Orange Bowl. Despite his injuries, Namath made All-America that season.

During those four years at Alabama, however, Namath was changing. He developed a Southern-type drawl; he added some polish. "He learned to take responsibility for his actions," said Knox, who knew him from the other side of the Beaver River.

In other words, Namath was still a wild kid, but now man enough to take the consequences. All who knew him from Alabama agreed he didn't change once he got to New York, where he became the idol of America's groovy, uninhibited under-thirties and the despair of staid Weeb Ewbank.

"I believe in living the good life, and this little war [between the leagues] has made it possible. What difference does it make what you do as long as it doesn't hurt anybody else?"

This was Namath's credo. He became a symbol of the now generation but refused to accept any role as an influence for the next. If Werblin, who had three younger sons himself, ever admitted any fault in Namath, it was at this failing.

After the Super Bowl, Namath made some television commercials. Their theme: *When you've got it, flaunt it!* And that's what Joe Willie did, from llama rugs in his overpriced, overdecorated apartment to closets full of the latest in clothes. He flaunted his new wealth. And he flaunted his vices, which actually were not much worse than those of any other young, red-blooded, single American athlete. But, in flaunting, he created his own problems. His mistake was in thinking the words "phony" and "discreet" were synonyms.

It took four years before his essential good will, generosity, indifference to pain, and physical courage won from his teammates the title of leader, a title that his physical skills should have earned him long before.

After the epochal signing, Namath fullfilled an earlier commitment to play in the North-South All-Star game, where he earned his team a 7–7 tie by combining with future Dallas Cowboy star Bob Hayes on a 53-yard scoring pass. Then he came to New York to meet the press. His introductory press conference was held in Toots Shor's restaurant a little later in the afternoon after Y. A. Tittle of the Giants had announced his retirement from pro football in the same building under the same spotlights. The significance of the two events was not overlooked. Namath was being given the city if he could take it.

Namath then entered Lenox Hill Hospital for one of the most completely reported operations in medical history. It was only a knee, but you'd have thought it was the first heart transplant, complete with live photographs and diagrams in several national magazines.

Namath's right knee was a mess. Modern medical practice calls for an immediate operation on knee injuries, and Dr. Nicholas was to have spectacular success with several Jets by following this theory. Namath's knee had been hurt in midseason at Alabama and became more mangled every time he tried to play on it and hurt it again. Time also worked against the damaged tissues, and then his left knee developed a bursitis condition and a tendency toward future injury because of unnatural stress as Namath favored the right. (In contrast to the Namath case, Terry Hanratty of Notre Dame hurt his knee during the 1968 season, his last for the Fighting Irish, but was given an immediate operation. His college career was not seen as the end of his future.)

Namath was on the operating table for one hour and thirteen minutes. Dr. Nicholas removed the cartilage, tightened the ligaments, and removed a cyst. When it was over, he said, "Namath has the knees of a seventy-year-old man."

After Namath recovered from the surgery in his $65-a-day corner room at Lenox Hill, Werblin almost literally took Joe into his family. They were together constantly as Werblin put his new property on display in all the best places, from the 21 Club to Shor's to the swinging parties at the Kentucky Derby. "He's the greatest, a wonderful young man. It's amazing how a room lights up when he walks in. That's star quality," Werblin would repeat to all listeners.

"It sounds like he's talking about a prize stud," one woman whispered after hearing Namath extolled at length over cocktails.

"That," her escort replied, "is just about it."

Namath not only would be the star of Werblin's stable, he would be the start of a fine line of football thoroughbreds. After Werblin signed Namath, he received wires and letters from colleagues throughout the AFL, congratulating him for his coup and thanking him for putting the AFL in the spotlight and making their job easier.

"Before any boy picks up a pen next year, he'll want to hear from us," Chuck Knox predicted.

12

Joe Willie's First Challenge

Jet football players had been drifting into camp all during the sunny July day. None of them was really in that much of a hurry to get to Peekskill, New York, a dull if picturesque little community. ("What's open?" Joe Namath once asked Matt Snell when he wanted to go out for a late snack. "Nothing," Matt replied. "That's why we're here.") However, the players had to report by 6 P.M. for the opening of training camp, and this year they approached the ordeal with a little edge of anticipation. Joe Namath, the fabulous rookie, was coming to town with that big $400,000 contract.

As the afternoon wore on, more players congregated in the courtyard of Peekskill Military Academy under the huge oak tree from which a British Revolutionary War spy had once been hanged. As each new car approached, conversations broke off and the early arrivals would turn toward the driveway.

Finally, at 5:55, five minutes before the deadline, a black convertible pulled up to the dormitory and four hundred thousand dollars' worth of football player got out. He grabbed his luggage and told the driver good-bye. "I don't see why he's so early. He's got five minutes to go," one veteran grumbled.

"Yeah, but at least he's left that big green car behind," another conceded grudgingly.

Joe Namath had arrived to start his professional career on perhaps the biggest spot in football history. All right, Mr. Four Hundred Thousand Dollars, let's see what you can do. Even the squirrels seemed to be wondering.

Namath wasn't the only rich rookie in the Jet camp. The pro football war was approaching its frenzied peak. Intrigue, controversy, and an apparently limitless checkbook had produced another outstanding first-year crop in Peekskill. The Jets had signed eleven of their twenty-one regular choices, including four of the first five and six of the first eight. The Class of '65 also included a future from 1964, defensive back Cornell Gordon; a future from the 1965 list, George Sauer, Jr.; and a free agent from Texas named Jim Hudson.

There was a story for almost every new player and a tale involving those who got away, too.

There was another expensive quarterback in camp besides Namath. The Jets on the second round had drafted John Huarte of Notre Dame, winner of the Heisman Trophy as the most outstanding player in college football. With Dick Wood and Pete Liske already gone in deals, Huarte was promised a full shot at the first-string job in competition with Namath and holdover Mike Taliaferro.

Huarte was a cool customer just oozing with that famed Notre Dame polish. He and his advisers sat down with the Jets and the NFL Philadelphia Eagles and he came away with a $200,000 contract from Sonny Werblin. Huarte, who hadn't received much of a chance to play at Notre Dame until his sensational senior season, actually was signed several weeks ahead of Namath. But Werblin kept the deal secret. He felt Huarte's signing for a big bonus might dissuade Namath from going with the Jets. Consequently, Huarte's announcement press conference was held several weeks after Namath's.

There had been no delay in announcing the signing of Verlon Biggs, a huge defensive end from Jackson State who was the Jets' third-round draft choice. Biggs was one of many players "kidnapped" by NFL "baby-sitters." Booze, broads, and blackmail were some of the weapons used by both sides in this war for talent. Biggs, transferred with several others from city to city, from hotel to hotel, in the days before the draft, proved impervious to all NFL pressure. George Sauer, Sr., almost wore out his airlines credit card following Biggs around the country, and Verlon was smart enough to slip off and call his college coach at each stop. The coach kept Sauer informed.

When Biggs refused to be pressured into signing with the NFL on draft day while still half-asleep and groggy from a late-night party, the older league declined to pick him at all. The Jets did and moved right in and signed him.

The Jets' fourth-round draft choice was Bob Schweickert, a good-looking kid from Virginia Tech. Like Gordon and Hudson, Schweickert had been a college quarterback, but he was ticketed for duty as a running back or flanker. Only 190 pounds, he became one of the Jets' spectacular big-money ($100,000) failures. He just didn't have the size or toughness to be a pro. Schweickert, incidentally, signed with

Two rich rookies: John Huarte (top) and Joe Namath.

the Jets over the 49ers because sportscaster Howard Cosell, whom he admired, recommended the New York team. Schweickert's biggest headline came when he helped the FBI expose an Army sergeant who was selling places in reserve units to potential two-year draftees. In the units, they would have to serve only six months' active duty.

The Jets lost some big names, too, the most noteworthy being Tom Nowatzke, a 235-pound fullback-linebacker from Indiana. That story has never really been told. The Jets had been romancing Nowatzke for several weeks after their secret "nondraft," trying to get some kind of commitment from him. But Nowatzke kept begging off, even though he insisted he had not pledged himself to the NFL, either. He promised to face the draft with an open mind unless, he hedged, "I'm drafted by the Detroit Lions." Nowatzke was from Flint, Michigan. He said he couldn't be blamed for wanting to play close to home.

The week of the draft, Nowatzke arrived in New York on an All-American college junket. Werblin met him at the airport and took both Nowatzke and his NFL baby-sitter to Shea Stadium. There he talked privately with the boy. The more they talked, the more Werblin was convinced that Nowatzke already had signed with the Lions. On their way into town from the stadium, Werblin threw a new bonus offer at Nowatzke, almost triple what they had been discussing. The big fullback, Werblin recalls, "turned green."

Why the Jets went ahead and tabbed Nowatzke as their second first-round choice nobody has ever satisfactorily explained. Within hours after the Jets made their selection, the Lions, to nobody's surprise, drafted Nowatzke No. 1 and, within minutes, produced him signed and sealed for a press conference.

If Werblin was convinced Nowatzke had already signed—as he kept charging until the fullback threatened a lawsuit the following year— why did he waste that precious high choice? "If there was a chance he hadn't signed, we had to take it," Werblin explained later.

Down in the seventh round, the Jets had two picks. They drafted and signed Jim Harris of Utah State, who became a rookie starter at defensive tackle alongside Biggs. And they drafted and failed to sign Archie Roberts, the Columbia quarterback. Roberts was grabbed off as a free agent by Cleveland, which produced a better scholarship package for him and his wife, in medical school at Cleveland's Western Reserve University.

Sauer's signing created tremendous controversy of a different nature. Young George had been redshirted one season at Texas. Although his college class was graduating, he still had a season of eligibility. But he ached to get on with his professional career. "I feel I've given Texas four years' hard work in return for my scholarship," he declared as he sought a contract.

Young Sauer's decision created a dilemma for Ewbank. Weeb had long followed a personal rule that he would never sign a boy with eligibility remaining, if his college coach wanted him back. And Darrell Royal, coach of the Longhorns, wanted him badly. "We've wet-nursed him through three years and toughened him up, and now, just when we're getting ready to capitalize on him, bam, he's gone," Royal complained.

But young Sauer, high-principled and studious, took the initiative in starting his pro career, just as he'd turned to football as a youngster at his own time and not under any urging from his Hall of Fame father. He moved out of the athletic dormitory and announced he would not play his final year of football at Texas under any circumstances. He then declined to take any of his final semester exams to assure that he would not be eligible the next fall anyway, quite a sacrifice for this bona fide student-athlete.

As proud as he had been when he called out his son's name at the draft earlier that winter, the elder Sauer was distressed at the turn of events. His life had been dedicated to college football, and he wanted his boy to continue working straight through to his degree. But when young George demonstrated how strongly he wanted to play pro football, his father backed him up.

(This case and another involving a Georgia tackle who signed a pro contract and then still played out his last year of college ball helped bring about the end of the redshirt draft after the following year.)

Except for some good games his senior year and that big touchdown catch in the Orange Bowl, young Sauer really hadn't shown that much pro potential. "Is he worth it?" Ewbank asked George, Sr., when the boy presented his contract demands.

"Yes, he is," the father answered.

Ewbank used to refer to Namath occasionally as "John," meaning Unitas. He liked to call George Sauer "a Raymond Berry with speed," referring, of course, to his all-time great receiver with the Colts. During a tense moment, Ewbank once looked down his bench and yelled, "Raymond, get in there." He was talking to Sauer, of course, but, knowing Ewbank, his confusion was the ultimate accolade.

The rookies who greeted the rest of the squad at Peekskill represented perhaps a million dollars or more in bonuses and maybe a couple of decades in no-cut contracts. "Don't worry, I'll be here after you've gone—I've got a no-cut contract," one rookie sneered at a veteran as they scrimmaged fiercely in the hot August sun. And the rookie was right.

At the close of the previous season, Werblin had talked frankly with all the veterans. He had warned them of the upcoming price war. He said the Jets would be forced to pay inflated bonuses to sign rookies. But he stressed that these rookies were vital to the league's survival and to the maintenance of jobs for the older players. As far as possible, actual salaries, he assured them, would be kept in line with what the veterans were receiving. Intellectually, the older players knew he was right. Emotionally, they couldn't accept it.

The tension mounted and the man in the middle was Namath. There was nothing in his contract about it, but part of his $400,000 was the fee for being the focal point of the discontent. The fact that he played the leadership position of quarterback had a lot to do with it. So did the army of interviewers seeking him out.

Huarte, meanwhile, spent only a couple of days with the Jets before reporting to the College All-Star camp in Chicago. If he ever had a chance to make it with the Jets, this finished him. Namath, excused from that early August charity game because of his knee operation, moved ahead of his rookie rival and Huarte never caught up.

Huarte's last great moment came against the NFL champion Cleveland Browns. He was the All-Stars' third-string quarterback, but after Roger Staubach of Navy was hurt and Craig Morton of California failed to move the team, coach Otto Graham called on Huarte. It was halfway through the third quarter, and the All-Stars trailed, 24–3. Huarte responded brilliantly, guiding the Stars to a pair of touchdowns to make the score a respectable 24–16. He was named the game's most valuable player, his last big honor. Later he was to fail at New York and Boston before becoming a little-used sub with the NFL Philadelphia Eagles.

Nobody ever came up with a definitive explanation for Huarte's lack of success. Mechanically, his passing fault was that he threw the ball sidearm, which made him shorter than his not-too-impressive six feet in height. In college Huarte was a scrambler; in the pros that's an invitation to disaster. Teammates confided that he would rush out of the pocket at the slightest pressure, whereas Namath would hang in until the final second and risk his lumps to get a completion. Finally, there was a feeling that he was more interested in his money, his investments, and his life after football. For better or worse, Namath was nothing but football player.

When Huarte returned from the All-Star game, Ewbank was committed to giving him a shot at the regular job, too. He, Namath, and Taliaferro took turns in workouts, which meant that nobody got enough practice. Huarte finally was given an exhibition start, but it proved an embarrassment. Only then was Ewbank able to concentrate on Namath and Taliaferro. Huarte was dropped to the taxi squad.

Namath had broken in with two touchdown passes in the Jets' rookie game against Boston, and further preseason tests showed his knee could take it. As he and Taliaferro shared exhibition game duty, Ewbank had to decide which would open the season.

Werblin, of course, wanted his coach to go with Namath. "He's supposed to be the best college football player of the year and possibly one of the greats of all time. Why can't he play right now?" Werblin demanded.

Ewbank had to say Namath wasn't ready. He knew Joe would be great, but he didn't rush him ahead of time. There's so much to learn about pro football, more than any rookie even realizes. On top of this, Namath had developed bad techniques the previous season by throwing with the bad knee. These habits had to be overcome, too. "Maybe he'll be ready in four-five games," Ewbank told his boss.

At least Namath realized he wasn't ready. After the final exhibition game, he was asked who he thought should open the season at quarterback. "Why, Mike, of course," Namath snapped back without a moment's hesitation. Ewbank was a lot less direct. "We'll start whoever looks best in practice during the week," he insisted. It was a phrase he was to repeat ad nauseam all season.

As the Jets prepared to open in Houston, Ewbank made his final squad cuts and the survivors called a private team meeting before one of the last practice sessions at Peekskill. Center Mike Hudock and safety Dainard Paulson, the offensive and defensive player reps, called the meeting to order. Coaches were asked to leave.

This kind of meeting was standard procedure with the Jets. Just before the opener and after the final cuts, they always called a "unifying" session like this. The purpose was to wipe away any lingering training camp animosities and to mold the surviving squad members—

many of whom had been viciously battling each other for jobs—into a unified team.

Several players got up and spoke their mind on various subjects as the meeting began. Namath's name wasn't mentioned, but he realized what was on everybody's mind. He rose to his feet, a little of the slouch gone from his shoulders. He'd known from the beginning this moment would come.

Namath said he felt an undercurrent of resentment among the older players. He had expected it. Sure, he was close friends with Werblin and, sure, he had that big car and the big bankroll. But he hadn't been "getting away" with anything, no matter what they thought. Maybe they felt he wouldn't put out because of that big no-cut contract. "Well, I'm not just in this for the money," he declared angrily. He was there to be a winner and to be a member of the team. To achieve those ends, he would do all he could . . . and more, if necessary.

He said nobody had said anything to his face, and he challenged them to get any bad feeling off their chests now. He'd like to hear what they had to say and if anybody didn't like his answers he'd be glad to step outside and settle matters. Namath looked slowly around the room. Nobody spoke. When he sat down he knew that now the veterans would at least give him a chance to show what he could do. When they went out for a beer, they'd invite Taliaferro along. But at least now they'd block for Namath. If he had said the wrong thing, or remained silent, they might not even have extended him that courtesy.

13

Winning the Job

As usual, Weeb Ewbank deferred until the last minute announcing his quarterback for the season opener at Houston. However, Mike Taliaferro was working out with the first unit during practice all week and that was sufficient hint. Later in the week Weeb made it official that Taliaferro would start with Joe Namath on the sideline telephone. Two rookies, Jim Harris and Verlon Biggs, would man the right side of the defensive line. A third, Jim Hudson, would have started at safety but he was ill with pleurisy.

For perhaps the first time the Jets felt big league as their charter plane circled the Houston airport on its landing approach. Gone were the financial horrors of the Titan days and the uncertainties of Ewbank's early seasons. This group had worked together for most of a full year, and even the rookies had been around all through training camp. There were no strangers showing up two days before the opener to play quarterback. The Jets were finally a team.

They descended, however, into a Titan-type fiasco. The elements and Judge Roy Hofheinz, who played God in the Houston Astrodome, had conspired against them.

The Oilers had been playing in Jeppesen Stadium, a high school field, since their inception in 1960, but they planned to move into Houston's new air-conditioned Astrodome for 1965. They trumpeted the move in advertising for season tickets, and the AFL schedule was laid out with this development in mind. What better way to open the season than with the league's showcase rookie, Joe Namath, in the latest showcase stadium, the fabulous Astrodome? The scorching heat of Houston in late summer was no problem—the dome controlled nature in every way.

However, at the last minute, Hofheinz and Oiler owner Bud Adams, two strong-willed Texans, found they could not settle on a rental agreement. Hofheinz, many felt, thought he could get an NFL fran-

Joe Namath on the sideline telephone.

Vernon J. Biever

chise if he could deliver the Astrodome. So he set conditions for renting the stadium that Adams would not meet. With two men like this, compromise was a dirty word. Adams took his football team to Rice Stadium, a beautiful facility seating 70,000, all of the seats exposed to God's natural sunlight.

The temperature that September 14 was listed as 98 degrees. It must have been well over 100 in the stadium cauldron. And to make matters worse, the kickoff was scheduled only 30 minutes after high noon for the benefit of television viewers back east. The game drew 52,680 fans, the record for an AFL opener, and it was a horror. Players were perspiring so much "it was like playing in the rain," one reporter noted. Their jerseys, hands, and arms dripped sweat, and it proved almost impossible to hold the ball. The contest degenerated into a game of fumble. The Jets bobbled the ball seven times, tying the all-time league high, and the Oilers added six fumbles for a combined AFL record of thirteen.

The Jets lost, 27–21, as tight end Willie Frazier caught three touchdown passes and the Houston coach made some cracks about the Jet theories on pass defense. The Oiler head coach was none other than Bones Taylor, the old Titan assistant. He had been an assistant under Sammy Baugh at Houston the year before, 1964, and this season had switched jobs with his old boss. Harry Wismer wasn't the only AFL owner to run his football team by a script out of *Alice in Wonderland.*

As Namath watched Taliaferro go all the way in the Houston hotbox, he felt an odd disquiet. He didn't resent that the veteran was starting ahead of him—that was what worried him. Maybe he was getting complacent and "sorry." This was the reason Namath withdrew into himself as he left the stadium, refusing for one of the few times in his life to sign autographs.

Houston's opening day attendance record lasted only one week as 53,658 paid to see the fabulous Namath make his Shea Stadium debut against Kansas City.

But, again, Weeb started Taliaferro and it proved a shattering experience for the sensitive twenty-four-year-old quarterback. Mike got off poorly, fell behind against the powerful Chiefs, and then heard a crescendo of boos tumble down from the towering stands. Baseball and football players agree Shea Stadium is acoustically one of the "loudest" parks in sports. Now Taliaferro knew what they meant. "We want Joe, we want Joe," the fans cried heartlessly . . . and Taliaferro knew what they were saying. He was trying his best, but he felt smaller and smaller under the weight of the jeers. After six minutes of the second period, Ewbank mercifully pulled Taliaferro and gave 'em Joe. The stands broke into a roar of recognition when Namath trotted out in his then-distinctive white football shoes, his No. 12 green jersey still out-of-the-box fresh.

The Jets were trailing, 7–3, when Namath entered the game. Taliaferro had completed only four of twelve passes for a mere 24 yards. While he didn't win, Namath did better than that with 11 of 23 completions for 121 yards and the Jets' only touchdown in a 14–10 loss.

That performance earned Namath a start the following week in Buffalo. The Jets lost, 33–21, but Namath showed he could move the team against the best defensive team in the league, completing 19 of 40 passes for 287 yards and two touchdowns. He started again the next week in a 16–13 loss at Denver. Two nights before that game he ran into Bronco star Cookie Gilchrist in a Denver restaurant. "Hey, come on over here," Cookie boomed as Namath walked in. "I've never been this close to four hundred thousand dollars before." Then he laughed, and so did Namath. The two are still friends.

After a week's layoff, the Jets played at home against Oakland. Namath started, fell behind, and Taliaferro took over in the third period to produce a 24–24 tie. Mike's teammates were jubilant. There wasn't any secret about which quarterback they wanted to succeed. Taliaferro got the next start and lost to San Diego, 34–9, as Namath came in to mop up. The rookie completed only two of five passes for 21 yards, but for the first time, he began to see the mystery of pro football unfold in front of him. All of the diagrams, all of the movies, all of Weeb's lectures, suddenly seemed to come alive on the field. It was a wonderful feeling. Namath at last knew he was on his way.

The defeat dropped the Jets' record to 0–5–1 for their first six games, and people began asking Werblin if Ewbank's job was secure. This was the last year of Weeb's contract, but Ewbank was safe. He had prepared Werblin for just such a faltering start when he received permission to trade away Dick Wood, his only experienced quarterback.

The next week Denver came to town and Taliaferro started. Again Namath mopped up, but this was at the end of a 45–10 victory.

The Denver game was critical in the career of Don Maynard. The Saturday night before, he'd dropped a potential touchdown pass against the Chargers when the game was still close, and the boos were so heavy and vicious his wife left the stadium. They were even worse when he dropped another one later on. "I lost them in the lights," Maynard explained later, to which Ewbank replied angrily, "Well, those lights didn't seem to bother the Chargers any."

For the third straight year, Maynard was in trouble with his coach. With the Titans, Maynard had got into the habit of nursing phantom or minimal injuries during the week. He never missed games, but Ewbank's first year he had to issue Maynard a "practice or be gone" ultimatum. The next year, Ewbank almost pulled Maynard out of a game for breaking his pass patterns and hinted that he might trade the nonconforming flanker if he didn't start running the routes as diagrammed. Now he was grumbling, "We might have to look for someone else if Maynard doesn't stop dropping the ball."

However, the next week, Maynard was still in the opening lineup even though Ewbank could have gone with George Sauer, Jr., who had won a starting job, and Bake Turner, possibly the best reserve flanker in football. Maynard caught only one pass against the Broncos, but it went for a touchdown.

After the game, Maynard went into Ewbank's office with tears in his eyes. "Thanks for having faith in me," he told the coach, and he went on to have an almost unbelievable last seven games in which he caught 45 passes for 736 yards and 9 touchdowns. (For the season he was third best in the league with 68 catches for 1,218 yards and 14 TD's. His second-half totals alone would have put him in the top ten.)

The next Sunday the Jets went back on the road, to Kansas City. The date was November 7, and gusting winds, a preview of the bitter prairie winter, sent papers swirling around Municipal Stadium. The Chiefs, as always, presented some of the most awesome physical talent in the league. The Jet game plan called for short passes, which might nullify some of their tremendous pass rush.

Taliaferro nodded as Ewbank gave him his final instructions and he went out to direct the Jet offense. But Ewbank could hardly believe his eyes as he saw Taliaferro trying to unload one bomb after another. "Throw short, throw short," Ewbank kept repeating at every opportunity, but Mike kept throwing long, as if compelled by some private desperation.

As the Jets headed into their dressing room at the half, they were trailing, 10–6. Taliaferro had completed 9 of 17 passes for 107 yards, not bad, but he had been intercepted twice. Ewbank was outraged as he confronted his starting quarterback.

"I thought I told you to throw short," he demanded.

"I have been," Taliaferro replied.

"Well, in that case, I guess the ball's just been sailing on you or something," Ewbank countered sarcastically.

That was the end of Mike Taliaferro as a Jet, although he wore their uniform for two more full years. From that moment, he was there to play only if Namath broke a leg in a game or by "falling off a barstool," as Taliaferro once noted bitterly. In the final six games of the season, Taliaferro was to throw only nine passes, of which he completed three and had two intercepted. In 1966 he saw only enough action to throw forty-one passes, and in 1967 that number dropped to twenty. Even in games when Namath was throwing interceptions by bunches, Taliaferro was left waiting on the sidelines like a jilted bride, holding a telephone instead of a bouquet. Only when the game got completely out of reach did Taliaferro play.

Namath, of course, had something to do with Taliaferro's eclipse, starting with that afternoon in Kansas City. Joe was the starting quarterback when the Jets went into action at their 25 after the second-half kickoff. On the first play Bill Mathis ran for three and then Namath passed to George Sauer for 10 yards and a first down at the 38. A 16-yard completion to Maynard gave the Jets a first down in Kansas City territory at the Chief 46. The home team was called for a personal foul on the next play, which moved the Jets to the 31, and after an incomplete pass to Mathis, Namath hit his tight end, Dee Mackey. When Mackey was about to be tackled at the 15, he lateraled to Maynard, who went the rest of the way for the winning touchdown. Jim Turner's conversion made it 13–10 and the Jet defense held on the rest of the way for a big upset victory.

With a crisp, controlled scoring drive, Joe Namath in three minutes and two seconds had won the starting job. The following week he led the Jets to a 30–20 victory over Boston, and he backed that up with a 41–14 rout of Houston in which he threw four touchdown passes.

That victory over the Oilers gave the Jets a four-game winning streak, a team record, and Namath was responsible for most of it. Only then did the veterans concede that he had the goods, that he could win for them and put money in their pockets. Of course, there was still resentment. They didn't like all the money he had and his swinging ways and especially his close relationship with the boss. But there was respect in their attitude, too.

All good things, including winning streaks, must come to an end, however. Once again injuries were cutting into the Jets' thin supply of talent. They lost at San Diego, 38–7, and, as they waited for their plane to Oakland, there was a chance meeting between Namath and the Yankees' Mickey Mantle. Star players in all sports, and all fields, are drawn to each other, and the two men paired off and headed for the cocktail lounge to chat.

"Man, that's a lot of green stamps in there," one Jet noted, referring to the high-priced athletes.

"Yeah, and not one good knee between 'em," someone mused.

Mantle and Namath were a lot alike despite the twelve-year difference in their ages. For both, sports was the only escape from a horrible, grinding future; the Oklahoma lead mine where Mantle's father toiled, the Pennsylvania steel mill—it was all the same. Both had to bear the cross of injuries; both played in constant pain. And both were gripped by a fatalism that convinced them life was temporary, why punish yourself to prepare for the long haul? Every day you didn't die, every game you survived without a career-ending injury, was a bonus.

Their conversation ended when the Jets' plane arrived to take them to Oakland, where the Raiders' 24–14 victory was noteworthy as the beginning of Namath's famous feud with Ben Davidson. Davidson was a giant of a defensive end, six feet eight, 285 or more pounds, who liked to ride his motorcycle on vacation trips through rural Mexico. Oakland boss Al Davis had rescued him from the NFL, where he'd failed to survive because they said he wasn't mean enough. So Davidson signed at Oakland, grew a big red handlebar mustache, and got mean. He really went to work on Namath that afternoon on muddy Frank Youell Field. As officials walked off one of several roughing-the-passer penalties against the Raiders, Namath matched the giant defensive end stride for stride, jawing up at his tormentor who outweighed him by some 100 pounds.

Later Joe was to reveal that Davidson had tried to twist his neck in a pileup and was one of the very few players he'd faced that year to go for his knee.

"Davidson's got no class," Namath sneered, the ultimate put-down.

"Well, I happen to think Joe's got plenty of class," Davidson replied airily when informed of Namath's remarks. "Remember, the field was pretty muddy out there and you might hurt yourself if you try to stop too suddenly. The best thing to do is just fall down . . . and it's a lot softer if you fall down on somebody."

But despite the punishment, the Raiders were high in praise of Namath, and their coach, Al Davis, called him "the kind of player who tips the field." Opposing players noted all the little inborn technical skills that Namath possessed. How fast he set up, how quickly he delivered the ball, how well for a rookie he picked up defensive changes. And his courage. He'd take his beating.

After Oakland, the Jets came home to close out their season against Buffalo. The 14–12 victory looked nice in the record books because it was the first time the Jets or Titans had ever won a closing game. It also enabled the Jets to clinch second place in the Eastern Division with their third straight 5–8–1 record. The record books didn't show that Buffalo had just clinched the Eastern Division title and wanted only to stay healthy for the upcoming title game against San Diego.

Still, Namath did throw a couple of touchdown passes to Don Maynard against the Bills, and his late-season efforts placed him third in the league in passing. He was also a runaway choice as Rookie of the Year, the first quarterback ever to be so honored since Bob Waterfield and Otto Graham broke in as pros some twenty years earlier. As the season ended, Namath's draft status was clarified. His wobbly knees made him 4-F, but he was required to take three full physical examinations before the Army, pressured by a nationwide furor, certified him as unacceptable.

To cap the great year, Namath was noted in the columns as dating movie star Mamie Van Doren, and he became the only rookie named to the AFL All-Star squad, which met the league champion Bills in Houston. San Diego veteran John Hadl started the game, but Namath played the second half and led the Stars from behind to a 30–19 victory. The only rookie was named the game's most valuable offensive player.

That vote just confirmed the judgment of his New York teammates. "The fellows are looking forward to next year," one said, "and wherever we go, Joe's going to take us there."

14

Merger

The usual newspaper crowd gathered in the upstairs dining room at Shor's shortly before five that February evening, expecting the usual menu of large drinks, small hors d'oeuvres, and a preview of the 1965 Jet Highlight Film. There was to be an added serving, however. Almost casually, bare minutes before the final deadlines of New York's afternoon papers, press aide Joe Cahill told writers that Weeb Ewbank had just been officially rehired for another three-year term as coach and general manager.

As Ewbank began putting his team together for the 1966 season, far more dramatic events were taking place behind the scenes, events that would prove more important to the future of pro football than anything that would take place on the field.

The war for college players had been just as bitter as ever following the midwinter draft. The older league again had its baby-sitters carefully organized to blitz the AFL upstarts. Pete Rozelle, commissioner of the NFL, was in the forefront of this campaign. He made sure that all club owners acted unselfishly for the good of the league. A baby-sitter might represent one club, but if his charge was drafted by another, he immediately would begin recommending that team and the NFL in general. Anything to keep the boy away from the American League.

Aggressive owners in the AFL found they had to make their own battle plans. The annual secret draft had to be carried on without the knowledge of their commissioner, Joe Foss. After that, each club was on its own. One, San Diego, made little effort to sign top draft choices. The Chargers apparently felt they were strong enough to sit out the bidding war and still be better than their AFL rivals. Others, like Denver, drafted top prospects who wanted to play elsewhere but refused to trade their rights to keep the boys in the league.

Werblin, of course, had just about the best signing record in the

Sonny Werblin (left) and the commissioner, Joe Foss.

league. Three straight years he grabbed off his No. 1 choice. He felt Foss should be on hand to organize the fight against the NFL for players and franchises instead of gadding about the world on big-game hunts. Werblin, who in a short time had become a power in the league, led the revolt to get a new commissioner.

Foss had survived such threats before, but in the early days the struggling league had needed him and his name for integrity more than he needed them. He'd done his job so well that now his name was no longer essential. On April 7, 1966, it was announced that Foss had "resigned" as commissioner.

The next day Al Davis, the Eastern slicker who almost single-handedly as coach and general manager had turned Oakland into a major league sports city, was named the new commissioner. Davis was only thirty-six years old when he got the job, but he already had compiled a tremendous football record. As a player, he hadn't even made the college varsity at Syracuse. As a coach, he was conceded to be a good handler of men. As a recruiter, he was the world's champion. He had the con and the cunning to win down in the gutter, and that's where the war for talent was being fought.

On May 1, 1966, less than a month after Davis took over, the war escalated to its most perilous and expensive level. Pete Gogolak, Buffalo's standout place-kicker, had played out his option during the 1965 season. On May 1, he became a free agent and he signed with the New York Giants of the National Football League. One player, Willard Dewveall, had jumped from the NFL Bears to the AFL Oilers back in 1961, but after that event the two leagues reached a gentleman's agreement not to let it happen again. They wouldn't sign jumpers, for this would create expensive chaos for both sides. For fear of antitrust action, this policy was never spelled out, but it did exist.

The Gogolak signing gave Davis the excuse he needed to declare immediate all-out war without waiting for the next college draft. He ordered his owners not to wait for college prospects but to go to work on established NFL stars who had not yet signed their 1966 contracts. They were to be persuaded to play out their options in '66, as Gogolak had done, and then jump to the AFL in 1967 for huge bonuses. Quarterbacks were to be the prime targets. Davis claimed he had 100 top NFL players ready to jump. Werblin, it was reported, had Green Bay defensive backs Herb Adderley and Willie Wood all set to sign one night at his apartment when he was taken ill after dinner.

It was at this point that the NFL realized coexistence was a necessity. Peace talks were opened, and exactly two months after Davis was hired as commissioner, the merger was announced. There would be a common draft and a Super Bowl. Oddly, Davis had not been informed of the negotiations. He and Werblin, the two men most successful in battling the NFL, were outspoken critics of the agreement, which called for an eighteen-million-dollar indemnity payment over twenty years by the league to the New York Giants and San Francisco 49ers for infringement on their territory by the Jets and Raiders. Werblin and Davis felt they had the NFL on the run and that a little patience would have brought much better terms.

There was irony in that it was the Giants who had opened the Pandora's box of merger by signing Gogolak. The Mara family had been one of the pioneers of professional football, and they had taken the emergence of the AFL and a rival team in New York more personally than most of their NFL colleagues. They didn't get that much immediate use out of Gogolak, either. Their 1966 record was so bad, 1–12–1, that a place-kicker was the last thing they needed, and in

1967 he went into the Army and saw only part-time duty. The Maras did get that huge cash payment, but many wondered whether this was worth to them the loss of their standing as the foremost and only pro football family in New York.

On July 25, Davis quit as commissioner and went back to Oakland as managing general partner, which suited the NFL, if not his AFL rivals, just fine. Amiable Milt Woodard, a longtime aide to Foss, became the new AFL president.

Ewbank, of course, had his own worries, which centered on showing improvement for the 1966 season. Those 5–8–1 records were getting tiresome. And when Werblin got tired of them, Weeb would be in trouble. The Jets faced major problems as they headed into Ewbank's fourth season. For the first time since the league was founded, they were in the position of giving up players to another team. Miami had just been awarded a franchise, and each established team had to surrender four men in the expansion draft.

The four Jets were defensive back Willie West, defensive end LaVerne Torczon, linebacker Wahoo McDaniel, and center Mike Hudock.

The Jets didn't really mind losing the first three. They couldn't use West at his natural position of safety because they had better men there, and he was overmatched at cornerback. Torczon, beaten out by Verlon Biggs, had been an All-Star with Buffalo in 1960, the AFL's first season, but his time was past. And McDaniel had outworn his welcome. (Reporting on the aftermath of a wild party in a motel near Shea Stadium where some of the players lived, an assistant told Ewbank the Jets involved numbered "two whites, two blacks, and one Indian." At least the party was integrated.)

The Jets admitted they took a chance on exposing Hudock, one of four Titan originals. The pipe-smoking veteran was thirty-one years old with a history of recent injuries. Ewbank didn't think the Dolphins would go for him. When they did, the Jets reluctantly were forced to play John Schmitt, a two-year member of the taxi squad. That's how great coaches are made. The mild-mannered Schmitt, with an incongruous inch-square thatch of white standing out in his brown hair, would become one of the Super Bowl standouts.

To replace McDaniel, the Jets had second-year pro Al Atkinson and $300,000 rookie Carl McAdams of Oklahoma. Atkinson had been drafted out of Villanova the year before by Buffalo, but he was trying to make the Bills at one of their strongest positions. When he was put on waivers just before the season opener, the Jets grabbed him.

Atkinson was desolate over this. Shy, quiet, and introverted, he had made friends at Buffalo. He would be among strangers in New York. But he made a name for himself with eye-catching open-field tackles on Jet special teams and, in the last two games of 1965, started ahead of McDaniel. Wahoo had been the best middle linebacker the Jets/ Titans ever had, which wasn't really saying a helluva lot. Atkinson was a potential All-Star. Wahoo was twenty-eight, Atkinson was twenty-two. In wrestling parlance, Wahoo lost three falls out of three.

Atkinson didn't say much —it took him two years to ask the publicity department to remove the words "exceptionally quiet off the field" from his biography, but Wahoo had done enough talking to take care of all the middle linebackers for a decade. A tackle in college, Atkinson was still learning a new position in training camp of 1966. He knew that McAdams, drilling with the College All-Stars in Chicago, would be coming back with his fat contract to try to beat him out of the middle linebacker's job. But every evening at Peekskill, Al would ask the coaches for an extra copy of the day's lessons so he could keep the rookie's playbook up to date. "Enjoy the game," he'd tell reporters before every kickoff. Why not? He did.

In addition to the four new Dolphins, the Jets also unloaded the second half of John Huarte's $200,000 contract by trading him to Boston. In exchange, the Jets got a Wichita State lineman named Jim Waskiewicz and veteran receiver Jim Colclough.

Why the Jets needed an old, slow receiver for their already well-stocked stable nobody knew. And when George Sauer, Jr., showed amazing improvement in training camp, Colclough was returned to the Patriots for a future draft choice.

The Waskiewicz deal—he pronounced it Was-CAV-ij, and radio announcers as well as typesetters were glad when he left—illustrated the kind of spontaneous college draft the AFL was running. Officially, the deal was for Colclough and a fourth-round draft choice. But the Jets knew in advance that they wanted the man Boston would draft fourth, Waskiewicz.

Nobody was surprised when the NFL declined to waste a draft choice on Waskiewicz, which was also the case with Bill Yearby, the Jets' No. 1 draftee from Michigan. The Jets lost their No. 2 pick, Kentucky tackle Sam Ball, to Baltimore and signed No. 3, McAdams, in competition with the St. Louis Cardinals. They also signed a sixth-round pick, halfback Emerson Boozer of Maryland State, in competition with the Pittsburgh Steelers, and a No. 8, tight end Pete Lammons of Texas, in competition with Cleveland.

Like McAdams, Yearby got $300,000 to sign and then both joined the College All-Stars in Chicago. Neither paid off anything near his contract price, although the Jets did get some return from McAdams.

Yearby reported back to Peekskill with bad knees, underwent several operations over the years, and his game action could be measured by the minute. It was $300,000 down the drain.

McAdams' career started under similar distressing circumstances and he didn't even make it back to Peekskill. As a collegian, McAdams had been rated on a par with Tommy Nobis of Texas as a middle linebacker and some said he was better. He had that love for physical combat common to all good football players, especially those on the defensive platoon. But late one night in Chicago he was out sightseeing with some teammates and he tripped or fell—or was violently pushed, according to some unsubstantiated accounts—off a curb and broke his ankle.

The ankle was put in a cast and then an infection developed. He needed an operation . . . and another . . . and another. The next year he reported to training camp and broke a toe. McAdams had the worst feet in football. He could have taken his money and gone home to a life of quiet in White Deer, Texas. For $300,000 he probably could have bought the place. But he elected to take the punishing route. By God, he would play football again. His nightmares were not of his injury or of getting hurt again, but of fears that fans and his teammates, especially, would think he was a quitter. He played a few games at the end of the '67 season and in 1968 became a valuable spare defensive tackle. Maybe he'd never be a linebacker again, but Carl McAdams had won his battle.

The Jets had a huge opening at tight end and they expected Yearby to fill it. But while Yearby was gone All-Starring, Pete Lammons was given a shot at the job. A round-cheeked Texan, Lammons was one of those guys you draft because he's a pretty good athlete and competitor and you figure he'll make himself a place on your team. That's just what happened. Lammons won the battle for the tight end job before Yearby even had a chance to don a uniform. When Yearby did report, Lammons was being touted for rookie of the year at tight end and his high-priced rival from Michigan was told to dress with the defensive players. Lammons was fearless except for one area. The idea of hospitals and surgery turned him to jelly. So he played hurt, game after game, and declined off-season knee operations. "That's what they pay you for, to show up," he would say after playing when coaches had counted him out. He may not have been All-Pro, but he certainly was all pro.

Walt Michaels will never forget the signing of Emerson Boozer. Boozer may have been unknown to most fans, but when he finished high school at Augusta, Georgia, he had 100 college offers. He decided on Maryland State, a Negro college, and made the Pittsburgh Courier's All-American team three years straight. The Jets and the NFL Steelers had both picked him in the top ten, and they both went after him.

Michaels was the Jet assistant given the task of signing Boozer, and they talked terms in the basement rumpus room of the home of Maryland State's president. As Michaels was completing negotiations with Boozer he looked up and saw three faces peering through the basement window—agents of the opposition, the Steelers. Michaels knew he had to have Boozer signed before they left that room.

A long-term contract in the neighborhood of $100,000 was decided upon. But as Michaels shoved the contract toward Boozer, Emerson's lawyer said they wanted the $20,000 bonus portion of the 100 grand immediately.

Michaels was stunned. Twenty thousand was a little more than he customarily carried around in his pocket, and he had no company checks with him. He pulled out his personal checkbook, looked at the balance, and gulped. He was only three or four zeros short. But he wrote out the check to Emerson Boozer, got the halfback's signature on a contract, and then put in a rush call to the Jet office. They'd better get $20,000 to cover that check over to Michaels' bank pronto. Michaels just knew it was being cashed as he called.

The Jets also moved into the free agent field. At the only game they personally scouted Boozer, a teammate, Earl Christy, had his greatest night, and he was signed to become eventually a kick returner on the Super Bowl team. Defensive back Randy Beverly, a New Jersey boy who'd gone to school out at Colorado State, joined the Jets with little fanfare and spent the season on a farm club. Lightweight linebacker Paul Crane of Alabama was a nondraftee pickup. And at midsummer, Ewbank answered a call from the defensive back he had first turned pro at Baltimore and then traded away, John Sample.

15

Calling Dr. Nicholas, Again

Joe Namath was coming home. The banners in downtown Birmingham, Alabama, heralded WELCOME AFL, and a league record exhibition game crowd of 57,205 crammed Legion Field to see the colorful Pennsylvanian, whom many Alabamans had adopted as their own, lead the Jets against Houston in their opening 1966 exhibition. Weeb Ewbank announced he would start his No. 1 quarterback against the Oilers, and Joe received a wild ovation when introduced. He was still the college hero.

Namath started slowly before the big crowd, missing four of his first five passes, but now, still in the first quarter, he had the Jets moving. Two of three completions for 34 yards and the Jets were inside Houston's 30. Here Namath called Matt Snell through the middle. The play gained two yards, and as Snell thought he heard a whistle he angrily threw the ball down. But there was no whistle, or at least the referee said it hadn't sounded. Ernie Ladd, Houston's economy-size tackle, picked up the ball and started to run.

Namath had already unhooked his chin strap for a breather before calling the next play. When he saw Ladd running, he turned to argue with the official about the call. Then he sensed Ladd, with defensive end Don Floyd as interference, thundering toward him. Floyd aimed a block at Namath, but Joe played off the 245-pound veteran. He avoided the full impact of Floyd's charge, but his delicate right knee, braced though it was, twisted under the fast movement. Namath went down in a painful heap, and as his teammates muttered about a "cheap shot" and threatened to "get" Floyd next time they met, Namath hobbled off the field.

Dr. James A. Nicholas, the Jet physician who had operated on Namath a year earlier, escorted his frightened young patient into the dressing room. "He was hurt. He was hurt and he was scared," the doctor noted, and he tried to convince Namath that the injury wasn't really serious, only a minor sprain. Later Namath came out to watch the second half, wearing his suit jacket and tie, polka dot Bermuda shorts because his regular pants wouldn't fit over the bandage, and sandals.

When the Jets returned to New York, X rays were taken and announced as negative, but Namath didn't play in the team's second exhibition game, or the third, or the fourth. Mike Taliaferro, who had replaced Namath against Houston and quarterbacked a 16–10 victory, led the Jets to a sweep of the card, a 4–0 preseason record. He looked good doing it, too.

When it came time to open the season, Namath was just starting to practice again and Ewbank conceded he owed Taliaferro a chance to hold the job. Since the opener was against the new Miami team, Weeb also had it in the back of his mind that he could beat the Dolphins with a second-string quarterback and give Namath another week's rest. So Taliaferro found himself again in the middle of the quarterback shuffle and all he asked was not to be embarrassed.

Ewbank, however, grew quickly disenchanted with Taliaferro—after exactly 30 minutes of play. The Jets led, 9–0, but Taliaferro wasn't moving the team and had completed only four of seventeen passes. Namath played the second half in a 19–14 victory.

The Miami game was played on a Saturday night, which gave Namath an extra half day's rest before the Jet home opener at Shea the following Sunday. The opponent was Houston, and Namath responded with his best pro effort. The sophomore quarterback was never more brilliant as a long-distance bomber. He completed five touchdown passes against the Oilers, including guided missiles of 67 yards to George Sauer and 55 yards to Don Maynard.

The final score was 52–13, the most points ever scored by a New York team in the AFL. Two omens occurred during the rout, though. Namath was not intercepted once by Houston, but he was to spend the rest of the season trying to explode similar bombs. Too often they simply blew up in his hands. And, late in the game, a rookie named Emerson Boozer was given his first chance to carry the ball. Included in his five carries was a 39-yard touchdown run.

Namath and the Jets were far from sharp the following week. Jim Turner had to kick three field goals for a 16–7 victory in Denver. The Broncos had just changed coaches, but not their style—they were still the roughest team in the league and linebacker John Bramlett, who had entertained Namath the day before the game, gave the Jet quarterback a good going-over. Ray Malavasi, the Broncos' new coach, even took a swing at Matt Snell when the Jet fullback was run out of bounds on one play. (Snell wasn't hurt, but Malavasi reportedly drew a league fine.)

Still, this was the Jets' third straight victory, and they consoled themselves by pointing out that it's a good team that can win when it plays badly. The Jets were in high spirits when they went up to Boston's Fenway Park, but their euphoria was sadly short-lived. Namath was being intercepted and Jim Turner was missing field goals. Going into the final quarter, Boston led the unbeaten Jets, 24–7. Fans were jeering at Namath and the Boston bench was joining in. "Louder, louder," Namath gestured as he defiantly cupped his hand to his ear and 27,000 Bostonians enthusiastically responded.

But Namath responded, too, with an unbelievable fourth quarter. Playing like a Unitas, he picked the Patriots apart. Short touchdown passes to Matt Snell and Pete Lammons brought the Jets within a field goal in the closing minutes. Now it was up to the defense, which took the ball away from the Patriots and gave the Jets one more chance. Completing seven of eight passes on the drive, Namath moved the Jets in range and Jim Turner kicked a 17-yard field goal with 32

George Sauer is on his way.

New York Jets

seconds left for a 24–24 tie. Overshadowed by Namath's clutch performance were earlier missed opportunities that cost a possible victory.

A record AFL crowd of 63,497 greeted the Jets at Shea Stadium the next week when they returned for a Saturday night game against the Chargers. The Jets had a 3-0-1 record; San Diego had won four in a row. This would be the Jets' big test.

The New Yorkers took a 7–3 lead, fell behind, 16–9, and then won it 17–16, on an eight-yard touchdown run by Emerson Boozer. Boozer hadn't carried the ball a single time the week before in Boston. It was a glorious victory for the Jets—the first time they'd beaten the Chargers since their days as Titans. And before a record crowd, too. The 4-0-1 record marked the team's greatest start, and it was all over but the travel arrangements to put the Jets in the first Super Bowl in Los Angeles.

But a shorter trip to Houston torpedoed those plans. Namath was intercepted four times and the Jets not only were beaten, they were shut out, 24–0. And this by a team they had routed by 39 points only four weeks earlier. Pressed for an explanation of this reversal, Namath snapped sarcastically, "Yeah, we were all out getting drunk the night before." Some listeners took him seriously. Namath had taken a bad situation and made it worse.

The Jets returned home the following week, but friendly Shea wasn't so friendly this time. The New Yorkers took a 14–7 lead at the half against Oakland and both touchdowns were scored by Namath, his first as a pro. He bootlegged left for two yards and later sneaked for one. But the Raiders rallied for 17 points in the final quarter and, unlike the Jets in Boston, they got a 24–21 victory out of it. The Raiders scored their winning touchdown with two seconds left when fullback Hewritt Dixon, stopped up the middle on fourth down from a foot out, slid off the pile around end. The TD had been set up by a 42-yard pass from Tom Flores to Art Powell, the old Titan. On both plays, Ewbank put the blame on Dainard Paulson, their former all-league safetyman. As the beaten Jets trudged through the runway, a fan deliberately spilled coffee on Namath.

The fans were just as ugly the next week. The Jets scored 20 points in the last quarter but still went down to a 33–23 defeat by Buffalo as Namath outdid himself with five interceptions. The Jet rushing game amounted to an embarrassing net five yards as fans wondered audibly whatever happened to Emerson Boozer. In a sidelight as the Jets fell out of the Eastern Division lead, Dainard Paulson, excoriated by Ewbank the week before, suffered a cracked jaw. This was to be the Swede's last year with the Jets. He lost his starting job and then was traded to Oakland, the team that had cost him his place in New York. The high-minded halfback was dropped by the Raiders on their last cut in '67, and another old Titan drifted out of the pros.

The Jets were heavy underdogs as they took their three-game losing streak up to Buffalo. But with 11 seconds to go in the first half, they were locked in a scoreless tie with fourth-and-three at the Bill three. Kicker Jim Turner and holder Jim Hudson came in to try the field goal from a sharp angle at the 10, but when Hudson got the snap he rose to his feet and looked for a receiver. It was the old fake field goal trick!

Ewbank said he and his staff had studied Buffalo films of similar situations all week and would have guaranteed the success of this ploy. But this wasn't Sunday afternoon at the movies. The play called for a screen pass to Matt Snell, but the Bills anticipated the trick and almost literally tackled the Jet fullback. Hudson had to look for another man and his pass to Lammons fell incomplete. So instead of going off with a lead, the Jets were still no better than even.

Early in the fourth quarter the Bills were in front by 7–3, but the Jets staged a 64-yard drive to find themselves with fourth-and-a-foot at the Bill 28 and ten minutes to go. What should Weeb do? Go for the first down and then a touchdown that would put the Jets out front, or take the safe field goal and then play for another field goal that would win the game? There was plenty of time, so Ewbank decided to go for the kick. Nobody could have faulted his reasoning except that he didn't count on big Jim Dunaway, Buffalo's 275-pound defensive tackle, turning into a halfback. Dunaway broke through, blocked the kick, then scooped it up and rumbled 72 yards for the touchdown that assured the Bills' 14–3 victory and the Jets' fourth straight loss.

Ewbank probably set a career record for second-guesses after this game, and to make matters worse, Matt Snell had suffered a separated shoulder in the fourth quarter. Before criticism of this game had died down, poor Weeb had to make some more decisions.

Throughout the first ten games of the season, Ewbank had been under pressure to make more use of rookie Emerson Boozer's obvious running talents. The Jets had never had a breakaway halfback (Tiller the Thriller didn't count), and fans were getting bored with Ewbank's pass, pass, pass, and cloud-of-dust-into-the-line offense. (It did little good to point out that the Jets didn't have the line blocking to blow out the opposition and make a running game go.)

Boozer, running in padded shoes to protect his bunioned feet—his feet literally never touched the ground—had proved immensely exciting in his brief exposure. He had a twisting, turning, slashing style with tremendous second effort. Some of his best runs were for short yardage on plays where he should have been thrown for big losses.

However, Weeb remembered a play in the Denver game. Boozer had missed an assignment, let Bramlett through on a blitz, and almost put Joe Namath out of business forever. If Weeb Ewbank had Man O' War on his team, the famous thoroughbred wouldn't get into a game until he learned how to block. As Ewbank remembered, Man O' War, like Boozer, wasn't so hot as a pass receiver, either.

Fortunately, Boozer remembered that play in Denver, too. He'd been assigned to go out for a pass, but if the linebacker was blitzing, his job was to stay home and block. As he went out, Boozer noticed Bramlett shooting in for Namath. "Instead of running the pass pattern, I felt like running off the field to the bench," Boozer said. Ewbank had the same idea as far as the bench was concerned.

But Boozer kept studying. He didn't always believe the coaches, but when he saw his mistakes on film he knew he had to be doing something wrong. His biggest helper was Bill Mathis, and when Ewbank decided to start Boozer against Miami the next week, it was Mathis who was benched.

Actually, Ewbank could have moved Mathis to fullback, the position he had played regularly until Snell had moved him out two years earlier. But he put Mark Smolinski in for Snell and kept Mathis behind Boozer. This way, he would make Boozer feel he really had been promoted—and he would have Mathis available at halfback in case the rookie's blocking broke down.

Fortunately, the Jets were playing Miami and they breezed to a 30–13 victory as Boozer carried 23 times for 64 yards, plunged a yard for one touchdown, and returned a kickoff 96 yards for another.

The Miami victory also marked George Sauer's self-proclaimed "best game as a Jet." He caught eight passes for 144 yards and took over first place in the league standings for receivers. Complete dedication, intelligence, and long hours of practice had transformed this promising rookie into a sophomore star. When he turned pro a year earlier, he had thought he would need more weight, but the next time around he trimmed off the 11 new pounds to 195 and earned a bonus in added speed. A study of films in the off-season by the coaching staff revealed that Sauer had most of his trouble catching passes over his right shoulder. The Jets had his eyes examined and learned he was terribly nearsighted in the right eye. This threw his depth perception way off. A $100 contact lens for use in games corrected the problem.

Back at the University of Texas and studying toward his degree, Sauer also worked out during the day with other pros from his school like Pete Lammons and the Giants' Ernie Koy. In their small apartment, he distressed his new bride by constantly practicing "air dribbles" to strengthen his hands. He'd palm a football, drop it, and then catch it with one hand before it hit the floor. Nobody who knew either man ever thought to hint that young George was with the Jets only because of his father.

After beating Miami, the Jets lost at home to Kansas City, 32–24, as the Chiefs clinched the Western Division title, and then they set out on their annual West Coast trip. The first stop was Oakland, where the Raiders had moved into a brand-new stadium. But, as happened the year before, they still played the game on a muddy field. Namath looked like an old man trying to catch a bus on an icy street as he skittered down the sideline on a 39-yard run to set up an early Jet field goal. Weeb Ewbank showed he could move just as fast as he raced along beside his quarterback screaming, "Get out of bounds, get out of bounds!"

This was a typical Namath game for 1966. He completed 20 of 42 passes for 327 yards and two touchdowns, one a 70-yarder to Billy Mathis when he caught the Raiders in a safety blitz. But he also suffered five more interceptions, several of which directly set up Oakland scores.

The Jets trailed, 28–20, going into the final minutes, but they were able to gain possession and Namath got them past the 50. Guessing the Raiders would be laying back to prevent the long pass, he called on Emerson Boozer for the draw play and Billy Boo ran and twisted 47 yards for the touchdown. With 53 seconds left, Namath then passed to Sauer for the two-point conversion and a 28–28 tie. Snell was back by this time, but Boozer was showing why he'd been shoved ahead of Mathis as the No. 1 halfback.

The tie eliminated the Jets from any chance at the Eastern title, but that wasn't the team's major worry as it moved down the California coast to San Diego. Paul Rochester, the fun-loving defensive tackle,

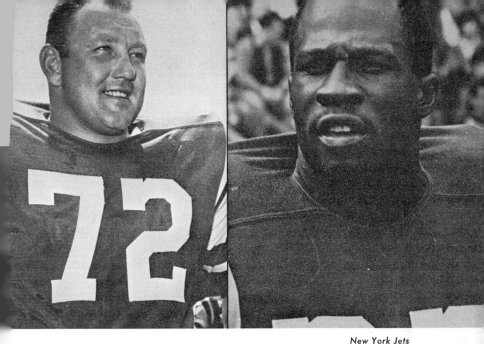

Paul Rochester (left) and Emerson Boozer.

had been left behind in a darkened hospital room, not only his football future but the sight in his left eye in jeopardy. Rochester had been injured on one of the first plays of the game. He had been just about ready to close in on Oakland quarterback Tom Flores when "the lights went out." Teammate Verlon Biggs, also reaching for Flores, apparently had stuck a finger through Rochester's face mask and into his eye. Rocky sat out a few series of downs, then went back to finish the game and even blocked an Oakland field goal attempt.

However, a hospital examination revealed the seriousness of his injury. His sight would be permanently impaired. But Rochester vowed he would play again. A Michigan State teammate of his, Fred Arbanas, continued to play tight end for Kansas City despite complete blindness in one eye. Rocky did have some vision left in his bad eye and, besides, he didn't have to catch passes the way Arbanas did. "Football is my life," Arbanas had said, and the game meant as much or more to Rochester.

Rochester had been orphaned in his teens, and his high school coach on Long Island had taken him into his home. Football had enabled him to get his college education at Michigan State, and football had opened the doors to a promising business career. During the Super Bowl season, football would help reunite Rochester with his runaway younger brother, a high school dropout. If this could help put the boy on the right path, as football had done for him years before, then the risk of playing on with only one good eye had to be worth it for Paul Rochester.

The Jets lost that game in San Diego, 42–27. Jim Turner had an extra point blocked for his first PAT miss as a pro. George Sauer watched Lance Alworth catch seven passes to move in front in their race for the receiving title, and Namath threw a couple more interceptions to help set up Charger scores.

After their 4-0-1 start, the Jets showed only one victory, one tie, and six losses in their last eight games. They would need a little help to get up for their season windup at home against Boston . . . and they got it.

The Patriots came in for the Saturday afternoon game with an 8-3-2 record. All they needed was a tie to clinch the Eastern Division title. Buffalo, 8-4-1, was scheduled at home against Denver the next day, Sunday. If the Jets won, the Bills could take the title by beating Denver. That week the Jets received 160 telegrams from Buffalo exhorting them to do their best against the Patriots.

Boston scored first, but the Jets quickly established control and led, 31–7, going into the last quarter. Namath threw a pair of touchdown passes to Don Maynard and a 77-yarder to George Sauer, the longest of his pro career. As the Jets ran out their 38–28 victory, Shea Stadium fans joined in a few jeering choruses of "Good-bye, Boston, good-bye Boston . . ." Giant coach Allie Sherman had been hearing the same refrain across the river at Yankee Stadium. The fans had merged long before the leagues.

In the Jet dressing room, Ralph Wilson, owner of the Bills, who would take advantage of their opportunity by beating Denver the next day, stuck out his hand to congratulate and thank Sonny Werblin.

"Okay, do it," the Jet owner commanded.

And Ralph Wilson, more times a millionaire than Werblin, dropped to his knees and salaamed in front of the Jet boss.

The victory gave the Jets a closing 6-6-2 record, their first breakeven season under Ewbank, but it meant much more than that. Achieved against a live opponent, unlike the previous season's finale over listless Buffalo, it was by far the Jets' best game of the year. It would send them all home on a high and hopeful note.

Namath, who led the league with 27 interceptions, did not have a single pass stolen by the Patriots. Maybe he would return in '67 as a consistent professional. Emerson Boozer, now an acknowledged pro standout who would play in the All-Star game as a rookie, ran 23 times for 117 yards. Although he didn't start and really didn't play much until the tenth game of the year, he finished tenth in the league in rushing. Matt Snell, healthy again, carried 22 times for 124 yards against the Patriots. Maybe the Jets at last had two runners who could take some of the pressure off their passing game. And George Sauer, the No. 2 pass receiver in the league, had emerged as a dangerous complement for Maynard.

The Jets appeared to be on the verge of great things, but first there was one little item of business. Remember that "minor strain" Namath had suffered in his right knee the first exhibition game of the season? Shortly before Christmas it was announced that he would have to undergo another operation on his knee.

After Joe's rookie season, he had requested another operation to

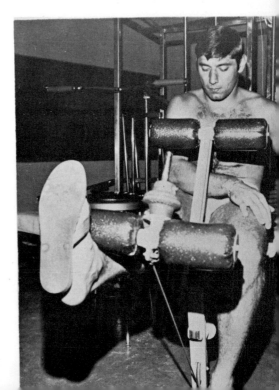

Joe Namath strengthens his knee after his second operation.

UPI

tighten up the knee so he could hopefully discard the heavy steel brace that hampered his mobility. Doctors said it wouldn't be worth the risk. But now there was further damage in the knee. In Lenox Hill Hospital, Dr. Nicholas and a team of surgeons went to work on Namath once again. They removed the other cartilage from Namath's knee and then—this was only announced after the operation—transplanted some tendons from the back of his leg to tighten up the wobbly joint.

They all said Joe would be back and be better than ever, but who could be sure?

16

Namath Goes AWOL

Joe Namath stood under some shade trees at the side of the Jets' Peekskill training field and told reporters his knee never felt better. The operation had been a success, and he now had more mobility than at any time since he was hurt. He'd never be a scrambler, but now, maybe, he'd no longer be rooted to one spot while passing. He said he was some 15 pounds heavier than the previous season and blamed it on a winter decision to quit smoking. He had bet $5,000 he could quit for five years and he gambled another $5,000 in hopes his mother would stop smoking, too. (At about this time, to help break the cigarette habit, he began dipping snuff.)

Some of the 15 extra pounds may have been hair. This season marked the debut of the "new," shaggy Namath. Hair curled down his neck and over his ears. Weeb Ewbank had tried to persuade Joe to get a haircut that morning because photographers were coming up to Peekskill, too. But it was a Monday and all the union barber shops were closed. "You wouldn't want me to go to a nonunion barber, would you?" Namath chided his coach.

Ewbank's staff had undergone its first change for this season. Chuck Knox, credited with developing such eventual Superstarters as Dave Herman, Winston Hill, and John Schmitt from the rawest material, had left to join the NFL Detroit Lions. Blond, smiling Ernie Zwahlen replaced him in charge of the offensive line.

As it turned out, the rookie crop was not too distinguished. For their No. 1 choice in the first common draft, the Jets had picked a "semisleeper" in Notre Dame lineman Paul Seiler. Seiler developed knee trouble during his rookie season, was activated for only two games, and then went into the service for two years. Unbelievably, the Jets were unable to sign their No. 2 pick, tight end Rich Sheron of Washington State, who went to Canada to play. Ewbank professed not to be distressed because Pete Lammons' fine rookie season had

The swinging world of Joe Namath.

left the Jets well off at tight end. But that never explained why he wasted such a high draft choice on a player he didn't need. The third pick, defensive lineman Dennis Randall of Oklahoma State, showed considerable promise until he hurt his knee at midseason. The following summer he was to walk out of training camp, quit pro football, change his mind, and then end up going to Cincinnati on waivers.

Down in the middle echelons of the list, though, were some pretty promising names. John Elliott, picked in the seventh round, became a Super Bowl starter and an All-Star after injuries and position shifts slowed his rookie development. Randy Rasmussen, No. 12, became a starter right away, then faded slightly out of favor before a title-game comeback in 1968. Mike Stromberg, No. 14, played a brief but vital role in the Jets' 1968 championship. And Jeff Richardson, No. 6, was a Super Bowl sub.

The rookies must have wondered what it was all about in the confusing hours before the Jets' first 1967 exhibition game Thursday night, August 4, against Boston in Bridgeport, Connecticut.

On Wednesday, Joe Namath, obviously upset by some news from home, walked into Ewbank's little office at the military academy and asked if he could leave camp after practice to go to New York for "personal reasons." Ewbank agreed, but with a game the next night, he told his quarterback, "Be back for curfew at ten tonight."

That was the last anybody on the Jets saw of Namath until the next morning.

Between the time he left Peekskill and the time he returned, it was established that Namath had been seen in several East Side Manhattan bars, including his favorite hangout, a rough and sleazy First Avenue place called the Open End, which was to be the scene of a couple of shootings the next summer. There, near the 4 A.M. closing hour, Namath ran into Charles Parmiter, sports editor of *Time* magazine. What happened next became the subject of conflicting lawsuits. Parmiter claimed Namath called him a "$100-a-week creep" and, with the aid of two friends, punched him around. Namath denied it and filed a countersuit charging defamation of character.

Regardless of what actually happened in that particular bar, the entire Jet family, especially his teammates, were annoyed at the way Joe had gone AWOL. The only possible exception was Namath's favorite owner, Sonny Werblin.

All that morning, players gathered in little groups in the Peekskill dormitory. They were angry. They thought the Jets had a good chance to go all the way to a championship, and here was Namath, their quarterback, leader and money man, taking off on a wild spree the night before the first exhibition game. Sure, the game didn't count, but patterns set in training camp would carry over into the regular season.

The players finally called a meeting. This wasn't a problem between Joe and his public or Joe and his coaches. This was between Joe and his teammates. They decided to demand a firsthand explanation. When the bleary-eyed and remorseful quarterback showed up shortly past noon, veteran guard Sam DeLuca met him at the door. "We want to talk to you," he told Joe. "We have a right to know why you left."

At 2 P.M., Namath, unshaven and red-eyed (some thought he might have been crying), stood before his teammates in closed session. Had he taken off just for a hot date, or had personal pressures and problems driven him to this?

"I'm sorry," Namath began to the circle of hostile faces. "I didn't realize this would have such a serious effect on you guys."

Then, although he never did spell out the exact problem, Namath managed to convince his teammates that family pressures and worry had driven him to cut loose for the night.

"He convinced us that he believed he had a valid reason for leaving and it had to do with his family, that he wasn't just running off for a date," DeLuca recalled later. "Whether it really was a valid reason, whether he was right, was unimportant. The fact that he believed it, that was important. That's what we wanted to hear from him."

Later Ewbank was called in. He told the players how Joe had come to him the day before and asked for the time off. To the players this was confirmation of Namath's statement.

After Namath's apology and plea to be reinstated, some of his teammates got up and spoke their mind. Johnny Sample summed it up, "You're the quarterback and the star of this team. With all the money you got, we expect you to be a leader, too."

(Later it was learned that Namath's older brother, Bob, had been stricken with a sudden paralysis in his legs. Joe's mother's brother had shown the same symptoms several years earlier before suddenly dropping dead. Joe's mother was worried sick, and Joe was, and is, very much a mother's son. There were also whispers of other family problems.)

That night the Jets, shaken but perhaps purged, left for Bridgeport to meet the Patriots. Namath had been scheduled to play the first half, but he quit after the first quarter. Remorse and a killing hangover hadn't benched him. On the contrary, he was playing so well the Jets had taken a 28–0 lead in the opening period and Ewbank wanted to look at some of his other players before the game turned into a rout.

When the Jets regrouped at Peekskill, Ewbank fined Namath $500. Obviously his teammates' acceptance of the apology helped mitigate the punishment for what was an outright defiance of Ewbank's "be back by ten" edict. Owner Werblin, though, volunteered that "if it was up to me I wouldn't have fined him," which was a pretty sharp kick in the teeth to 39 other members of the squad, many of whom would have been run out of camp for the same infraction. Never had Werblin's double standard for stars and spear carriers been more glaringly apparent. This, of course, was Werblin's big mistake in running the Jets and a partial explanation of why, during his tenure, Namath was never fully accepted by his teammates and the Jets never won a championship.

Werblin viewed pro football as an extension of show business, dependent on star attractions who, simply, were different from other mortals. What Werblin forgot is that the rolls of Actors Equity are jammed with the names of out-of-work actors who can fill all the supporting parts ten times over. If a gal in the chorus doesn't like the star's special treatment, she can be replaced by someone just as talented and possibly more so. But the man playing right guard on the Jets was there because he was the *best* right guard available, not because he was a pretty blond with big bosoms who slept with the producer. Guards and tackles might not excite the box office but they were integral to a winning team. They knew it and they took pride in that knowledge. Werblin's flaw was not acknowledging that pride. And Namath suffered for it.

After Namath's escapade, Werblin recognized that his star needed a lift. This would be the last year of Joe's $400,000 contract. Why not sign him to a new one right now? Joe's Birmingham lawyer, Mike Bite, was called up to New York, where a new three-year deal to run through 1970 was hammered out. Dick Young of the New York *Daily News* later pegged the terms as a continuation of the $25,000 salary, plus three more years of deferred payments of $35,000 a year. It was a good deal for both sides. Namath, with knees that could fail on any play, was assured six more years of financial security. Werblin, by signing Namath so far before the termination of his first contract, was able to get Joe for a much more reasonable figure than if the quarterback was about to become a free agent.

The signing was kept secret. Late in the '67 season and during the subsequent winter, Werblin must have enjoyed reading all the speculations on how much money Namath would demand for his next contract. Guesses ranged to $1,000,000 and more. The actual value was about $205,000.

Two weeks after the 55–13 rout of Boston in Bridgeport came the game some of the veterans had been waiting to play since 1960— their first test against an NFL team, the Philadelphia Eagles.

Larry Grantham had been suffering from a knee infection for several weeks (John Elliott, the rookie from Texas, was outstanding as his sub), and he vowed he would get back in uniform to play this game. The Jets were almost as fired up for this one as they would be for the Super Bowl seventeen months later. Only 22,000 fans were present in the U. of Cincinnati's Nippert Stadium, but all New York, at least, was waiting eagerly to learn the outcome.

With Namath at quarterback, the Jets were a winning team for the first 25 minutes of the game. They were leading, 13–3, when Namath stepped up into the pocket to throw a pass and his left knee could be seen to buckle visibly as it hyperextended. It was diagnosed as a sprain—he'd suffered a similar injury in training camp two weeks earlier—and Namath left the game for good. If it had been a league game, he might have returned, but Ewbank was taking no chances. The Eagles rallied to take a 17–13 halftime lead and won going away, 34–19.

In their victory, the Eagles battered the right side of the Jet defense, much as the New Yorkers were to do to the Colts in the Super Bowl. Grantham, coming off the sick list too soon, should not have been playing right linebacker. And right end Verlon Biggs and right tackle Jim Harris just were not in shape. Both had reported to camp overweight, Biggs at 297, Harris at 294. Those were the official weights. Some reports had both well over 300. Ewbank wanted each to lose 25 pounds, but they didn't make it and they resented Ewbank's making a public issue of their poundage. Neither lived up to his rookie and sophomore form during the ensuing season.

Biggs, in particular, was disappointing. Although line coach Wal Michaels was careful not to overburden him with complicated techniques of defensive play, Biggs had been one of the league's outstanding rookies in 1965. All Michaels did was point him at the quarter back, and Biggs' strength and speed took care of the rest. Dr. Nicholas was amazed at Biggs' physique and performance in various strength tests during his rookie physical examination. "Do you lift weights or something?" the doctor asked.

"No," Verlon replied. "I just live."

Biggs had been hampered by a mysterious virus his second pro season and even had to spend some time in the hospital. But he seemed to be progressing as a pro. The Jets hoped to get an outstanding third year from their silent but lethal defensive end. But he ended the season being benched.

After losing to the Eagles, the Jets beat Houston of their own league, 13–7, but this exhibition marked the end of Sam DeLuca's pro career. A freak play at the line of scrimmage tore up the ligaments in DeLuca's knee, and even as the classy veteran guard hobbled off the field, the doctor was telling him, "That's it, you're through for the year." Both of them knew that probably meant forever. DeLuca was thirty-one years old.

The Jets, in fact, had already begun to make plans to replace him. Everybody thought top draftee Paul Seiler would get his job, but instead, Ewbank reached down to freckle-faced Randy Rasmussen to play the position. Rasmussen was from the tiny town of Elba, Nebraska, attended the little school of Kearney State, and made a small college All-America team two straight years. You couldn't carve the country out of farmboy Rasmussen with a surgeon's knife. All he needed was a blade of grass between his teeth to play Huck Finn— if, that is, you can imagine Huck weighing 255 solid pounds.

In the same game in which DeLuca was hurt, backup quarterback Mike Taliaferro suffered a severe injury to his right shoulder. Ewbank scanned the waiver lists to see who else was available, but then decided to go with his third-string quarterback and place-kicker, Jim Turner. Ewbank had a favorite saying whenever he was asked why he didn't get more insurance at quarterback. "There's nothing wrong with Turner," he'd parrot almost automatically. "He's the most accurate passer we've got, just throwing short in practice, and he's got a better arm than any of the guys who were here when we took over."

What he really meant was that the Jets would sink or swim with Joe Namath.

17

The 100-Proof Halfback

When Weeb Ewbank took over the disorganized Baltimore franchise in 1954, he promised Colt owners and fans a championship by his fifth season. He delivered, too, and in fact almost made it a year ahead of time. On his arrival in New York, he made no promises, but he indicated the same timetable would be in effect. The 1967 season was Weeb's fifth in command of the Jets, and he cautiously conceded, "This year we've got a chance to go all the way." Jet players, owners, and fans agreed with him, and there was a sense of anticipation—of great things to come—as the team embarked for Buffalo and the season opener.

A record crowd of 45,748 was whooping it up in decrepit War Memorial Stadium at the start, but the hometown fans soon had reason to turn sullen and surly. With Namath completing two touchdown passes to Don Maynard, one a 56-yarder, and Jim Turner kicking a 32-yard field goal, the Jets amassed a 17–0 lead going into the final quarter.

The Jets went into that period with a fatal weakness, however. During the third period, cornerback Cornell Gordon had intercepted a Buffalo pass and was heading upfield on the return when hit with a blindside block tackle by Elbert Dubenion. The blow severely damaged Gordon's knee and the Bills quickly went to work on his replacement, Solomon Brannan.

After they turned into the final quarter, Buffalo quarterback Jack Kemp twice hit Art Powell (the old Titan and Raider) with touchdown passes, and now the Jets were back on their heels, their momentum gone, with only a 17–14 lead. Curley Johnson, their punter, was having a poor day, and the Jets couldn't even kick out of danger. With only 2:27 to play, Mike Mercer kicked a 51-yard field goal to bring Buffalo even, and with only nine seconds left, he booted a 43-yarder to win, 20–17.

Bunions never stopped Emerson Boozer.

It was a shocking, demoralizing defeat, made even more ominous by the loss of Gordon and fullback Matt Snell with knee injuries. Gordon never did undergo surgery, but his knee was placed in a cast and he didn't play again until the final game of the season. The Jets also hoped to avoid surgery for Snell, but after two weeks, the knee didn't come around and Dr. Nicholas had to operate. Since it was cartilage, not ligaments, there was hope Snell could return for the last third of the season.

Jim Turner, the Jets' place-kicker, had long pointed out the unique on-the-spot nature of his solitary job. "You're either the hero or the goat. You make it or you don't," he maintained. Except for blocking to provide the opportunity, you got no help from your teammates and you had nobody to blame. In the Buffalo debacle, Turner was the goat. He had made a 32-yarder, but he also missed field goal attempts from the 16, the 35, and the 40. Asked about place-kickers in the crowded dressing room, Werblin in his disappointment snorted, "We don't have one." Turner overheard, and the sensitive temperamental specialist never forgave him.

The Jets were idle with a bye after the Buffalo collapse, and Werblin and Ewbank scanned the land of pro football limbo, tax squads and waiver lists, for a kicker. They even attempted to deal for Oakland's venerable George Blanda, a fine kicker who could also double as quarterback. But nothing developed and the Jets ended up claiming Booth Lusteg from Miami on waivers. League rules specified that a claimed player must be placed on the active roster, so the Jets went into their final days of preparation for Denver with both Lusteg and Turner in uniform.

Lusteg's story was one of the all-time weirdos, which is one reason Ewbank kept Turner around as a precaution. (He also wanted to see how Turner would meet the challenge and whether he could rise above it.) Weeb had met Lusteg before, back in 1964 when Lusteg was living in Flushing, Queens, near Shea Stadium, and teaching high school math. He attended the Jets' public tryout at Macombs Dam Park in the Bronx and looked promising enough to earn a further try-out at training camp. That lasted only until he was asked to kick against a rushing line. Turner, then a rookie, won the job, and Lusteg, then known as Jay, spent two seasons in the Atlantic Coast Football League, a minor pro circuit.

In 1966, Lusteg showed up at the Bills' camp and asked for a try-out. He now was calling himself Booth, his middle name, and he told them he could also play defensive halfback. He'd learned that pro teams like specialists who can fill in at other positions (like Turner). He also figured nobody would be interested in a twenty-seven-year-old rookie from the U. of Connecticut who had not played football in college. So he told everybody he was two years younger and had attended Boston College, which his twenty-five-year-old brother had done.

Lusteg became an instant sensation with the Bills as he backed up his boast that he knew more about place-kicking than any man alive, including Cleveland's legendary Lou Groza. He won the place-kicking job and soon became the league's most exciting kicker. This proved his undoing. Reporters quickly ferreted out his real name and background. Lusteg's demise as a kicker coincided with their revelations. In the Bills' eighth game of the season, Lusteg kicked four field goals in one game—against the Jets in Shea Stadium—and added three extra points to take over the league scoring lead.

The very next week, he missed four out of six field goal attempts, and in the Bills' last five games after that one, he kicked only three out of nine. Even though Lusteg tied for second in the league in scoring and tied Kansas City's Mike Mercer for the most points by kicking, 98, the Bills jumped at the chance to reassert their rights to Mercer during the off-season.

At Buffalo, and again at Miami, Lusteg lost out in head-to-head duels for the place-kicking job. Carrying a little blue bag that contained his kicking tee and shoes, Lusteg was greeted with open hostility by the other Jets, although Turner was quite cordial. To Turner's buddies, though, Lusteg was an interloper, a threat. Ewbank determined that Turner and Lusteg would participate in a kickoff the next few days before they played Denver. The winner would kick in the game.

The first few rounds of the kickoff were held on Randalls Island, a dusty, rutted city-owned field the Jets used for several weeks after the start of classes forced them out of Peekskill and until the baseball Mets would vacate Shea Stadium. After Lusteg had finished his warm-up kicks in solitude at the end of the field, Turner trotted by a reporter. "He missed five out of eight, put that down," Tank hissed out of the side of his mouth.

At the end of each practice session, the two kickers alternated at various distances behind a line of scrimmage. "Hey, aaaata boy, Tank!" "Way to go!" "All riiiiight!" Shouts of encouragement filled the air every time Turner kicked one through the goalposts. Every Lusteg effort was greeted with stony silence. By the time the team left for Denver, the pressure was beginning to tell, and Turner out-kicked his rival in two workouts in the Bronco stadium, too.

The night before the game, Ewbank announced that Turner had won back most of his job. He would kick off and try extra points. Lusteg would kick field goals. Shortly before the kickoff, Ewbank made another announcement. Lusteg claimed he had a bad ankle and would not kick at all. As soon as the Jets got back to New York—they rallied from a 17-point deficit to beat Denver, 38–24—Lusteg was gone. Turner, who the next year would break every place-kicking record in the book, had conquered the challenge.

Back home the next week, the Jets defeated Miami, 29–7, as Namath passed for three touchdowns and 415 yards, the second straight game in which he had set career and club records for pass-ing yardage.

The following Saturday night, Oakland, undefeated in three games, came into Shea. The Raiders were being touted as the strongest team in the Western Division, and Namath added a little frosting to the match-up by accusing them of playing "dirty football." He had the scars to prove it, too. The Jets were leading the league in offense, the Raiders in defense, but this game the Jet defenders had to carry the burden. Namath failed to throw a single touchdown pass, but he was superb in directing the Jets' controlled offense. Meanwhile New York's front four put on its best rush of the year and harried Oakland's new quarterback, Daryle Lamonica, into four interceptions and his poorest effort of the season. The Jets won, 27–14, and their performance against a strong and tough opponent helped erase at last the shock of that opening game defeat in Buffalo.

The Jets now had a 3–1 record after three straight victories, and Houston, the next week's opponent at Shea, was 2-and-2. The other teams in the Eastern Division all had lost three times. If the Jets could hand the Oilers a third defeat this early in the season, the race would be just about over. Houston would join the also-rans in build-ing for next year with rookies, and the Jets would be able to win go-ing away. The Oilers knew this, too. By a quirk in the schedule, they only played the Jets once this season, and this would be their only chance to get back into contention.

Through most of the first half, it looked as if the Oilers might as well begin preparing for next season. As more than 62,000 fans shouted encouragement, Emerson Boozer ran five yards for a first-period touchdown, and 56 seconds into the second quarter, Namath passed 30 yards to Don Maynard for another score. Jim Turner's 10-yard field goal halfway through the period gave the Jets a 17–0 lead. "Oh-oh, now we're in trouble," press box comedians gagged, recalling the Buffalo collapse.

Their fears appeared groundless, however, as the home team once again drove into Houston territory in the closing minutes of the half. With only seconds to go, Jim Turner lined up to kick a field goal from the 34 that would have made it 20–0. The kick never got past the line of scrimmage. Pat Holmes, Houston's fine defensive end, broke through to block the kick, and Ken Houston, a swift rookie defensive back, scooped it up and ran 71 yards for an Oiler TD. Instead of going off at the half 20 points ahead, the Jets were in front by only 17–7.

Namath had not been intercepted a single time in the first half, but his game fell apart completely after the intermission. On the third play from scrimmage, Namath's pass for Maynard was intercepted by Miller Farr and returned 51 yards for a touchdown that cut the Jet margin to a slender 17–14. After the Oilers kicked off, the Jets drove to the Houston 21. Again Namath aimed for Maynard, again Farr intercepted, this time at his 13, and he returned 67 yards before Namath horrified Werblin, Ewbank, and most of the assemblage by making a saving tackle at the Jet 20. But five plays later the Oilers got the touchdown anyway on a pass from new quarterback Pete Beathard to Monte Ledbetter and they went in front, 21–17.

The Jets retaliated with a 27-yard field goal by Turner to pull within a point, but once again Namath was intercepted and once again an Oiler defender, Ken Houston, ran all the way, 43 yards, for a touchdown. The Oilers had scored 21 points in the third quarter as John Wittenborn's conversion gave them a 28–20 lead. Namath had been intercepted three times and each theft had led to a Houston touchdown. Although Mike Taliaferro had been reported physically able to play some weeks earlier, Ewbank had said his arm wasn't strong enough and declined to put him on the active list. Turner was his only other quarterback and Weeb didn't dare use him. He stuck with Namath as boos echoed through the stadium.

The Jets tried desperately to rally in the fourth quarter, but twice more Houston interceptions foiled Namath's attempts to strike back. However, with just over five minutes to play, Beathard was hit by onrushing Gerry Philbin as he tried to pass from his nine, and linebacker Al Atkinson intercepted the misdirected football at the 15. He returned to the three, and on the first play Boozer burst over for the score.

The Jets now needed a two-point conversion to tie, and Namath was throwing for Don Maynard all the way. Two Houston defenders, Larry Carwell and W. K. Hicks, were climbing all over Maynard. Yellow flags flew for two counts of pass interference, but the slender flanker still held the ball. The score was tied at 28–28 with five minutes to go.

At this point, the Oilers changed quarterbacks again. Beathard, who had replaced rookie Bob Davis just before the half, was new to the team. He had reported after a big deal with Kansas City just days before the Jet game. So Oiler coach Wally Lemm went to experienced Don Trull, whose trade to Boston would be announced minutes after the game. He figured Trull was his safest bet to run the clock, avoid a fumble, and at all costs, prevent a loss.

With 44 seconds left, the Oilers stalled at the Jet 45 and Wittenborn tried a 52-yard field goal. He was way short, and now the Jets were at their 15 with 34 seconds to go. On the first play, Namath sent Boozer over right tackle on a trap. Booz gained 21 yards, but fans booed what they thought was a play-it-safe-for-the-tie call. Then Namath passed short to Pete Lammons, who was run out of bounds at the Jet 39, stopping the clock with 11 seconds to go.

Time remained for only one play, and Namath elected to go for broke. He'd throw for the sky, and even if the Oilers intercepted, odds were against another runback into the end zone. George Sauer was to be Namath's receiver, and Joe sent the blond end deep and far as he let the desperate pass fly. But W. K. Hicks got there first for Houston's sixth interception against Namath and headed upfield from the Oiler 25. The Jets appeared frozen in their cleats. Seconds seemed to pass before they reacted to the dangerous situation. Hicks was flying, but at the Jet 35 the mass of bodies met. Out of the tangle, Hicks lateraled to Ken Houston, who in turn lateraled to Larry Carwell, who once again started for the Jet goal.

It was impossible. The clock had already run out and this was like some psychedelic nightmare. Offensive and defensive roles were reversed. Garland Boyette, a 240-pound linebacker, was leading interference for Carwell as a blocker, and Namath, fragile knees and all, was hobbling to cut them off. He might not have made it in time, but Maynard, sprinting as if he was back running the hurdles for Texas

Western, made a dive at Carwell and ticked his heel just hard enough to slow him up. Playing off Boyette's block like a professional defensive back, Namath brought Carwell down in the dirt of the baseball infield at the four-yard line to save the tie. For long seconds after the play, he lay there, face down. Even though Houston had not won, Namath and the Jets had lost. Joe's six interceptions were a club and personal high and tied the league record. The Oilers' 245 yards in returns was an AFL record.

The tie in itself was not too damaging, except that the Jets had blown a chance to wipe out their last opposition for the Eastern Division championship. What did hurt were the psychological factors. The Oilers now had renewed hope that their new quarterback, Beathard, could still help them make a run for the title. Loss of a 17-point lead for the second time and Namath's wild interception performance were demoralizing. As Ewbank finally prepared to activate Mike Taliaferro, one Jet noted, "Maybe we ought to activate Ray Abruzzese [Namath's old Alabama buddy who was now a spare safety with the Jets]. He could line up behind the backs when we're on offense and tackle those guys when they run back the interceptions."

The schedule came to the Jets' rescue at this point. They next drew expansion Miami and beat the Dolphins, 33–14, as Namath sat out the second half with a Charley horse. The following week the Jets rallied from a 20–7 deficit late in the second period to beat Boston, 30–23.

The victory over Boston closed out the first half of the Jets' season and they were still on top of the Eastern Division with a 5–1–1 record. They had a full game in the standings on Houston (4–2–1), and Boston, Buffalo, and Miami were out of it with five losses apiece.

The brightest note of the first half of the season was the brilliant performance by Emerson Boozer, who had emerged as one of pro football's most exciting climax runners. Maybe he didn't have sprinter speed and maybe he didn't have fullback power, but give him the ball inside the 10 and he'd get you six points. Because of Ewbank's emphasis, he also had developed into a pretty good blocker and a dangerous pass receiver, even though he still dropped a lot of balls in practice.

When he first joined the Jets as a rookie, Boozer didn't know what to expect. But after his fine 1967 finish and off-season workouts with the Colts' great Lenny Moore, he had true confidence. As a rookie he simply assumed he'd be able to do whatever they might ask; now he knew what was demanded and knew he could meet the test. He had learned what it meant to be a pro.

All that remained from those uncertain rookie days were his bunions. Boozer refused to have them cut off, despite the discomfort they gave him. They helped his balance, he insisted, and he promised: "When they hurt too much to run, then I'll have them cut off." Boozer liked to point to the case of fullback Billy Joe, who was AFL Rookie of the Year with Denver in 1963 while suffering from bunions but just another runner after the operation. By an ironic twist, Joe was now a Jet teammate. Boozer didn't want to follow Billy Joe's route from city to city.

Boozer had been shut out from the end zone when the Jets opened at Buffalo, but with Snell injured, he became the team's only real running threat. Against Denver in the next game he scored three touchdowns on short runs, and the next week against Miami he scored three more. The first came on a one-yard plunge, the next two on passes from Namath. That made six touchdowns in two games, and the next three weeks he added two more a game for a total of twelve in his last five outs. It was an incredible performance, and as the Jets wound up the first half of their season, he scored a single touchdown against the Patriots, his thirteenth.

Every touchdown record in football was in Boozer's grasp after the first seven games, as he led the league in scoring with 78 points. No other nonkicker had ever won that title, but he had a lead of 22 points on the field. The Jet record for touchdowns by rushing was seven, and Boozer already had beaten that by three in half a season, all of his running scores coming from inside the 10. He was also only one short of receiver Don Maynard's overall club record of 14 TD's.[*]

Ol' Booz was a 100-proof halfback with a white lightning kick. As the Jets gathered in the lobby of the Hilton Airport Inn in Kansas City to await the buses that would take them to Municipal Stadium to start the second half of their season against the Chiefs, somebody asked young George Sauer about the game plan.

"Very simple," Sauer deadpanned. "It's Boozer into the end zone."

---

[*] Other records in Boozer's reach: AFL—most touchdowns rushing, 13, by Cookie Gilchrist and Abner Haynes, both in 1962; most touchdowns overall, 19, by Haynes in 1962. NFL—most touchdowns rushing, 19, by Jim Taylor in 1962; most touchdowns overall, 22, by Gale Sayers in 1965.

18

Flop of the Year

The Jets found a sloppy track when they arrived at Municipal Stadium. That was bad news. Kansas City was a big team, maybe the biggest in football. Beef and power pay off on a muddy field. Ernie Ladd, six feet nine, 313 pounds. Buck Buchanan, six feet seven, 287 pounds. They provided the beef of a defensive line that would be looking for Namath all afternoon.

From the very beginning it was a war, and for a while the underdog Jets held their own. They scored first on a short Jim Turner field goal, trailed at the quarter, 10–3, but then tied at 10–10 during the second period after a 70-yard drive that included a 13-yard first down scramble by Namath. As his quarterback bounced off Kansas City's All-Star linebacker, Bobby Bell, Weeb Ewbank appeared to be in a state of shock.

But Kansas City power began to assert itself. Verlon Biggs had to be lifted from the game, and assistant coach J. D. Donaldson gave the big end a sidelines lecture for what he was letting the Chiefs do to him. Don Maynard caught a pass and then his ribs seemed to buckle as two Kansas City defensive backs crunched him on the tackle. He was done for the day. Buchanan, giving rookie guard Randy Rasmussen his worst game of the season, smashed Namath for a loss. It was still the first half, but already, on both sides of the line of scrimmage, uniform pants showed flecks of blood mixed with the mud.

Just before the break, a Willie Mitchell interception set up Jan Stenerud's second field goal, and the Chiefs went off leading, 13–10. It was still a ballgame.

Within five minutes of the second half, however, the Chiefs had two more touchdowns. They drove 69 yards after the kickoff for one score with Mike Garrett biting off huge morsels of yardage, and two plays after the touchdown, Willie Mitchell intercepted a Namath pass and ran it in from the 27. A two-point conversion gave the Chiefs a 28–10 advantage.

Namath, limping from a bone chip in his ankle incurred a week before, was under heavy pressure. Twice, with the Jets pinned deep in their own territory, Ewbank let Mike Taliaferro try to wedge it out. But Pete Lammons was hurt when tackled after catching a pass and fumbled to set up still another Kansas City touchdown, and two other Jets (Earl Christy and Solomon Brannan) were chopped up on the kickoff. Forget the scoreboard—the Jets were taking a terrible physical beating.

The Jets trailed, 35–10, going into the fourth quarter, but now they got a little drive going after Buchanan had started them off on the wrong foot by batting a pass back into Namath's face. (He was to do this four times during the game.) However, Namath passed to Bill Mathis for nine to the Jet 39, and he ran Boozer for three yards and a first down on the 42.

Short passes were the only way to beat the Kansas City rush, so Namath called Boozer on a swing pattern to the left. Boozer caught the little lob near the sidelines and headed upfield. He was looking for the linebacker. That's the man he had to beat on this play. And, sure enough, here came Sherrill Headrick in pursuit at an angle from the middle of the field. Headrick caught up to Boozer at the Chief 39 after a 19-yard gain and leaped on his back to ride him out of bounds. Mitchell, the cornerback, was racing up to help. Boozer never saw Mitchell driving in low to crunch against his planted right leg. Surprise —and then pain as the ligaments tore apart—sent shock waves through Boozer's body. Trainer Jeff Snedeker and equipment manager Bill Hampton helped him off the field.

By the time Boozer settled on the bench, the initial pain had subsided. Emerson thought it was just another of the bumps and bruises that go with the game. The Jets were driving toward a touchdown and Boozer wanted to go back in. Dr. Nicholas squatted in front of him on the bench. He took the injured leg in his hands and waggled it from side to side. That's when Boozer knew he was hurt. Hurt bad.

The 42–18 rout was played out to the enjoyment of a record Kansas City crowd (46,642), but it was a grim group of Jets that headed back to New York. Boozer and Dr. Nicholas would not be going home from the airport. They would head directly for the Hospital for Special Surgery.

Dr. James A. Nicholas had gained great public notice for the operations on Namath's knees, but the young orthopedic surgeon had been recognized as one of the leaders in his specialty long before that. The late President Kennedy was one of his patients, and he had become associated with the Jets when they were still known as the Titans.

The skillful surgeon saw his work with athletes as only part of a crusade. Through them, he could help publicize his more basic work, the necessity for orthopedic awareness among citizens in all areas, especially those involving children. Quite often, he felt, the arthritic knee of a man of fifty was the legacy of an improperly treated "minor" childhood injury. He believed that all youngsters should be given an orthopedic examination to determine when they were physically developed enough to participate in contact sports. The study of athletic injuries provided him with a controlled area for his research. But he was proud of his football players, too. Of 40 players on the Jets' Super Bowl squad, he had performed 36 operations on 28 of them.

Dr. Nicholas had a theory about knee operations. He felt that the sooner surgery was attempted, the better was the chance for recovery. On their arrival at the hospital, Dr. Nicholas made preparations to operate on Boozer that morning.

(The doctor didn't reserve such emergency treatment for stars. Pete Perrault was a utility lineman with the Jets for several years, a fringe player in every sense of the word. Half the season on the taxi squad, half the season on special teams. A good guy to have around because he could finish a game at several positions. And a good guy, too. Pete Perrault tore up his knee in a night exhibition out of town one year. Dr. Nicholas took him from the airport to the hospital, and it was after midnight when they checked in. Instead of even waiting until the next morning—a couple of hours' sleep wouldn't refresh him that much— the doctor ordered Perrault wheeled right into surgery. The 3 A.M. operation saved Perrault's career and Pete was able to come back and play long enough to qualify for his AFL pension. For a guy who never made Namath-league or even Boozer-league money, this was important. That operation didn't make the national magazines, but the players knew about it. And Pete Perrault would always be grateful.)

Boozer's ligaments had been badly mangled and the odds were slim that he'd ever play again. The early operation, though, gave him a chance. From now on, determination and hard, painful therapy would mark the route for his comeback.

The loss of Boozer left the Jets in shock. Matt Snell was just preparing to come back from his own knee operation, and Ewbank's plans had called for the fullback to break in easily against the Patriots two weeks later. The Jets would have a bye after the Boston game, so Snell then would have two more weeks for rest and therapy before heading into the final four games.

Boozer's injury radically changed all that. Although Ewbank hedged and Snell was skeptical, there was no question Matt would be on the field to face Buffalo that coming Sunday even if they had to push him out on roller skates. There had to be somebody in the lineup who at least *looked* as if he could run with the ball.

Snell, his knee certified as healthy, was there at the kickoff, all right, and he carried the ball three times in each half as the Jets avenged that opening loss to the Bills, 20–10. (Rookie Dennis Randall joined the Nicholas Knee Club in that game.) A week later Snell carried only twice and caught a pass before being led off early with a concussion in a 29–24 victory at Boston. The Jets almost blew a 29–3 lead in this one.

The open date gave the Jets a chance to regroup and take stock. They had four games to go, Denver and Kansas City at home, then Oakland and San Diego on the road. They were 14-point favorites over the Broncos, but would be hard-pressed in the last three. With a 7–2–1 record, they held a one-game lead in the Eastern Division over the 6–3–1 Oilers. But Houston had the easier closing schedule in which two games against Miami sandwiched home encounters with Oakland and San Diego.

The Broncos, who had lost 10 of 12 games, would be the Jets' last cinch opponent, but as they went out for the kickoff, the New Yorkers noticed a terrible omen. For the first time since Werblin and his associates had bought the team, it was raining at gametime in Shea Stadium. A total of 61,615 tickets had been sold, but only 32,903 fans showed up on the miserable day. The Giants were on television from Cleveland that afternoon, which made it an easy decision for the wise stay-at-homes.

The first period was scoreless, but in the second quarter Namath reverted to his Houston form. Four times he was intercepted and every one helped set up a Denver score. In between, the Broncos' Floyd Little ripped off a 72-yard punt return for another touchdown. It was the first scoring punt return of the season in the AFL, which showed that those plays, like interceptions, just shouldn't happen. In baseball, that would have added up to five errors for the Jets, five unearned runs for the Broncos. At one point, Denver scored two touchdowns and a field goal in less than three minutes, thanks to Little's return and Namath's generosity. When the halftime gun mercifully sounded, the Broncos had scored 26 points in the second quarter and the Jets, with their touted offense, had failed to get on the board.

Namath came out firing in the second half. He threw 42 passes in the final 30 minutes, and three of them went for Jet touchdowns. But he could never make up those four interceptions. With Boozer gone and Snell still not effective, the Jets found that Namath's wing and their pregame prayer couldn't carry them. They lost, 33–25, and out in Houston under the weatherproof Astrodome the Oilers beat Miami, 17–14, to pull into a tie for the Eastern Division lead.

There were other problems besides the Oilers and the schedule as the Jets started work for their rematch with Kansas City. Joe Namath's right thumb had been injured against Denver. The Jets tried to keep it quiet, but Namath wasn't working out. Guess who found out about it first? The bookmakers. They took the game off the boards (refused to take any more bets) until it was determined whether Namath would play. Namath didn't work out until Friday, and within minutes after he walked off the field healthy at the completion of his first practice, the game was back on the boards. That's why pro football tries to make coaches report all injuries. The high rollers and bookmakers have their own sources of information and pay well for it. Nothing escapes them. Pro football commissioner Pete Rozelle, following the lead of his predecessor, the late Bert Bell, figures the public should be let in on these facts, too. The coaches don't always agree.

When Paul Zimmerman of the New York *Post* uncovered Namath's injury, Ewbank tried to minimize it. But after the season, Namath confided, "They thought it was broken."

Still, Namath was in the pit against the fearsome Kansas City pass rush the following week, as Ewbank came up with another surprise. Jim Harris, a three-year starter, was benched at defensive right tackle, and John Elliott, the blond rookie from Texas, took his place.

The big holes were in the offensive line, though, as Buchanan and Ladd took turns pouring through against Sherman Plunkett. Namath, who never did throw long with his thumb heavily taped, spent most of the afternoon picking himself up. Once Ewbank offered to put Talia-ferro into the game, but Namath shrugged him off. He wouldn't be driven out. But the Jets had no offense, and Kansas City shut them out until the last nine minutes in a 21–7 victory.

This game provided two freak plays, one of which affected the out-

Joe Namath is disconsolate in defeat.

UPI

come. The score was still 0–0 late in the first half, Kansas City was pinned back on its own two-yard line, and Jerrel Wilson was punting from the end zone on fourth down. In a thousand-to-one shot, Wilson's punt hit his own deep blocker, Curtis McClinton, right on his hip pads. The Jets were all set to take possession at the KC 10 in easy touchdown or at least field goal range when officials started marking off a penalty. The Jets' Carl McAdams had been called for a personal foul, the play was nullified, and Kansas City started all over with first down at the 17.

Eventually, the Chiefs had to punt again, and the Jets took over at their 20 with time in the half for a couple of plays. Earlier in the week, the Jets had picked up Abner Haynes on waivers from Miami. Haynes had been the AFL's first big-name star as a rookie in 1960 for the Dallas Texans and later moved with the team to Kansas City. By now he was at the end of his career (he would retire after the season), but the Jets thought he might give them a little help at running back.

The first play after Kansas City's kick was a hand-off to Haynes. But as Li'l Abner headed around end, he saw the massive figures of Ladd and Buchanan looming up in front of him. In panic, he lateraled back to Namath and so let his fragile quarterback get tackled for the three-yard loss. If Namath had been hurt, Haynes might have been retired by the Jets a few games earlier than he'd planned.

The day wasn't a total disaster, however. Out in Houston the Oilers were being beaten by the Raiders, 19–7. The Jets were still in a tie for first place, but they weren't feeling very comfortable about it. They had lost two in a row and three of their last five. They would have to win the championship on the road—not a very pleasant prospect.

The Raiders had clinched the Western Division title with their victory over Houston, but the Jets knew better than to expect a complacent team waiting for them. The only game Oakland had lost all season was to the Jets that October night in Shea Stadium. The Raiders wanted to avenge that solitary defeat, and a victory would give them a shot at finishing up with the best record in AFL history.

More to the point, they preferred that Houston win the Eastern Division championship. They knew that on a good day Namath could beat any team. They feared his arm. They did not want to face it for a third time in a championship game with big money and a Super Bowl invitation in the balance. Besides, they always enjoyed rubbing Joe's nose in the mud.

The Jets went out to the West Coast early in the week to avoid bad weather in New York and on Saturday before their game in Oakland relaxed in motel rooms to watch Houston's Saturday game with San Diego on television.

What they saw was a 24–17 Houston victory that dropped the Jets a half game out of first place. During the half, TV announcer Curt Gowdy mentioned that the Oilers were using modern videotape scouting equipment in the next booth to provide instant films of Charger formations. Later he amended this to say the machine was being used only to record the halftime band show. Ewbank in California and Werblin in New York both bolted upright at Gowdy's initial comment. Use of electronic scouting equipment was prohibited, and the Oilers had been called on this before during the exhibition season. Werblin fired off an angry protest to AFL president Milt Woodard, but the Oilers were cleared of the charges and the result stood.

The next afternoon the Jets went out to see what they could do on their own about overtaking the Oilers.

Both teams were fired for a top effort. An Oakland fumble gave New York its first break, and Namath passed 29 yards to Maynard for a touchdown. Oakland scored on a George Blanda field goal and New York led, 7–3, at the quarter. The Jets stayed in front, 14–10 at the half, their second touchdown coming when Snell fumbled on a plunge from the one and Namath picked up the ball and ran it in.

Both front lines had been putting a tremendous rush on the passer, and the Raiders went back after Namath with fire shooting out of their face masks in the second half. On the Jets' second series of the third quarter, Isaac Lassiter, the underrated defensive end who actually was a much better player than his mustachioed running mate, Ben Davidson, broke through on Namath. Lassiter weighs nearly 300 pounds and he was like a wild elephant in his black jersey, thundering after the quarterback, forearm first. He cracked Namath head-on in the face just as Joe released the ball, and the flattened quarterback never did see linebacker John Williamson intercept on the Jet 31.

After Williamson's three-yard return, the Raiders needed only seven plays to get the easy touchdown that put them on top for good, 17–14. On the next series they got another one when Daryle Lamonica passed 47 yards to tight end Billy Cannon for a TD after Oakland had recovered a Jet fumble. That made it 24–14.

The scoring pass to Cannon actually had been set up late in the first quarter when Jim Hudson, the Jets' strong safety, went out with a dislocated hip. Solomon Brannan got the call to replace him. It was a second chance for Brannan. He had come in at cornerback for Cornell Gordon in the opener at Buffalo, and his poor performance opened the way for unsung Randy Beverly to claim and win a job. Now Brannan was getting a shot at safety, but he proved incapable of handling Cannon on this big play and several others.

As the third quarter ended, the Jets were driving and a 32-yard pass from Namath to George Sauer set up a first-and-goal at the Raider 10. Mathis hit the right side for two and then Namath moved to the right side on a roll-out. He had a clear path to the end zone, but he hesitated just a split second too long looking for a receiver. By the time he started to run, the defense was reacting. Although he literally threw himself at the goal line, he was stacked up at the one. Neither Mathis nor Snell could punch it over on two tries from that point, a spot that would have been virtually automatic for the missing Boozer.

The Jets had missed their last chance to get back in the ballgame. Buoyed by the goal line stand, the Raiders exploded for another quick touchdown to go ahead, 31–14. The big margin meant that Namath now had only one weapon left, the long pass. And that meant that the Raiders could mount an all-out pass rush. Joe was in for more lumps.

A holding penalty set the Jets deep in their territory after the kickoff, and Namath was scrambling as the Raiders chased him out of the pocket. With Namath running, Davidson was able to escape from Winston Hill's block and he lumbered after the hobbling quarterback. Namath got the pass away (it fell incomplete), but Davidson literally launched himself at the Jet quarterback, a lethal, 287-pound flying missile. His left fist and forearm came cracking up under Namath's face mask and sent Joe and his helmet flying in different directions as Jet guard Dave Herman gasped in shock.

Officials threw their flags for a roughing-the-passer penalty, and while they were pacing off the 15 yards, Namath, dazed and glassy-eyed, rested on his hands and knees like a fighter taking the count. If he'd been a fighter, Namath wouldn't have made his feet by the count of 10, and even if he had, the bout probably would have been stopped to save him further punishment. But somehow he rose and wandered this way and that until his head cleared. The helmet was retrieved and Namath strode back into the huddle. The 53,000 fans in the stadium, plus millions watching on television around the nation, including hardened football veterans, marveled at Namath's courage. He stepped up in the pocket and threw a nine-yard completion to Pete Lammons on the very next play. And he stood right in there, never flinching against the Oakland rush, and passed for two more touchdowns and a two-point conversion in the 38–29 loss.

After the game, doctors said Namath was probably suffering from a broken cheekbone. "How'd you get it, Joe?" one reporter asked. "Was it when Davidson hit you?"

"Naw," Namath replied defiantly. "I got it this morning biting on a piece of steak."

With the defeat, the Jets lost any chance to win the Eastern title outright. The best they could do was tie. Hopefully, Ewbank declined to put Hudson on the inactive list. Perhaps he'd be okay for a play-off, if there was a play-off. Gordon, who'd said he'd been ready for a month, would be activated to play safety against San Diego in the last game of the season the following week.

Sunday night after the Oakland battering, several of the Jets decided to take off for Las Vegas. Their time was their own until Monday night when they had to join their teammates in Escondido, California, a small town only 20 miles from San Diego. Namath, all shaved and dapper despite a swollen and discolored cheek, led the group to Vegas. A cracked cheekbone wouldn't stop him from playing the next week— why should it stop him from playing now?

When Namath returned to Escondido, a special face mask, which he would continue to wear the following season, was rigged to protect the injury. X rays, finally taken on Tuesday, confirmed the fracture.

Once again the Oilers were scheduled on a Saturday, this time in Miami. If, somehow, the Dolphins could score an upset, the Jets would have a chance to force a play-off by beating the Chargers the next day. Since the Houston game was being played at night, there would be no national television and no local broadcast. So the Jets arranged for Henry Goldberg, son of a Newark, New Jersey, sports columnist who lived in Miami, to call them long distance from the Orange Bowl press box and provide a running account of the game. An amplifier was attached to the receiver in the private dining room of the Jets' Escondido motel and the team filed in to hear its fate being decided across the continent.

As the Oilers pulled away to their 41–10 rout, there became less and less for Goldberg to say. Late in the third quarter, Jet players began to start drifting out. Houston, which had won only three games in 1966, became the first team in AFL history to move from last to first in one year. The fact that they had expected the night's result didn't lessen the Jets' disappointment. George Sauer sat off to one side and cried. "To think," he said, "after everything we've gone through, it was all for nothing."

Later that night, somebody in the celebrating Houston party sent the Jets a telegram. It read: GOOD LUCK, SONY (*sic*), ON YOUR GAME WITH THE CHARGERS. WE SAVED SECOND PLACE FOR YOU. THE HOUSTON OILERS.

The misspelling of Sonny Werblin's name was believed to be deliberate. Sony is a firm that makes electronic equipment and it was thought to be a reference to Werblin's videotape charges the week before. Ewbank tucked the telegram away in his briefcase. He would find a use for it one day.

The next afternoon was December 24, Christmas Eve, the kind of balmy, 80-degree southern California day Easterners can never reconcile with the Yuletide season. Both teams were playing for fun, records, and 1968 paychecks. The Chargers had a chance to finish second in the Western Division, but as the Jets knew so well, second place meant no financial rewards and a lot of disappointment. Namath, as he had done the year before against Boston, closed out his season with a near-perfect performance. He threw for four touchdowns (three to Maynard) and did not have a pass intercepted.

For the season, Sauer, who made the All-Star team, and Maynard finished one-two in the AFL in pass receiving. Namath, who had broken the AFL one-year record for passing yardage against Oakland the weekend before, ended up with 4,007 yards for the season. No pro player had ever broken 4,000 before or even come within 250 yards of it. But Joe also had been intercepted 28 times and he had more physical problems, this time with his "good" knee, the left. Back in that exhibition game with the Eagles, he had suffered a slight tendon tear. After another fine performance in the AFL All-Star game, Namath's knee was placed in a cast for several weeks. Immobilizing the knee helped relieve some of the old bursitis condition, but not the torn tendon. For the third time in as many years, Namath had to enter the hospital for a knee operation. Compared to the other two, however, this was a hangnail.

Sitting in the back row of the press box as the Jets played San Diego, Werblin found little to enjoy in the 42–31 rout that gave his team its best record ever, 8–5–1. What he recalled were the big leads the Jets had squandered and losses in three of the last four games of the season that had cost the Jets the title. He remembered those other late-season collapses. He wondered out loud why Ewbank had waited so long to find replacements for the slumping Biggs and Harris.

"Well, at least we didn't fold in this one," he grumbled after the final gun.

In his disappointment, and though he denied it later, Werblin those final weeks strongly considered replacing Ewbank as coach while retaining him as general manager the following season. But he wisely elected not to make a precipitate move—not until he'd come up with a replacement. "It's not like baseball. You don't make a change just to be making a change," he declared. "I haven't given any thought to whether Weeb will come back or not come back. I'd have to see who's available and then make a decision. If I make a change it would be before the draft."

Since Ewbank was still under contract, this was hardly a ringing vote of confidence.

However, before he could mount a search for a new coach, Werblin had other matters to attend to. He was only president of the Jets, not the sole owner or even a majority stockholder. His partners were unhappy, all of them. That situation had to be resolved, and fast.

19

The Last Supper

The Werblins were entertaining. The guest list had more names than a training camp roster. The booze was flowing and the steaks were rare. A five-piece combo played show tunes. Every by-lined sportswriter, editor, and columnist in New York was there. So were their wives. Sonny Werblin believed in inviting the wives to his press parties. "Invite them and the guys have to show up," he'd say, and that night's turnout on only short hours' notice proved his point.

The party was held on a Friday night in May at Lüchow's, a downtown restaurant specializing in German food. Limousines hired by Werblin lined up outside to take the boxing writers and columnists uptown to the light heavyweight title fight between Bob Foster and Dick Tiger at Madison Square Garden. The cars would wait and bring them back, too. No rush. The party wouldn't be ending soon. That's the way Werblin did things. He threw great parties, probably because he and his wife, Leah Ray, liked to go to great parties. They had more fun than anyone else.

But this one wasn't just a party, it was a wake. Sonny Werblin was leaving the scene, and by request of his partners. They had bought him out. The deal had been completed 24 hours earlier. Sonny could have remained as a stockholder in the club, but he knew he would be voted out as president. Backed against a wall by a platoon of newsmen between cocktails and the main course, Werblin, his voice, as always, never rising, lashed out at his former associates: "When it was a failure, nobody else came around. You didn't see them in Kansas City when it was fourteen below and your feet stuck to the metal floor. But the moment a profit appeared, we were running things by committee . . . and I know you can't run any venture by committee."

He said the Jets, after five years, in 1967 had just turned their first profit, $180,000.

Werblin said he might be back in sports some day, but only with a

New York-based franchise. "I'm strictly a New York guy," he wise-cracked. "Everything else is Philadelphia."

The rupture between Sonny and his partners was a gradual thing. It didn't just erupt with the first black-ink entry in the ledger. In the beginning, Werblin's partners did indeed make some road trips to distant places with the team. As the years passed, they were seen less. Was it because they tired of the grind, or were they made to feel less than welcome, less than equal co-owners with the flamboyant Werblin? Probably a little of both.

Most observers commenting on the dispute said that Werblin's partners—Don Lillis, Phil Iselin, Townsend Martin, and Leon Hess—objected to Sonny's headline monopoly. This could not have been true. All four men shunned personal publicity in their other endeavors before, during, and after the Werblin regime.

Nor did they really want to usurp Werblin's one-man rule of the franchise. When he was overthrown, they virtually had to flip a coin to see who would replace him as titular head of the team. The loser was stuck with the job.

What they did want was a feeling of being a part of things. They didn't want to hear about big trades from friends who'd read about them in the papers first. They wanted to go into the dressing room and be greeted by the players. As the team grew in value, they realized they were paying more and more for their position of privileged outsiders.

The American Football League offices used to be in a building owned by Leon Hess, by far the wealthiest member of the syndicate and one of the nation's richest men. When he had time, Hess would drop by AFL headquarters to pass the time of day and talk football. "I want to find out what's happening with my money," he'd explain wistfully.

"You buy a football team to have fun," Lillis complained. "All I get out of it is a couple of box seats to the game and a free lunch. For the money we've got in this club, I could buy a lot of tickets."

Frustration with the team's inability to win a title didn't help, and the other owners weren't as enchanted as Werblin with Ewbank, either. First indication that all was not happy aboard the Jet ship came with postseason rumors the team was up for sale. Madison Square Garden, then spreading out in the sports world, was reported to be one potential buyer. The National Broadcasting Corporation, possibly anxious to emulate the rival Columbia Broadcasting System, which had purchased the baseball Yankees, was another. There were whispers that Lillis was the partner pushing the sale. If a deal had been completed, the syndicate might have received $10,000,000 for the Jets, ten times their original investment.

Everybody knew Werblin didn't want to sell. He loved the team and he had three sons, any or all of whom might want to go into the football business one day. He didn't need the money, and unlike his equally wealthy partners, he was having loads of fun. After years of operating backstage, he basked in the spotlight.

As the sale rumors receded, there were new reports that Werblin and his partners were involved in a battle for control of the club. Sonny was fighting for his life in football, and decisions about a coach became secondary. The date for the college draft came and went with Ewbank still on the job.

The key number in this intramural war was $7,000,000. The five partners agreed on this as the club's value. Werblin could buy them out or they would buy Werblin out. They actually thought Werblin would come up with the dough, and for a long time, Sonny was tempted. But then his estranged partners said they wouldn't go for any buy-now, pay-later deal. They wanted the payoff in a lump sum. With, among other things, the security of those three sons obviously in mind, Werblin at the last minute elected not to mortgage himself to the million laughs of pro football. He sold out. On the basis of the known figures, it was estimated he received $1,638,000. Roughly eight times his $200,000 investment. Each of the remaining partners was listed as becoming an equal 25 percent owner.

Of course, Werblin left a little bit of himself with the football team, but the association lingered both ways. During Super Bowl week, there were more stories written in a sympathetic vein about outsider Werblin missing his greatest moment than about all the owners of both clubs combined. (And as a nonfootball person, Werblin was even allowed to bet on his team, which put him several thousand dollars up on his old partners.) As Werblin had confided during his farewell dinner, "You know, I'm in a great spot. If the Jets win next year, everybody will say it was my team. If they lose, it will be because the new owners screwed it up."

Actually, the greatest tribute to Werblin was that he wasn't missed, except at party time. He had built so well that the Jets would continue without missing a beat no matter who was president. The Gotham Football Club, Inc., was established and would prosper.

Although Werblin's departure broke suddenly on a Tuesday night, May 21, there was one small hint in Sunday papers of the nineteenth. A minor item reported that Joe Namath, whose $400,000 contract had come to an end after the 1967 season, had been signed by the Jets for another three years. This was the weekend of the Preakness, middle event in horse racing's Triple Crown series, and the Namath announcement was buried under a welter of stories about the race and other spring sports events. Werblin normally might have been expected to have provided a Hollywood setting for Namath's signing, picking a day when there was no competition for newspaper space. A lot of people wondered what was up.

Months later, Werblin told Dick Young, sports columnist of the New York *Daily News,* why he'd done it this way. "I had just decided to sell out and the whole thing would be wrapped up in a few days. I had signed Namath a long time ago and it suddenly dawned on me, why should I let them have the pleasure of announcing it?"

Lillis, generally assumed to have forced the issue, was named president in the new alignment. The first thing he did was assign Ewbank full responsibility for operation of the club. "If you die over a weekend," he told Ewbank, "don't let me know until Monday." The second thing he did was tell Ewbank, "I want to win and I want to win this year." The third, fourth, and fifth things reportedly were to try to get either Vince Lombardi of Green Bay or Al Davis of Oakland to succeed Ewbank if Weeb didn't "win this year." (The lure for both men was supposed to be part ownership of the club, and he almost did sign up Davis.)

Lillis, a sixty-six-year-old widower and self-styled "meatball golfer," had been a 145-pound end in high school. "If I was thirty pounds heavier I'd have been an All-American," he said, but he also insisted, "I don't pretend to be a football expert and it's too late to learn. I don't see where the team will need me except to make a decision if something's wrong from a business point of view."

Lillis said "business acumen" would be his contribution to the Jets, and he had plenty of that. A college dropout ("After a few months, I quit. I wanted to go out and make some money"), he became a multimillionaire. He owned a seat on the stock exchange and he was a limited partner in the investment banking firm of Bear, Stearns & Co. He was a member of the board of nine corporations.

His background as a sports promoter centered on years as president of Bowie Race Course. It was there that he instituted winter racing to enable the small Maryland track to compete against the larger wheels in the East. "If our heating plant isn't enough for the fans, we'll have beef tea and whiskey to keep 'em warm . . . and you can keep that beef tea," Lillis remarked.

Given a free hand with the Jets, Ewbank immediately posted some new rules. Reporters no longer were allowed in the training room where players went for their therapy, and all reporters had to be out of the dressing room on game days an hour before the kickoff. (Werblin would have allowed writers in the huddle if he thought it would help publicize his team.) Ewbank also said hard liquor no longer would be tolerated by any passengers on charter flights after games, only beer in rationed amounts.

When Lillis was named president of the Jets on May 23, 1968, he already was a very sick man and had recently been released from the hospital after a siege of emphysema. Five weeks after his appointment, he went back into the hospital for an appendectomy. On July 23, with the Jets already in training camp, Lillis passed away. Cause of death was listed as a heart ailment.

The Jets were stunned by the news, although few of the players really knew him. Practice was held as usual that day. Ewbank figured the unpretentious Lillis would have preferred it that way—"That's the kind of man he was." The team attended the funeral.

On August 6, sixty-three-year-old Phil Iselin, as expected, was named president. Lillis' stock was left to his daughter, Mrs. Reynolds Springborn, who was named a vice-president. Iselin, white-haired, blue-eyed, and dapper, had made himself a millionaire from possibly even more humble beginnings than Lillis. Iselin, in fact, was a high school dropout. He had quit school at fifteen when his father, who ran a restaurant and bar in Port Washington, Long Island, encountered financial reverses.

Iselin worked at a variety of jobs until he found his métier at twenty-one as a dress salesman. At twenty-five, he owned his first factory and he built his Korell Corporation into a twenty-million-dollar-a-year giant in the garment industry.

Iselin got into sports by accident. He and his wife, Betty (they have a grown son and a daughter), owned an estate called Sous Bois in Oceanport, New Jersey. In 1946, Amory L. Haskell, a well-known horseman, called on Iselin one day and asked if he would object to having a racetrack built nearby. Iselin not only failed to object, he embraced the project and became a moving force in creating the prosperous "Resort of Racing," Monmouth Park. When Haskell died in 1966, Iselin succeeded him as president.

Iselin was known in racing for his many innovations at Monmouth, including closed-circuit television for the film patrol, a Turf Club for grandstand patrons, and spiffy jockey quarters that included a swimming pool. The track was his first, and really only, sports love. The Jets were second, stimulating but still a chore that he seemed to enjoy more before he became the boss. His slight interest in boxing was a family duty. Son Jimmy presided over Peers Management, which sponsored heavyweight contender Buster Mathis.

Iselin, like Lillis, promised to keep his hands off the football team. The Jets were only a week away from their first exhibition game, and he couldn't make any changes even if he had been so inclined. However, he too made it clear that if the Jets did not win the Eastern Division championship he and his associates would have to take a long look at the entire situation. Ewbank had been that route before. In any language, the assignment was "win or else."

20

"We Can Win It All"

Joe Namath's East Side apartment was being redecorated. They were taking the llama rug from the living room and laying it in Ray Abruzzese's bedroom. The place was a mess. "Let's talk downstairs," Joe said.

At a back table in a little luncheonette, Namath talked of the upcoming 1968 season. "I want it to be the best one I ever had," he said. "I think we can win it all, and if I have a halfway good season I know we'll do it. I have confidence now that I can do it. Last year I thought I was ready and I wasn't.

"A championship," he concluded. "That's the whole thing. Everything else is incidental."

This appeared to be a more mature Namath who would be greeting his fourth pro season. His latest operation seemed to have been a success, but in any case, he knew pain would be his companion from now until long after he played his final game. "You get used to it," he said. "Not to the pain, you never get used to things hurting. But to watching yourself, to watching how you walk up stairs or how you sit down. Nobody knows what it feels like. How do you explain what kind of pain . . . an ache, a throb, or what?"

The absence of Werblin was not the only change when Namath and his teammates reported for work in July. The team had moved its training base from Peekskill to Hofstra University in Hempstead, Long Island, where they would be billeted in a brand-new high-rise dormitory. There would even be coeds around. The bachelors' eyes lit up at that news.

Ernie Zwahlen, who had been with the Jets only one year, left to join the coaching staff of the San Francisco 49ers. J. D. Donaldson, one of Weeb's original assistants, also dropped out. J. D., always a gentleman, went back home to Ohio to work for Paul Brown of the new Cincinnati Bengals. Except for J. D., the Jets lost little of conse-

Joe Namath stirred up a lot of controversy over his acceptance of a mink coat in training camp and for failing to suit up for an exhibition game in Houston, even though he insisted he was injured (right).

quence to the expansion team. Quiet Buddy Ryan and big, jovial Joe Spencer took over as the new line coaches.

One reason the Jets moved to Hofstra was the school's plan to install Astroturf on its football field. This would provide perfect conditions for preparing for an exhibition game against the Oilers in Houston. But a strike of maintenance employees at the college stalled all work on the field and it never did get finished before the season.

Pickets ringed the campus. Sometimes the strike scene got a little nasty. Tacks often were strewn in the parking lot, and many a Jet found himself with a mysterious flat tire. Walt Michaels, the bulky defensive coach, almost ran off the road when his tire buckled on an expressway. The next day he returned to one of the picket stations carrying a baseball bat. Walt Michaels almost never gets angry. When he does he is awe-inspiring. He didn't have to issue a second warning.

The strike wasn't the only problem Ewbank faced in his first season as general manager in fact as well as name. Emerson Boozer, his best and possibly only halfback, was in the Army for a six-month hitch. The Army had grabbed him earlier that month, which would have finished him for virtually the entire season. Ewbank tried to keep the matter quiet and covered up Boozer's absence as long as he could. He felt Boozer would be discharged as soon as the leg was fully examined. (He'd felt the same way about Paul Seiler, who was still in military uniform.) Weeb feared publicity might force the Army to keep Emerson, but though the story eventually was widely printed, Boozer received a discharge in mid-August. He'd spent about half of every day in the service undergoing therapy on his bad knee, which was not a very good deal for the government.

Ewbank had issued weight ultimatums to four of his linemen: Verlon Biggs, Paul Rochester, Sherman Plunkett, and Jim Harris. Biggs, who had been two weeks late reporting the season before, came in early this time and at the lowest weight since his rookie season, 274. Weeb was overjoyed. Rochester, Plunkett, and Harris didn't make it, and Weeb said they would have to repay the Jets for their training camp expenses (about $15 a day) until they cut down. Rochester made the weight in 24 hours.

Weeb had liked what he saw of John Elliott at defensive tackle at the end of the 1967 season and that's where he decided to place the fine athlete from Warren, Texas. Elliott didn't have a tackle's size. He had reported as a rookie at 243 pounds, but he wore down to 229 by the end of the season. Ewbank knew Elliott had the strength and quickness to play the interior line position, where he would furnish outstanding pass rush and pursuit on running plays. Looking at Elliott's frame, Ewbank gambled that the blond Texan, now a year older, would be able to hold at 240 to 245 through a tough season.

With Elliott set at defensive tackle, Ewbank moved Harris to offense. If Jim, whose off-season work as a child guidance counselor belied his brash and flashy style, had reported in shape, he would have had Plunkett's job. But when he and Plunkett both came in overweight, Ewbank publicly fined, demoted, and cut them, in that order, and handed the starting job to rookie Sam Walton.

The Jets had led off their draft with what looked like four straight winners. They liked their No. 1 pick, fullback Lee White of Weber State, so much that Ewbank even offered Matt Snell around for trade during the off-season. Steve Thompson, a defensive lineman from Washington, drafted in the second round, was probably one reason Biggs reported in shape. Walton was drafted third, and Gary Magner, the fourth pick from Southern Cal, looked like a cinch to make the club as a spare linebacker.

Walton, though, was the only one of the four to have a starting job opened up for him. Sam was from Memphis, Tennessee, and he'd gone to East Texas State on a basketball scholarship. He didn't go out for football until he learned that he couldn't eat at the school training table for free until the beginning of basketball season. At six feet six and 270 pounds, Walton figured he'd better not risk starvation so far from home. Slow-moving and slow-talking off the field, he was a cat in uniform. The Jets figured they could teach him what he had to know. Sherman Plunkett helped him a lot before he was cut, and then Winston Hill took the rookie under his huge wing. Scrimmaging daily against tough and agile Gerry Philbin accelerated his education.

The rookies, as usual, reported early. As time approached for the veterans to sign in, Ewbank found himself with a problem at quarterback. Mike Taliaferro was demanding to be traded. He didn't want to spend another demeaning year as Joe Namath's caddy. Sid Gillman, astute coach of the Chargers, had once said that a young quarterback's skills start eroding if he doesn't get a chance to play after four years. This would be Mike's fifth season. He had to give himself a chance.

Mike Holovak, the Boston coach who had taken John Huarte off the Jets' hands, had always liked Taliaferro. He still wanted him. When Ewbank said he'd be willing to take Babe Parilli in exchange, Holovak agreed to the deal.

Parilli was an outstanding addition to the Jets. He was thirty-eight years old and entering his fifteenth season as a pro. He had played in the National League and in Canada and was an AFL original. He started with Oakland in 1960 and was traded to Boston the following year, where Holovak restored his confidence and turned him once again into a winner. On any list of all-time great AFL quarterbacks, Parilli's name had to be included. For years Holovak never hired a backfield coach and handled most of those chores himself. He wanted to make sure the job would be open for the Babe when Parilli retired.

But the Boston team, victim of penurious management, deteriorated. Parilli, as the quarterback, became the on-field target. Maybe

Babe Parilli (left) and Sam Walton.

he wasn't the star of old, but he deserved better of Boston fans who churlishly cheered during one game when he was injured and had to be helped off the field. Holovak felt Parilli had earned the right to bow out not with boos but with a champion. He agreed to the deal.

Nobody will ever really know how much Parilli's example helped mold the new Namath. Sure, Joe was maturing on his own, but it had to help him just watching Parilli's behavior on and off the field. The Babe had been one of Namath's schoolday heroes. Joe could remember as a student in grammar school admiring a "Babe Parilli Helmet" in the window of a Beaver Falls Army-Navy store. Parilli also had played for Bear Bryant, at Kentucky, and Joe recalled how the coach would absentmindedly call him "Babe," just as Ewbank sometimes referred to him as "John" for Unitas.

One of Namath's problems in those first years had been his relationship with Ewbank. To Joe, the only great coach was Bear Bryant, an inspirational hard-driving figure. Ewbank was cut from a different pattern, one which did not necessarily inspire awe in his quarterback, and Joe showed it. It took Namath four years to learn that success can respond to many masters. Who knows whether Parilli's acceptance of a respectful player-coach relationship under Weeb might not have helped Namath by example?

Many credited Werblin's absence for Namath's new attitude, but this was not completely the case. Where Werblin's absence helped was in the attitude of the other players toward Namath. They no longer needed to resent, rightly or wrongly, his entrée to the boss.

Before the season opened, Ewbank made one more brilliant pick-up, a move that was to have tremendous impact later in the year. Bob Talamini, an AFL original, had become unhappy at Houston. A jolly, easygoing guy, he felt he had never been tough enough at the bargaining table. Before the 1967 season he had signed a two-year contract. But then he came up with another outstanding season, made All-AFL for the sixth time, and helped the Oilers to their surprise division championship. He felt he deserved a new deal, if only in reward for the years he had signed for less money than he wanted. But the Oilers' front office balked. When Talamini's wife was injured in an automobile accident, that gave him the jolt he needed to announce his retirement. His values had changed. Football was his profession, not the fun game of college. If he was going to make the sacrifices, and demand them of his family, he would be paid for it.

During the exhibition season, Ewbank learned that Talamini really wanted to continue his football career. When the Jets played in Houston, the two men got together for lunch and then Weeb went to the Oilers to see if they could work a deal. The Houston club was willing, and so, for a third-round draft choice, Ewbank was able to pick up a twenty-nine-year-old six-time All-Star. Talamini had given Houston eight dedicated seasons, but the Oiler front office marked his departure with waspish innuendo. Talamini was to remember.

These new veterans weren't a factor when the Jets opened up with a rookie game in Baltimore on July 30. This was an emotional moment for Ewbank, his first appearance in Memorial Stadium since he was fired by the Colts after the 1962 season. Ewbank is short and dumpy and presents a most distinctive appearance. But when he walked out on the field, the audience gave no sign of recognition. Only when his name was announced was he given a loud welcoming cheer. Then all his old players with the Colts, with the exception of Johnny Unitas, who had talked privately with him earlier, lined up at midfield to shake his hand. It was a touching scene.

The game, though, was not too special. The Jets, playing without top draftee Lee White, who was off with the College All-Stars, lost,

27–14. Steve Thompson, the promising rookie, hurt his knee and underwent surgery. It was only a cartilage, though, and he had hopes of returning late in the season.

Two weeks later, the entire squad went down to Houston for their first exhibition game and another tempest. The Jets, somehow, perhaps as a legacy from Harry Wismer, never developed the knack of nipping a bad situation in the bud. Just before the game Namath complained that his knee hurt too much to play. He and Ewbank could be seen arguing as the Jets went through their warm-ups. Rumors spread that Namath was demanding a $3,000 fee from the club for all exhibition appearances. Although this was denied by all parties, even Namath's teammates, playing for their $100 a game, were wondering. Ewbank said the argument concerned whether Namath should get in uniform to operate the sideline telephone. "I thought it would look better," Ewbank explained. Obviously his relationship with Namath, though improved, was far from perfect.

The Jets lost this one, 28–14, but five days later they beat Boston, 25–6. Namath was on the bench against the Patriots, too, but he had some distinguished company in Emerson Boozer, just out of the Army.

A week later, returning to Birmingham, where his name helped draw another crowd, Namath was in the lineup as the Jets scored their first victory over an NFL team. The victim was Atlanta by a 27–12 score, but the second of the Jets' top rookies, Gary Magner, was kayoed for the season with serious knee damage.

After losing, 13–10, to expansion Cincinnati in a substitute for their canceled dream game with the NFL Giants, the Jets closed out their exhibition season before the biggest crowd ever to see an AFL team in action, 84,918, in Cleveland's huge Municipal Stadium. The crowd, a record for the Browns too, was there to enjoy another of Cleveland owner Art Modell's famed doubleheaders. The Jets, first AFL team to be invited to the lucrative affair, played the NFL Detroit Lions in the opener while the Browns met the Green Bay Packers in the second game. Weeb Ewbank activated rookie Harvey Nairn, a track star from Southern University, just for this game. "I want him to see what it's like to play in front of eighty thousand people," the coach explained, planning for several years in the future, when the inexperienced Nairn might be ready as "my next Don Maynard."

Emerson Boozer, nursing his knee after the Army call had negated long months of dedicated and solitary therapy, got his first start

Jets' Gerry Philbin closes in on a quarterback, Bob Griese of Miami.

against the Lions. Booz was leery of this moment. His leg was healed, the doctor kept repeating to him, but the mental scars lingered. These were the hardest wounds to cure. It would take a full year.

With Namath at quarterback, Boozer was called upon early. When Alex Karras, the Lions' great defensive tackle, pitchforked him with a vicious block tackle near the goal line and Boozer got up asking to carry the ball again, the Jets knew he was physically sound.

A one-yard plunge by Matt Snell, with Boozer leading the blocking, put the Jets in front, 6–3, and the AFL team completely dominated the first half when regulars on both sides were in the lineup. Those few who picked the Jets in the Super Bowl would remember these 30 minutes and the fierce, unrelenting rush the AFL team put on Detroit quarterback Bill Munson. Gerry Philbin, the agile and combative Jet end who channeled his deep, violent instincts into football, eventually put Munson out with a rib injury.

The final score in this most satisfying Jet victory was 9–6, and the triumph assured the AFL of an edge over the Nationals in preseason exhibition games.

The Jets opened their season in Kansas City the following week, and Ewbank had a lot on his mind under both of his hats as the team's charter plane droned westward. As a coach, he had to decide on a replacement for Al Atkinson at middle linebacker. Atkinson, who was developing into All-Star material, had suffered a severely bruised shin against the Lions and it was more serious than it sounded.

In his other role as general manager, Ewbank found himself with five top players still unsigned for the upcoming season—Don Maynard, George Sauer, Matt Snell, John Sample, and Verlon Biggs. The Jets from their first practice had been pointing for this opening game at Kansas City. Ewbank would have liked all the loose strings knotted before the kickoff. Even though the five could play under the option clause on last year's contracts, nobody really liked the idea, especially the players. If they got hurt, the Jets could pay them off on the basis of last year's salary, less 10 percent. They were at the mercy of Ewbank's generosity, and although he swore he would protect them, they were never sure. For some reason, Ewbank as a general manager did not always inspire trust in his players on financial matters.

On the plane trip to Kansas City, Ewbank got Sauer and Maynard to agree to terms. But the next morning, only hours before the kickoff, Sample announced he would not step out on the field without a contract. He, too, was brought into the fold in the bare minutes between the pregame meal and the bus trip to the stadium.

Snell and Biggs, however, went against the Chiefs without new contracts. Ewbank wasn't worried about his silent end because Verlon hadn't signed until more than halfway through the previous season. But Snell, who seemed to be on the verge of a bad mood much of the time, was a different story. He said if he chanced one game without a contract, he would gamble all the way and play out his option to become a free agent. If he had a good year, he would be king of the hill.

It wasn't all bad news, though. In a brief squad meeting after their final light workout on Saturday, the Jets named their captains for 1968. John Sample was reelected head of the defensive platoon, and Joe Namath, accepted at last, was chosen to lead the offense. Namath, almost tearfully, called it as great "as any honor I've ever had."

21

"I Stink"

Summery, sunny weather and a record crowd of more than 48,000 greeted the Jets in Kansas City for the opening game of the 1968 season, and the contest developed into a minor classic. Jim Turner kicked a 22-yard field goal and then Joe Namath passed to Don Maynard for two touchdowns and a 17–3 halftime lead for the visitors.

However, after six minutes of the third period, Noland (Super Gnat) Smith buzzed off on an 80-yard punt return and Jan Stenerud kicked his second and third field goals. That brought the Chiefs to within a point at 17–16, in the opening seconds of the fourth quarter. It looked like the old fold days of 1967. Even after Turner and Stenerud traded off field goals, the Jet victory was very much in jeopardy with 5:56 to play and the score 20–19.

With Stenerud, a Norwegian who had come to Montana State on a ski scholarship, perhaps the best long-distance kicker in the league, the Jets would have to protect their fragile lead for almost six additional minutes. Six minutes in which they had to control the ball, score, or back Kansas City so deep in its own territory that even Stenerud's ICBM's couldn't get the Chiefs on the board.

This was the situation as Stenerud moved up to kick off after his fourth field goal. He dug his instep, soccer style, into the football, which lofted deep toward the sideline. Earl Christy, the good-natured Jet kick returner, drifted under it and there was a gasp from the crowd as he fielded the kickoff and promptly stepped out of bounds at the five-yard line. What a blunder! He should have let the ball go. If it had gone out of bounds, Stenerud would have had to kick over from five yards farther back. If it had rolled into the end zone, the Jets would have taken possession at their 20.

The situation looked even more grim when Emerson Boozer lost a yard on the first play and then Namath's pass to Maynard was broken up by Emmitt Thomas. It was now third-and-eleven on the Jet four. If the Jets could not make a first down on the next play, they would have to punt and Kansas City would get possession about mid-field. A few plays would easily put Stenerud in field goal range. Namath marshaled the Jets in the huddle and daringly called for the exact same pass to Maynard that had failed on the previous down. This time it worked. Maynard pulled it in for a 17-yard gain and a first down at the Jet 21.

On first down, Namath passed to Maynard for eight more and then Matt Snell cracked left guard for five yards and another first down to the Jet 34. Bill Mathis ran for one, and Namath passed to Sauer for 16 and a first down at the Chief 49. At last the Jets had made it to the other half of the field.

They had controlled the ball for almost four minutes, but 2:04 still remained, which added another dimension to their problem. Now if they lost the ball and Kansas City scored to go ahead, the Jets would have no chance to regain the lead.

Snell ran for three, Boozer lost a yard, and again Namath was faced with a third-down play at the KC 47. But again he went to Maynard, who had established mastery over Thomas, and the Jet flanker beat his man for a 19-yard advance to the KC 28. Only 1:38 remained. There was still no safety in the clock. The Jets had to squeeze every second and avoid errors like a fumble, interception, or long penalty. Boozer hit right guard for one yard. Snell went at right tackle for two. Then Boozer lost three back to the 28. Less than a minute remained and the Jets had only one play left. They walked in slow motion up to the line, and officials threw their flags. "Delay of game!" The Jets never took a penalty more gladly. Only five seconds remained as they once more went up over the ball. The official play-by-play tells it best: "Snell leans forward slowly, no gain. *End of game.*"

Hank Stram, congenial and inventive coach of the Chiefs, was stunned. "That last drive by Namath was fabulous," he raved. "I felt there was no way they could go from their four and maintain possession to the end of the game. I'd have given hundred-to-one odds against it."

The manner of the victory was just as important as the result. The Jets had gone out on the road, their usual graveyard, lost their momentum, almost blown a big lead, and still pulled themselves out of a self-inflicted crisis to save the afternoon. Perhaps this season would be different.

When the Jets arrived at the airport, they learned that their charter flight had been delayed. Hubert Humphrey was using the plane for his Presidential campaign and it would be late getting to Kansas City. Normally this would have been cause for loud and sulky complaints by the players, especially since it was Sunday and the airport bar was closed. But nobody griped tonight. Players laughed and joked with fans who happened to wander into the private dining room where they ate their sanitary airline dinners off little trays at long crowded tables.

Off in the corner, though, one player sat quietly, under mild sedation, his right leg propped stiffly on a chair. It was Lee White, the Jets' No. 1 draft choice. On the third series of downs, he had been injured covering on a punt at almost the same spot where Boozer had been hurt the year before. His ligaments were ruptured and he would be out for the year, the third of the Jets' top four draft choices to undergo knee surgery.

White's injury strengthened Snell's contract position and he knew it. With White hurt and Boozer still an uncertain quantity, Matt would nail the Jets to the bargaining table right now rather than waiting to play out his option. By that time, everybody might be healthy again. As the Jets flew east, Snell talked loudly to reporters about what he considered past ill treatment by the club. He said he might not even play the following week if he wasn't signed. Although he lamely tried to claim he had been misquoted, Snell still was demoted from the starting lineup in a surprise move by Ewbank only minutes before the kickoff against Boston the next Sunday. That game, incidentally, was being played in Birmingham, Alabama, since the Patriots had been frozen out of their home field by the baseball Red Sox.

Al Atkinson, who hadn't played against Kansas City, was replaced for the second straight game by Mike Stromberg, a commercial artist in the off-season, who turned in another outstanding job before being hurt himself late in the game. (He, too, got a knee and was out for the year.) Carl McAdams, who had been spelling Verlon Biggs and Paul Rochester in the defensive line because of the 84-degree heat, moved back to take Stromberg's place. The onetime big bonus disappointment earned his money that day, and he writhed in pain from heat cramps as the Jets returned from their 47–31 runaway.

Snell finally signed his contract the day after the team returned from Birmingham, and the Jets were loose and confident as they resumed workouts for their third straight road game at Buffalo. Why not?

They were 19-point favorites over a Buffalo team that had lost its two top quarterbacks, Jack Kemp and Tom Flores, to injuries. The Jets hadn't won in Buffalo since 1962 (the strike victory), but this looked like the time. The Jets were 2-and-0 with Al Atkinson healthy again while the Bills were 0-and-3 after losing to expansion Cincinnati.

Earl Christy, whose mental error had almost cost the Jets their opener in Kansas City, partially atoned in Buffalo as he took the opening kickoff and raced 87 yards to the Buffalo seven to set up a quick and easy Jet touchdown. (Christy's dream was to run a kick back all the way in a league game. He didn't make it all year.)

The Jets led, 7–0, and they'd hardly broken a sweat, but now it appeared as if their 1967 Buffalo nightmare was showing up on re-runs like an old television show. Namath threw long to Don Maynard, but Tom Janik intercepted at the Buffalo 27, and his 37-yard return set up a field goal by Bruce Alford. It was the Bills' first field goal of the season. A 60-yard drive, a Buffalo touchdown, and the Bills held a 10–7 lead. Worried? Not the Jets, especially when Ralph Baker, the colorless but efficient linebacker, recovered a Bill fumble on Buffalo's 10.

Namath was confident he could get a quick score and went right to the air. Two passes fell incomplete and then he threw to Curley Johnson, who had come in at tight end when Pete Lammons pulled up lame. This one was caught all right, and went for a touchdown, but a touchdown by the wrong team. Janik picked off his second interception of the game on the goal line and sprinted down the sideline 100 yards for the TD. "A cardinal sin," Namath said of his faulty pass that had prevented his team from at least settling for a field goal.

Buffalo, leading, 17–7, almost broke the game open right then. On the Jets' first play, Butch Byrd intercepted a Namath pass and raced into the end zone, but the Bills were offsides and the score was nullified. The Jets then were able to wrap two touchdowns around an Alford field goal and went off at the half one point in front, 21–20.

But it became 23–21, Buffalo, going into the final quarter after Namath's fumble had set up another Alford field goal.

Even though there was plenty of time, Namath tried to win it all on one pass. Again he threw long and Byrd intercepted at the Buffalo 47 and ran it all the way in for a touchdown. A penalty didn't save the Jets this time. Sixty-two seconds later it happened again. Booker Edgerson intercepted Namath and ran it back 45 yards for the score to make it 37–21. Babe Parilli, riveted to the sideline telephone as Ewbank declined to make a change, looked sick to his stomach.

Still, Weeb had his reasons. *Joe's the one who can get us there,* he thought—and Joe nearly did it. He got the Jets one touchdown, was intercepted by Byrd again on the next drive, and then Paul Crane's second blocked punt in as many weeks set up another easy Jet score in the closing seconds. Despite Namath's impossible performance—five interceptions, three run back for touchdowns, plus a sixth interception and fourth TD runback nullified by penalty—the Jets were beaten by only two points, 37–35. This would be the only Buffalo victory all year.

After the game, Ewbank kept his dressing room door shuttered for several minutes longer than usual. His muffled voice could be heard in the corridor delivering an out-of-character tongue-lashing. He told the players they had taken the Bills too lightly, but Namath didn't buy it. "It's all the dumb guy sitting right here," he said, referring to himself while new president Phil Iselin, so different from Werblin, was asking Ewbank diffidently, "Is it all right if I come in now?"

Later, John Namath, Joe's father, talked to Murray Janoff of the Long Island *Press* as his son hobbled down the steep steps from the dressing room. "Look at him—he can hardly get down the stairs. I want him to give up football. I can't stand to watch him play anymore," the distraught father said.

But Joe wasn't quitting. The same determination and complete confidence that made him throw the risky pass also made him a winner. Pain was only a minor opponent. "I've had days like this before and I'll have 'em again. Even good pitchers get knocked out of the box," Namath shrugged.

Aside from the loss, there were two disquieting developments at Buffalo.

Pete Lammons, the tight end, had suffered a pulled groin muscle and wouldn't be able to play against the Chargers the following week. And Sam Walton, the rookie tackle who'd looked so good up until then, had been battered and humiliated by Buffalo end Ron McDole. On one play, Walton finally threw his arms around McDole in an illegal tackle to keep him away from Namath. A full stadium—but not a single official—saw the infraction.

At his weekly press luncheon, Ewbank publicly chastised Walton for his performance but promised the rookie another chance against San Diego. And he said that Curley Johnson, normally a punter, and fullback Mark Smolinski would share duty at tight end until Lammons recovered. For Smolinski, captain of the special teams, this was a cliché come true. A fine blocker and good man on teams, Smo was no Whirlaway running with the ball. Over the years critics who rapped the Jets' weak running game made Smolinski their target. "How can he keep a guy like that around?" they'd ask and answer themselves that it was probably only because Smo was one of Weeb's old boys, a member of his Baltimore Mafia.

Weeb would always point to Smolinski's blocking ability—no blitzer ever got through him—and to his work on special teams. Then, several dozen times a year, he'd point out, "And he's also a fine receiver. Why, I almost made a tight end out of him in Baltimore." After eight years as a pro, Smolinski was finally making one of Weeb's aphorisms come to life.

Johnson, however, would get the start before a record 63,788 that Saturday night in Shea when San Diego rolled in with a perfect 3–0 record.

The Jets couldn't get much of an offense going in the first half, but interceptions by Randy Beverly and Cornell Gordon set up two Jim Turner field goals and Tank added a third after a drive that included three straight completions from Namath to the virtually ignored Curley Johnson. (Curley hurt his right knee when tackled after the third catch and played no more that season except as a punter. He underwent postseason surgery.) The Chargers scored on a touchdown pass from John Hadl to Lance Alworth, and the Jets led, 9–7, at the half.

The Jets dominated most of the third quarter but still needed a break to expand their lead. Driving from their 44 to the Charger 8, Namath found himself at third-and-two under a heavy rush from Scott Appleton. Just as he was hit, he elected to throw the ball away over the end zone to avoid an interception and retain possession for a cinch fourth-down field goal. But as the ball flew wild, Kenny Graham committed pass interference on new tight end Mark Smolinski in the end zone. The Jets got an automatic first down at the one and Snell hurdled over for a 16–7 lead.

The big lead lasted only 42 seconds and one play. Gary Garrison beat Randy Beverly, who had a terrible night, to complete an 84-yard touchdown pass play with quarterback John Hadl. But Dennis Partee's conversion kick was wide right, and the Jets led 16–13. In the fourth quarter a 37-yard punt return by Speedy Duncan helped set up another

San Diego touchdown, and with 5:45 to play, the Jets trailed by 20–16. A field goal would do them no good. They need a touchdown.

The Jets started what they knew would be their last drive at the 25, and Namath completed three of four passes to Sauer, Maynard, and Smolinski for a first down at the Charger 40. But here the Jets stalled. Two passes misfired and on third down Namath aimed for Maynard and missed again. But officials called Charger defensive tackle Steve DeLong for roughing the passer. From fourth-and-ten at the 40, the Jets moved to first-and-ten at the 25.

A 19-yard completion from Namath to Smolinski set up a first down at the six. Boozer ran for three, Namath passed incomplete to Smo, and then Boozer ran for two more. It was fourth-and-goal at the one. Lammons replaced Smolinski at tight end. Perhaps the Chargers would think he was in to catch a pass. Actually he was there to block, since he'd had a lot more practice at the position than Smolinski. On their last thrust, the Jets sent Boozer over the left side of the line and the halfback dived over Lammons, Hill, and Rasmussen for the touchdown with 1:43 left.

It didn't seem like much, but the 103 seconds left plenty of time for explosive San Diego to overcome the Jets' 23–20 lead. The lightning bolts on Charger helmets were significant. The visitors drove back with the kickoff and had first down at the Jet 32 when Gerry Philbin rushed Hadl and John Sample saved the victory with a goal line interception. Hadl had committed the same "cardinal sin" of which Namath had been guilty the week before at Buffalo. Twenty-nine seconds remained when Sample stole the ball and Hadl should not have been gambling when he still had time and was close enough to try to kick a field goal for the tie.

The 23–20 comeback victory made up for the Buffalo debacle, and now the Jets had easy Denver coming in. They'd be 20-point favorites over the Broncos, one more than against the Bills. A year ago Denver had come into Shea Stadium as a heavy underdog and it had rained to presage the Broncos' stunning upset. This time it was coach Lou Saban's birthday, but it would take more than omens to beat the Jets this season.

When the Jets used a 60-yard pass from Namath to Maynard to set up Boozer's short scoring sweep the second time they got the ball, their fans were sure of it. Even when the Broncos drove back to tie at 7–7, their confidence remained unshaken.

But when Pete Jacquess intercepted Namath only minutes later in the second quarter to set up an easy Bronco score for a 14–7 lead, a lot of people began to wonder. Could this be 1967 all over again? This was the Broncos' fifth game of the season and they hadn't intercepted a single pass all year before this. How come they started on Namath?

A field goal by Jim Turner brought the Jets up to 14–10, but another interception of Namath stalled any chance to regain the lead by halftime. Fans booed as the home team killed the clock on its last play before the intermission.

Only 47 seconds after play resumed, the Broncos picked up another TD when Steve Tensi passed 72 yards to Eric Crabtree. That made the score 21–10, but although Turner kicked another field goal, Namath was intercepted three more times for a total of five as he tried too desperately to get the Jets back in the ballgame. Fans were jeering, but they are changeable as the weather. The boos turned to cheers as Namath made one last effort in the final 90 seconds to bring the Jets back for a chance to tie with a TD and a two-point conversion. However, a critical holding penalty set them back and Namath's fourth-down pass from the four bounced off the goalpost to assure Denver's shocking 21–13 victory.

The Jets had now lost two of their last three. Although they still led the Eastern Division, their 3–2 record was far from impressive. And Namath had thrown 12 interceptions in his first five games. At this rate he'd have his worst year for interceptions since turning pro. He should have been going in the other direction.

Shaken more than after any previous bad game, Namath pleaded with reporters to leave him alone. "I've always talked to you fellows before, no matter what," he said, "but not this time, please. Just say I stink. I ———ing stink."

Ewbank, with some justification, blamed a breakdown in pass protection for Namath's poor performance. However, he couldn't explain why Namath scorned short passes and other maneuvers that could nullify an all-out pass rush. Chief victim of the breakdown was Sam Walton, the rookie, who'd been sick before and during the game. Rich Jackson, a part-time deputy sheriff, gave Walton an even worse going-over than McDole had two weeks earlier. For a while, Ewbank tried Jeff Richardson in Walton's place but it made no difference. Eventually the fullback was assigned to help double-team the 255-pound defensive end. That helped a little.

There was, however, an element of humor in the defeat. As the Jets were driving toward what they hoped would be a tie, they found themselves without any more time-outs and in desperate need to stop the clock. With Rasmussen, Herman, and Talamini, they had three good guards and could afford to lose one. Talamini was given a card in Actors Equity. On the first play of that final drive, Namath passed to George Sauer at the sidelines. Talamini went into his swoon to fake an injury that would stop the clock, but Sauer managed to make it out of bounds, which served the same purpose. So Talamini quickly jumped to his feet before the officials could notice.

On the next play, though, Sauer couldn't get out of bounds, so Talamini, like Bernhardt playing Camille, died again. Jeff Snedeker, the Jets' trainer, came running out. "What hurts? What hurts?" he yelled dramatically.

"Look, don't give me a hard time," Talamini whispered out of the side of his mouth, "just grab somethin'."

While Snedeker worked on one leg, Dr. Nicholas came out and absentmindedly began ministering to the other one. As he was being helped off the field, Talamini took three steps before he remembered to limp.

"I was all set to pull the same thing against Buffalo two weeks ago, but we never got the ball back," Talamini confessed. "I hate to be known as the guy who takes the gas, so I'm not saying anything more. All I know is after the game there was a message to call Operator 36, Cecil B. DeMille, in Hollywood."

22

Only Heidi Beat Them

Tuesday after the Denver loss, Verlon Biggs reported to Shea Stadium with the beginnings of a goatee on his chin. "What's the big idea?" his teammates asked.

"I'm not shavin' it off till we win the division championship," Biggs replied.

"Hey, great idea," Jim Hudson agreed. "I'll grow one, too."

To Hudson, team unity was almost an obsession. Biggs in all his years with the Jets had been a solitary figure, trailing along in the shadow of the ebullient and more sophisticated Jim Harris. With Harris gone, the shy and silent Biggs was beginning to peek out of his shell. Hudson saw the beards as a way of helping Biggs finally become a full-fledged member of the group. It wouldn't hurt the rest of the team, either, as they tried to rally from their disappointing start.

Quite a few other Jets tried to grow beards, which had to be kept unobtrusive because of previous league rules against them. Paul Rochester started one and quit. The beard made him look like Burl Ives. Cornell Gordon's beard wouldn't grow, but he did manage a mustache. Al Atkinson and George Sauer tried, but you couldn't even see theirs. Bake Turner, the guitar-playing Texan who hoped for a career in show business, had grown a mustache for a television appearance. He kept his, and in the end it was Biggs, Turner, Hudson, Gordon, and John Elliott. After a couple of weeks, Elliott trimmed his beard. He said it itched under his chin strap.

About this time, too, Joe Namath began cultivating his famous Fu Manchu mustache. He wouldn't say a word about it in public, but as the outline of the droopy mustache filled out, it became obvious he was joining the club. By coincidence, it appeared Namath's mustache would be full grown just in time for the Jets' game in Oakland, where he would face Ben Davidson and his handlebar, lip to lip.

The beards, of course, were only a surface symptom of a new

Verlon Biggs and his beard.

New York Jets

determination gripping the entire team. The poor start finally made them grow up as pros. They realized that skill and fancy footwork didn't win championships. Toughness—physical and mental toughness—was also required. They finally became aware that more than "bad luck" had cost them the championship in 1967. As Casey Stengel once said, "People who complain about bad luck usually have bad luck all their lives."

For Namath particularly this was a time of crisis. Both leagues were full of second-rate quarterbacks who threw hot and cold. Consistency was the mark of the winners. Which would he be? "Sometimes you're playing a game and you feel great. It all opens up and you see everything unfold and you don't make a single mistake. And sometimes it seems as if there are ninety people scrambling in front of you," he once explained. Of his 28 interceptions in 1967, he threw 10 in two games. Of his 26 touchdown passes, 10 came in three games. This season it was the same old pattern, only worse.

In the week after the Denver loss, Namath took a long hard look at himself. He finally realized that his interceptions were hurting the team. Although his swinging life style didn't change, Namath turned conservative on the field. He became aware of his own fallibility, like a prizefighter who's been knocked out for the first time. Like the champions, he came off the canvas a better man. This week was Joe Namath's professional turning point.

From here on, Namath individually and the Jets as a team showed consistent improvement, game by game.

While the Jets were drawing themselves together for the championship run, coach Weeb Ewbank was making some changes, too. A breakdown in pass protection had assisted Namath's downfall against Denver, and he laid his plans to provide more blocking. No longer would it be everybody out for the pass. Running backs would be kept in to block. Billy Mathis, it seemed, began to play more. (Emerson Boozer, still not trusting his knee, kept coming up with various bumps and bruises he blamed on missing most of training camp and the exhibition season.) And Ewbank went out of his way to praise Matt Snell's blocking ability. "As good a blocking fullback on pass protection as I've ever coached," Ewbank lauded.

Ewbank had been faced with a touchy situation at guard with the acquisition of Bob Talamini from Houston. Randy Rasmussen had been the regular on the left side, and although he had gone downhill in the last weeks of his rookie season, he made a strong comeback in 1968. He was still, according to Ewbank, "a number one" at guard. Attempting to get ready too soon after joining his new club, Talamini had pulled a leg muscle in training camp. That set him back and enabled Ewbank to defer facing a decision between the newcomer and Rasmussen. But now Talamini was ready, and he'd been practicing all along only at Rasmussen's left guard position.

The schedule provided Ewbank with his excuse to make a change. The Jets next were slated in Houston, and he knew Talamini would be primed for a top effort against his old team. "They had to make excuses for losing me so cheaply, so the front office said a lot of things about me I didn't like. Remember, my family was still living in Houston and they read all about it," Talamini said grimly.

Ewbank stressed that Rasmussen hadn't "lost" his job by any means. "We've got three number one guards," he'd repeat, and he pointed out that Rasmussen, more familiar with the Jets' system, would be more valuable as a swing man at both left and right guard than the newcomer. This was to be an important factor later in the year.

Because of the time difference between Houston and the East, the Jets learned during their game that Boston had already beaten Buffalo. They would drop into a first-place tie with the Patriots if they

Randy Rasmussen

Bob Talamini

lost, and prospects didn't look too bright as Namath started out by missing on ten straight passes. Still, he wasn't intercepted, either, and the Jets took a 2–0 lead on a safety when Paul Crane blocked his third punt of the season. ("What do we call that play? We call it a punt block," he deadpanned afterward.) After a Randy Beverly interception, the Jets drove 60 yards for a touchdown. Namath completed his first pass on this march after almost 24 minutes of play, and he turned running back to sneak over from a yard out for the TD. Babe Parilli then passed to Mathis for a two-point conversion and the Jets went off at the half with a 10–0 lead. Jim Turner's 12-yard field goal on the first play of the fourth quarter boosted the Jet margin to 13–0.

However, on the next series, Verlon Biggs broke through to level Houston quarterback Bob Davis, and the blow ended up hurting the Jets more than it hurt Davis. Pete Beathard, the Oilers' regular quarterback, had been sidelined with appendicitis, so Houston picked up one of its old players, Don Trull, as a free agent after he had been cut by the Patriots. Trull, an unorthodox scrambler, had embarrassed the Jets before while with both Houston and Boston, and he was to do so again. In less time than it takes to climb to the top deck of the Astrodome, he had directed the Oilers on two drives and passed for two touchdowns to give the home team a 14–13 lead.

Only 4:19 remained to play, and after watching critical penalties and poor pass coverage cost his team, Weeb Ewbank on the sidelines was mentally preparing his "We beat ourselves with mistakes" post-mortem for the press.

But Namath and his teammates weren't thinking in those terms. Starting at his 20, Namath completed three straight passes to George Sauer for gains of 14, 9, and 13 yards and a first down at the Oiler 44. Then, with Houston concentrating on his wide receivers, he passed to Emerson Boozer over the middle. The pass was low and Emerson had to turn and pick it off his shoetops. But he made the catch and stumbled forward for a 17-yard gain to the 27. As long as he made catches like that in games, Boozer could continue to miss the easy ones in practice.

Since just over two minutes remained at this point, Jet strategy had to change. The New Yorkers now were in position to kick a winning field goal. However, if they scored quickly, the Oilers would have a chance to retaliate. Namath, who had completed four in a row, discarded the pass and turned to a time-consuming ground game. If the ground attack was halted after three downs, Turner could still kick a field goal. On first down, Namath sent Boozer for two and then Boozer followed a Dave Herman block for 15 more yards and a first down on the 10. Matt Snell hit left tackle for eight yards and then blasted the same area for two more yards and a touchdown, behind a block by Rasmussen, who was in for Talamini at that point. Turner's PAT made the score 20–14, but with 48 seconds left, Houston still had time.

Normally subs and expendables go on the field for kickoffs and punts. The work is dangerous and that's why they're known as suicide squads. Coaches euphemistically call them special teams, and Allie Sherman of the Giants, trying to give the subs a feeling of importance, calls them his "money" teams. Ewbank, like many coaches, has a refinement of his special squad. He calls it his "championship" team. With the game in the balance, when a long runback can be fatal, this group of regulars, most of them graduates of special teams, enters the game.

Buddy Ryan, an assistant coach, keeps the chart showing which players should be on the field in different situations—offense, defense, punts, field goals, goal line stands, onside kicks, etc. The list runs three deep to provide for injuries, and every player is supposed to know when he should be on the field. There's a heavy fine if he's not. As the Oilers moved on the field to receive the kickoff, Ryan looked up and down his bench for members of the unlisted championship squad. Gerry Philbin was sent out on the field, and Al Atkinson and John Elliott and Larry Grantham, regulars all. "They're pros, they know when they're needed," assistant Walt Michaels noted, and they were all ready. Ryan wanted to send Carl McAdams out, too, but couldn't spot him in the crowd. Jim Hudson went out but came back. "It seemed like there were seventeen guys out there. Everybody wanted to play and it wouldn't have been fair to chase one of the guys off. They'd been doing a good job," the safetyman, always mindful of squad morale, pointed out.

So Hudson watched from the sidelines as Curley Johnson kicked off. Zeke Moore fielded the ball at his five and returned to the 27, where he ran into an explosive tackle by Philbin. The blow forced a fumble, and Bill Rademacher recovered for the Jets, to assure the 20–14 victory. The Jets had now won four games, three of them directly traceable to late control drives by Namath, who, for the third straight game, did not throw a touchdown pass.

When the Jets reported back to Shea Stadium to prepare for a home game against Boston, the beards and mustaches were really beginning to take shape and the defensive linemen talked openly of their get-the-quarterback pool. Considered illegal by the league office, this one was Biggs' idea, too. He had started it for the second game of the season and won the first pot. All of the defensive linemen— Biggs, Elliott, Philbin, Rochester, and swing man McAdams—contributed $10 apiece. Defensive line coach Buddy Ryan, Ewbank, and Mike Martin, son of one of the owners who worked in the front office, added $10 each, too. Nobody collected in a defeat, or if the opposing quarterback was not thrown for a loss or if there was a tie for honors. Mike Taliaferro, their ex-teammate, didn't know it, but he was the subject of a $210 bounty that weekend.

Both Taliaferro and his sub, rookie Tom Sherman, underwent a brutal rush that afternoon as the Jets romped to a 48–14 victory over Boston. They were thrown a total of seven times for 50 yards in losses, and Philbin, who made four tackles and forced two fumbles, won the pool. Namath, though, for the second time in the season, jammed his right thumb and held an icepack to the finger as Babe

Parilli directed the final stages of the rout. Billy Joe, the Jets' most popular sub, ran for three touchdowns in the final period as seven-year-old John F. Kennedy, Jr., son of the late President, watched from the winners' bench. The youngster applauded after every touchdown, enjoying not so much the action as the little Jet-plane car that whizzed up and down the sidelines after home scores.

Namath didn't throw a touchdown pass against the Patriots, either, to make it four straight games, and his shutout string ran to five as the Jets avenged their earlier loss to Buffalo with a 25–21 victory at Shea. The Jet offense, in fact, didn't score a point in this one, the only New York touchdown coming when Johnny Sample returned an interception 36 yards.

The rest of the points came on field goals, and the one conversion, by Jim Turner. It was Turner's greatest day as a pro, and it started inauspiciously with boos. Jim missed his first attempt from the 26 and his second try was blocked. He was 0-for-2 and the Jets trailed, 7–0.

But then Turner went to work in earnest. He kicked a 32-yarder, made the PAT after Sample's touchdown, and added field goals from the 9, 32, and 27 to give the Jets a 19–7 lead going into the final period. The Jets, however, continued unable to win any game the easy way. Kay Stephenson completed his second touchdown pass of the game, and Hagood Clarke reeled off an 82-yard punt return. In less than three minutes, the Bills had scored twice and taken a 21–19 lead with only 6:18 to go.

Just under three and a half minutes remained when the Jets' comeback drive stalled at the Buffalo 28. Turner and Babe Parilli, his holder, moved out on the field. Turner was enjoying a record season and he gave a generous portion of the credit to Parilli. "The greatest holder in football," Turner said extravagantly. "He always spots the ball down with the laces just right, facing away from me." Parilli, the old pro, also served to steady Turner, a moody, high-strung specialist who would tighten the springs of inner tension until they almost snapped by gametime. After a bad game, it would always be days until Turner smiled again.

Parilli knew just how to jolly Turner along. A sometimes place-kicker himself, he'd tell Turner as they walked on the field, "Boy, this is an easy one we've got there. Bet I could kick it myself."

But this time Parilli was silent. Not a word passed between him and Turner. The game was in the balance with this kick, and a title was in the balance with every game. "If I said I didn't feel the pressure, I'd be lying," Turner confessed later, but he made good from the 35 and the Jets were back in front, 22–21. It was the first time in Turner's career that he had kicked a field goal that actually decided a game, bang-bang, just like that.

A couple of plays later, Al Atkinson intercepted a pass to set up another Turner field goal from the 27, his sixth of the day. "It's the most I ever made since we played an intrasquad game in Jersey City one year and I did the kicking for both sides," he recalled in the steaming clubhouse.

Turner's six field goals in one game tied an AFL record set by Gino Cappelletti of Boston in 1964, and Jim pointed out that Parilli was the holder then, too. Of course, the six broke Turner's own club record and his eight attempts established a league mark. His 19 points in one game was a club record.

(Before the year was out, Turner also was to set a pro record with 34 field goals and 145 points by kicking alone. His toe was to provide the margin of victory in 6 of the Jets' 13 victories, including the AFL championship game and the Super Bowl. In the latter, he outscored the Colts himself, ten points to seven. The margin of victory was nine.)

The week after Turner's display, Houston came into Shea. The Oilers had emerged as their only competition for the Eastern Division lead, and the Jets still remembered the way Houston caught them at the wire last year.

Weeb Ewbank made sure they didn't forget. A huge facsimile of a check for $25,000 made out to "each Jet player" was put up on the bulletin board. This was a reminder of the Super Bowl rewards that lay beyond the division championship. Thumbtacked nearby was a newspaper article. The headline asked: WILL THE JETS BLOW IT AGAIN? And in a prominent place was Weeb's copy of the scornful telegram he had received from the Oilers the season before: . . . WE SAVED SECOND PLACE FOR YOU.

Jet players also held a private meeting before the game in which the captains demanded "sacrifices" the rest of the way. But Ewbank knew it takes more than psychology to win a football game.

Two weeks earlier he'd come up with a new wrinkle against the Patriots, a shift into an unbalanced line, which helped ruin the rhythm of Boston's famous blitzing defense. For the Oilers, he devised still another offensive set. Tight end Pete Lammons and halfback Emerson Boozer were spread out wide. The usual outside receivers, George

Sauer and Don Maynard, were "slotted" in the gaps between the wide men and the interior line.

Houston's cornerbacks, always the speediest men in the secondary, automatically went to cover the outside men, leaving Maynard and Sauer with a tremendous advantage over their defenders. In seven minutes, before Houston could make adjustments, the Jets had picked up 10 quick points on the way to their 26–7 victory. Even cold wet weather, which had kept almost 25,000 ticket holders home, failed to dampen Jet joy at this important and emotional triumph.

And soon after the Jets had scored this record-tying fourth straight victory to move within whispering distance of the Eastern title, Jet owners got together informally with Weeb Ewbank. This was the last year of his second contract, but they indicated the coaching job was his the next season if he wanted it. Or, if he wished, he could return under the new contract simply as general manager. The decision was his. Weeb said he'd let them know after the season.

The Jets now were faced with their annual West Coast trip. Before they left, Ewbank confided that he'd settle for an even split in the two games. The players, grim and determined, agreed to a $5,000 fine for breaking curfew, 1,000 percent more than the usual $50. (Incidentally, in addition to the regular $50 fine for missing curfew, the club also had a $500 levy for making bed check and then sneaking out again.)

Memories of last year's brutal beating in Oakland seemed fresh as yesterday as the Jets came in for their landing over San Francisco Bay. This was not a football game, this was a crusade. Al Davis, the Oakland boss, and coach Johnny Rauch made sure to keep the Jets on edge. Locked in a three-way tie with Kansas City and San Diego for the Western Division lead, the Raiders needed this one, too.

For his part, Rauch maintained the mystery of whether Daryle Lamonica, who had missed the previous game because of injuries, would be ready to play quarterback against the Jets. Davis played the rest of the psychological game. The Raiders' new offices were decorated with blowups of football action photos. Occupying a place of honor was the famous picture of Davidson cracking Namath's cheekbone. "What a thing to be proud of," Ewbank said disgustedly when told about it. But when he went to pay a courtesy visit to the Raiders, the picture was quickly taken down and hidden behind a door.

It had been raining before the Jets arrived, but nobody bothered to put a tarpaulin on the field until the moment the Jets showed up to practice. Workmen were getting ready to unroll the covering when Walt Michaels confronted them. "You put this thing on the field and I'll stomp it full of holes," he warned, and so the Jets were given leave to work out.

The Jets' motel was near both the stadium and the Raider offices. One night Davis stopped by as usual to pick up an early edition of the morning paper. He chanced to see Namath, whom he'd known and admired since Joe was a college sophomore. They chatted and Ewbank joined them. "You know what he told Joe?" Ewbank exclaimed. "He said, 'I can't tell you who it is, but there's a guy on our team who's promised to get you Sunday. You'd better be careful.' That's the kind of stuff you pull in high school."

The Jets, of course, saw plots in the rising sun and spies behind every blade of grass, but this was the emotional tenor of the game, which started out with a personal foul call against the Jets on the opening kickoff. From then on it was a flurry of violence and yellow penalty flags, arguments and fights, and brilliant football. The Jets went out front, 6–0, on two Turner field goals, but Lamonica, taped like a mummy, completed a short touchdown pass and the Raiders led, 7–6, at the quarter. It was 14–12 at the half as Namath scored for the Jets on a one-yard keeper around right end, but Parilli's pass for a two-point conversion was incomplete.

The Jets regained the lead at 19–14 in the third quarter, but the Raiders drove back. With third down at the Jet 13, Lamonica threw a little flare pass to fullback Hewritt Dixon, who was tackled by safetyman Jim Hudson at the 11. But an official charged that Hudson had illegally grabbed Dixon by the face mask. The Jets already had been called an inordinate number of times for this infraction, and Hudson became enraged, especially, he claimed later, when the official started cursing him. (Hudson plays the game with such wild-eyed fervor, that he once was accused of taking pep pills. The charge was entirely without foundation. The Jets shuddered at the thought of Hudson hopped up even more by an outside stimulant.)

The Jet safety was yelling at back judge Frank Kirkland, who advanced on Hudson, shaking his finger as John Sample tried to move his teammate away from the official. Hudson then was thrown out of the game and he gestured to the crowd as he was escorted off the field.

The two penalties against Hudson—face-masking and unsportsmanlike conduct—moved the ball to the three, and Charlie Smith ran it over on the next play to put Oakland in front, 22–19.

In addition to Hudson, the Jets had lost linebacker Larry Grantham with a neck injury on the very same play, but the visitors were far from finished. Don Maynard had found himself a pigeon in rookie cornerback George Atkinson and the veteran flanker knew he could get free any time. As the fourth quarter started, the Raiders were threatening. But Paul Crane, in for Grantham, tackled Smith hard to force a fumble, and Gerry Philbin made a saving recovery at the Jet three. It took only two passes from Namath to Maynard to cover the 97 yards and the Jets were back in front, 26–22. (The 50-yard scoring pass was Joe's first in seven games. The Jets had won five of the six in which he had been shut out.) The Jets increased their lead to 29–22 when Turner added a 12-yard field goal with 8:49 to play.

With Fred Biletnikoff victimizing Sample, the Raiders came back for a tying touchdown, but the Jets reestablished their lead when Turner kicked a 26-yard field goal to make it 32–29 with only 65 seconds to play.

With all the penalties (19 for 238 yards against both teams as the Jets' 13-for-145 set a club record), the game was running late. Most pro games last two and a half hours; this one was three hours long and not over yet. It was 7 P.M. in the East, and the National Broadcasting Company had scheduled a classic children's movie, *Heidi*. Somewhere in television land a minor executive decreed that children shall not be disappointed. He pressed a magic button and the Jet-Oakland game disappeared. On came the Swiss orphan girl and her goatherd, and all over the nation irate football fans had to restrain themselves from destroying their television sets. In New York, thousands of listeners rushed to radios in hopes of recapturing Merle Harmon's account of the final 65 seconds of play. The NBC switchboard was deluged with so many calls, a network spokesman said, "the fuses blew out." When the network tried to recover its fumble and return to the game, it was over. Back in New York, millions of Jet fans, including Ewbank's wife, Lucy, went happily to dinner secure that their team had won. Some even called friends in Oakland to gloat.

In the Oakland Coliseum, however, shocking events were transpiring. With Hudson out of the game, the Raiders went to work on his successor, rookie Mike D'Amato, just as they had done the year before when Hudson was injured. D'Amato couldn't handle Raider halfback Charlie Smith on pass defense. Lamonica passed to Smith for 20 yards to the Oakland 42, and then the Jets were hit with still another face-masking infraction. That moved the ball to the Jet 43, and on the next play Lamonica again threw to Smith, who ran all the way in for the touchdown. George Blanda's conversion put the Raiders in front, 36–32, with only 42 seconds left to play, but the Jets still felt they had a chance. Namath was passing brilliantly and Maynard was still getting free on every pattern against Atkinson. All they needed was a halfway decent kickoff return.

Earl Christy had to be thinking about that, too. What a time to break his first touchdown runback! Mike Eischeid's kickoff was one of those hard-to-handle squibbers. It bounced in and out of Christy's hands at the 15 and Earl recovered at the 10. Instead of falling on the ball, or tucking it close and heading for the safe sideline to stop the clock, Christy tried to spin and twist upfield against a mob of Raider tacklers. But as he was thrown down at the 12, the ball squirted out of his hands toward the end zone. Preston Ridlehuber, a third-string Raider fullback, picked up the fumble and ran it in for a clinching touchdown in a 43–32 victory. These would be the only points he scored all season, and he flung the ball happily into the crowd. In a span of nine seconds, less time than it takes to run the hundred-yard dash, the Raiders had scored two touchdowns and won the game. Television and the Jets had blown the whole bit.

The Jets, forgetting 93 yards in penalties against the Raiders, felt cheated after the game. Dr. Nicholas and Walt Michaels both tried to berate the officials. The Jets, who'd lost their poise during the game—as Ewbank was to remind them later—didn't regain it after the final gun, either.

A battered and demoralized group flew that night to Long Beach, California, where they would drill for next Sunday's game in San Diego. With them, on crutches, was Billy Joe, whose knee had been injured in the Oakland game. He would undergo surgery in Los Angeles, and every member of the team walked by his seat to express sadness at the injury. "I've never known a player to face an operation with a better attitude," Dr. Nicholas said.

Grantham, who had suffered a neck injury, was left behind temporarily in an Oakland hospital. Paul Rochester remained with him. Two years ago their roles had been reversed when Rocky suffered his eye injury in the same city. Verlon Biggs was suffering from a bumped knee, and Joe Namath had a recurrence of the old sprained thumb, plus a sore foot where one of his teammates had stepped on him. Johnny Sample had the flu, but he got no sympathy from Jet coaches. They thought he should have spoken up before the game so they could have prepared a substitute and not after Biletnikoff had caught all those passes.

As they flew south, Ewbank had to raise his voice himself to cut off a shouting argument between his two top assistants, Clive Rush, who was in charge of the offense, and Walt Michaels, master of the defensive platoon.

Michaels was especially distraught over the defeat. For one thing, his defenders had played their worst game of the season. For another, he held a special grudge against the Raiders and Al Davis. Walt had been an assistant at Oakland when Davis moved in in 1963. Al Davis, a guy who'd never even really played college football, had then fired Michaels, the four-time All-Pro linebacker. An emotional guy beneath his supercalm façade, Michaels still lived the game through and with his players. He was crushed by the defeat.

The Jets were listless and picky as they resumed their workouts in Long Beach, and Ewbank wisely gave them free rein. They didn't even have to report in until noon on Tuesday and no curfew was imposed either that night or Wednesday. A couple of nights on the town was what the little doctor ordered. Their position in the standings was not as good as it had been, but it was far from precarious. It was no time for the coach to begin shouting and cracking the whip. He had to appear unshaken. If he didn't get down on them, they wouldn't get down on themselves.

On Thursday the Jets were put under a midnight curfew, and Friday and Saturday nights the deadline was set at 11 P.M. By this time Weeb figured they'd better be ready to play. Their road uniforms, lost en route from an Oakland cleaners, also arrived. That was a good sign.

The Jets were tight and silent as they gathered in the San Diego Stadium's roomy clubhouse. Steve Thompson, who had been hurt in the rookie game, was back on the roster, putting on a game uniform for the first time as a pro. The pants were too big; he had to change them. He was no more nervous than the rest of the team.

Then Namath could be seen walking to the washroom. He had a razor under his arm. Was this farewell to Fu Manchu? Was he going to shave his mustache? Reporters edged toward the washroom door. In the tense moments before the kickoff, Namath was nonchalantly trimming his mustache as if for a *Johnny Carson Show* appearance. Then he went out and destroyed the Chargers by throwing a couple of touchdown passes in a 37–15 runaway. San Diego, still in contention for the Western Division championship, had been relaxed and loose all week before meeting the Jets. Their spirits had been high. You never can tell.

The victory assured the Jets of no worse than a tie for the Eastern Division championship. They could win it themselves by beating Miami at home the following Sunday, or they could ease in earlier on Thursday if Kansas City beat Houston on Thanksgiving Day. Every year the club threw a Thanksgiving Day dinner for the players and their families at Shea Stadium. This was one time none of the wives would mind if their husbands watched television during a meal. If the Chiefs beat the Oilers in Kansas City, there would be champagne to wash down the turkey.

The Jets were eating their dessert, pumpkin pie, when the final seconds ticked off in Kansas City's 24–10 victory. In came the champagne from the back room. Weeb Ewbank grinned happily as his players showered him with the bubbly beverage. A division title, this was the goal. In their secret hearts the Jets may have dreamed Super Bowl, but they knew winning the AFL East had to be the first step.

A championship for dessert. (From left) Jim Turner, Cornell Gordon, Weeb Ewbank and Curley Johnson watch Houston lose.

New York Jets

Anything else would just be so much pumpkin pie and whipped cream. "I've waited nine years for this moment," said Don Maynard, one of the three surviving original Titans.

The next day, Cornell Gordon, Bake Turner, and Jim Hudson shaved off their beards and mustaches for a photographer. They each received $250 for the stunt, plus the electric razors to keep, from the manufacturer whose product they'd used.

As the Jets approached the pennant clinching that would make it all a moot point, AFL president Milt Woodard got around to writing them about their facial adornments. He said they presented a poor image to the youth of America. Biggs went ahead and shaved his beard, but Namath was outraged. His mustache was nobody's business but his own. What was so bad about hair? "The greatest man who ever lived had long hair and a beard," Namath pointed out. But soon after, for a $15,000 fee, he shaved his mustache as part of a television commercial for another razor company.

Woodard's letter was insignificant compared to another the Jets received at about this time. This one was from pro commissioner Pete Rozelle and it contained his ruling as an aftermath to the Oakland imbroglio. Dave Anderson of the New York *Times* broke the story and it was a dandy. The Jets as a team had been fined $2,000 for their actions after the game, namely complaints about the officiating from Ewbank and Michaels and the uninvited visit to the officials by Dr. Nicholas. Michaels was fined an additional $150 himself for chasing the officials and Hudson was fined $150 for his gestures. He and John Elliott, who had been kicked out of the game near the end, also received automatic $50 fines for being ejected.

"The matter," said Ewbank, "is closed." But the official who had ejected Hudson was taken off a New York assignment and given a game elsewhere. There had been threats, AFL supervisor of officials Mel Hein admitted.

The Jets now faced three closing games before meeting the still undetermined Western Division champion. Ewbank planned to devote the time to getting his team healthy. Namath would play the first half in each game.

In their final two home games, the Jets showed the pride that had made them champions. The week after a clinching, most teams merely go through the motions. Against Miami, the Sunday after their uproarious Thanksgiving Day party, the Jets fell behind, 17–14, in the final quarter, but Babe Parilli hit Don Maynard with two quick touch-

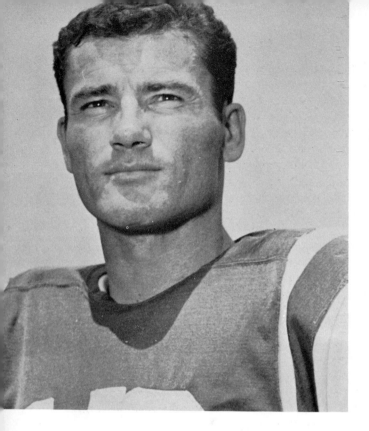

Don Maynard

New York Jets

down passes and the Jets were able to "win it on our own" as they had hoped, 35–17.

Maynard caught seven passes for 160 yards and three touchdowns in this game and became, for sheer yardage covered, the greatest pass receiver in pro football history. Raymond Berry, Weeb's old star at Baltimore, had set the old record of 9,275 yards, and Maynard passed him by 57 during the Miami game. For Maynard, playing better than he ever had before, it was a crowning achievement. He had been kicked around plenty during his long career, as witness the fact that he had been the receiver for no less than 26 different quarterbacks as a pro. He had been together with Namath longer than with any of the others. It showed.

The next week the Jets beat Cincinnati, 27–14. Five different Jets were injured in this game, the most serious being Maynard, who pulled the hamstring that would bother him through the Super Bowl. The game meant nothing, but when the Bengals blocked a punt and got a first down at the Jet two, New York's defensive line rose up in a magnificent goal line stand and four times threw them back. "They showed what they were made of," Weeb said proudly.

The final game of the season came on December 15 in Miami. The Jets won this game easily, 31–7, as Maynard watched from the sidelines in civilian clothes. During the half it was announced that Joe Namath had been voted by his teammates as the Jets' Most Valuable Player. Although the key man, quarterback, and supposed leader for three years before this, Namath had always finished way down in the voting. This election showed how Namath had changed . . . how his teammates had changed . . . and something about why they'd be playing for a championship. The honor was a companion piece to Joe's election as captain before the first game of the season. Nobody could blame him any longer for losing games. Intercepted twelve times in the first five games, he was intercepted only five times in the next nine. The Jets won eight of them.

When they returned to New York that night, members of the defensive platoon quickly grabbed up copies of the early editions of Monday's papers. Noting the scores and statistics of the other games, Larry Grantham let out a little whoop. The defense, so often maligned, had led the league. The only disappointment was individual and minimal. George Sauer, catching only two passes against the Dolphins, had come up two catches short against Lance Alworth of San Diego in his bid to repeat as AFL receiving champion.

The weekend results also left the Jets' play-off opponent undecided. The Chiefs and Raiders had finished in a tie and would play off for the Western Division title in Oakland the following weekend.

Not wishing anyone permanent harm, the Jets were pulling for a major war in Oakland. "I'd like to see 'em tie and go four overtimes," Ewbank said complacently. The Eastern champs wanted to see their opponents come in bloody and bruised while they were rested and healthy from a free weekend. As cold professionals, they were pulling for Kansas City. They felt certain they could stop the Chiefs' offense. They rated Oakland's Daryle Lamonica as more dangerous than Kansas City's Len Dawson. But as champions and men with pride, the Jets wanted Oakland to win. They wanted another shot at the Raiders, this time in their own backyard.

23
Revenge

The Jets didn't bother to send a coach to Oakland to scout the Western Division play-offs between the Raiders and the Chiefs. Weeb Ewbank and his staff could watch at home on television and they'd get the movies. Weeb did have a West Coast scout in the stands, though. If somebody left the game, the Jet coach wanted to know if the player was limping, and on what leg.

The Raiders prepared for the game with their usual mystery and even changed practice fields. Paul Zimmerman, enterprising reporter for the New York *Post,* actually found the field, but when he got closer for a better look, he was thrown out. The Raiders' kicking coach, Bugsy Engelberg, obviously hired for kicking out reporters, was assigned to escort Zimmerman from the vicinity. Since Engelberg is barely over five feet tall and Zimmerman is a strapping six-foot-two former college football player, that only added to the humiliation.

The Chiefs spurned the usual Oakland motels and irritated Raider boss Al Davis by staying in San Francisco's posh Mark Hopkins Hotel on Nob Hill. Davis maintained that AFL teams should never stay in NFL territory. This was the last time Kansas City was able to one-up anybody in Oakland.

That Sunday the Raiders broke to a 21–0 first-quarter lead, and with Daryle Lamonica completing five touchdown passes, rolled up a 41–6 rout. At one point, as the second quarter began, the Raider defense stopped Kansas City on seven straight plays inside the 10 and forced the Chiefs to settle for a Jan Stenerud field goal. After the game, Lamonica picked up the tab for his teammates' champagne party.

When the Raiders made plans to come to New York for the title game, their itinerary was dictated by two considerations unique to their organization. Since the Chiefs had gained prestige by staying at the Mark Hopkins, the Raiders would have to find a better hotel in

John Elliott, whose shift to tackle helped firm Jet defense, stops Oakland's Hewritt Dixon as Jim Hudson comes up to help out.

New York. And Oakland had to figure out a way to keep its players away from the inquiring press, which in most cities objected to being fed whatever the home team thought expedient. (Oakland cornerback Kent McCloughan underwent a knee operation in secret on Wednesday before the play-off with Kansas City, and on Friday local newsmen were still speculating that he might be activated against the Chiefs.)

The first problem was easily solved. Davis booked his team into the famous Waldorf-Astoria Hotel. Oakland Coach Johnny Rauch had said he was willing to practice "in any vacant lot," but everyone knew it would have to be a vacant lot with a fence. He and Davis bristled when told the league would order their players be produced for pregame interviews. So, for security and privacy, they waited until the last minute and flew into New York Friday night before the Sunday title game.

As the Jets staged their final workouts, Ewbank was faced with a couple of more important decisions. The Jets had been victimized at three positions in their *Heidi* loss to the Raiders—strong safety and left cornerback on defense, right tackle on offense. Assuming Jim Hudson had learned his lesson and would not get thrown out of another game, strong safety was rated as secure. But what to do about left corner, where Fred Biletnikoff had enjoyed such a big day against John Sample, and right tackle, where Isaac Lassiter had given rookie Sam Walton another painful lesson? What would happen when identical match-ups were presented in the championship game?

Ewbank pondered long about benching Sample, his defensive captain. During the week he worked both Cornell Gordon and Sample with the No. 1 unit. But in the end he decided to stick with the veteran, issuing but one warning: "We want you to take the post pattern away from Biletnikoff. The first time he runs one against you, out you go."

Ewbank was certain Sample would respond under pressure, but he wasn't so sure about Walton. The youngster had been asked to do a lot his rookie season. Would it be unfair, as well as unwise, to ask more? More critical, whereas Ewbank had a man he could throw in for Sample, it would take several line changes to replace Walton. This couldn't easily be done during a game.

A turning point for Walton had come during the *Heidi* game. Forgetting his fundamentals, giving ground too quickly under Lassiter's pressure, Walton had been the teammate who stepped on Namath's foot that afternoon. During workouts the next week, Ewbank and offensive line coach Joe Spencer had conducted a special seminar in blocking techniques for Walton. Ewbank, short, dumpy, and gray-haired, squaring off to demonstrate blocking form against Spencer and Walton, both twice his size, provided a ludicrous tableau. Just as strange was the need for such lessons with a third-round draft choice ten games into the season.

Walton seemed to improve as the Jets won their last four, but Ewbank wasn't satisfied. Like an old-line boxing manager, he was interested in styles. McDole, Jackson, and Lassiter were of a piece, big and powerful. They used their muscle. This was the style that had beaten Walton every time. The nifties didn't bother him. Weeb elected to make the change. Dave Herman, normally a guard, had finished up the Oakland game at tackle against Lassiter and survived. Ewbank decided to give him another shot. Herman would play tackle from the beginning and Randy Rasmussen would be a starter again at right guard. Herman was short and stubby, not really big enough to play tackle. Against a slicker like Kansas City's Jerry Mays, he'd have trouble closing in to make his block. But power guys like Lassiter (and Baltimore's Bubba Smith) would come to him. And Weeb knew Herman would not be outtoughed.

As for Rasmussen, he had played well early in the year and it had taken a veteran six-time All-Star to move him out. He'd responded well despite the benching and was ready when needed in reserve at both guard positions. Randy had played most of the final game against Miami when Herman was hurt, and he'd finished that *Heidi* game after Herman's move. In Sunday's championship, he would go up against lantern-jawed Dan Birdwell, toughest of the Oakland bullyboys, who was just completing his finest season.

Cold weather had forced the Jets into an armory for their final workout, and the thermometer read 37 degrees at kickoff time at Shea Stadium. However, frigid winds gusting across Flushing Bay and swirling around the jam-packed oval made the stadium even colder, a snowless version of the Russian front.

Davis and the Raiders made the first gamesmanship move when they had a plastic windbreaker erected over their bench. But the ploy was trumped. AFL president Milt Woodard ordered the barrier taken down. It blocked the view of some customers in the twelve-dollar field-level seats.

With 62,627 fans—the most ever to see an AFL title game—roaring encouragement, the Jets broke from the gate like quarter horses, and it was their Southwestern speedburner, Don Maynard, who started them. Even though his leg was hurting, Maynard resumed his torment of George Atkinson and the Jets ate up 56 yards on four plays for a 7–0 lead. The touchdown came on a 14-yard pass from Namath to Maynard, and Jim Turner kicked the point after only 3:39 had elapsed.

Late in the period, Turner kicked a 33-yard field goal, and with fans cheering the Jet defensive unit whenever it left the field, the home team took a 10–0 first-quarter lead.

However, as they changed sides, the Raiders were driving. Biletnikoff was catching passes on Sample, and 48 seconds into the second period, he ran that old post pattern and pulled in a 29-yard touchdown pass from Lamonica as Sample missed the tackle. The touchdown closed the gap to 10–7, and on the next series, Gordon went in for Sample. It was the first time in his long pro career that Sample had ever been benched during a game.

When the Jets got the ball back, Namath was rushed out of the pocket and scrambled around end for a 14-yard gain before escaping out of bounds. Three plays later, he wasn't so lucky. Ben Davidson and Isaac Lassiter, the fearsome ends, broke through and mashed Namath into the frozen ground for a seven-yard loss. Namath had suffered a bruised coccyx earlier in the season and it still bothered him. As he was being propelled toward the hard turf, he stuck his left hand behind his hip pads to ease the blow. When he got up he saw the ring finger of his left hand had been dislocated. And his right thumb, once again, was badly jammed. The dislocated finger looked like a snake. Namath couldn't even bear to look at it. But on the sidelines, trainer Jeff Snedeker popped it into place and taped it to the middle finger.

Raiders Dan Birdwell (53) and Carleton Oats chase Namath out of the pocket.

Barton Silverman

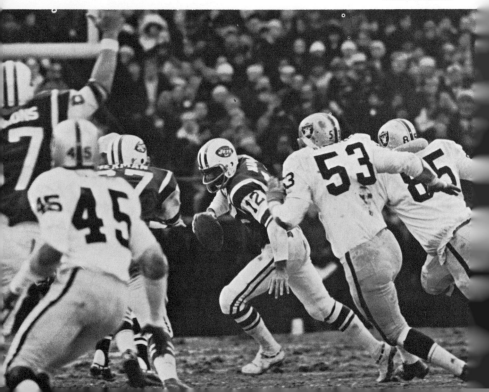

Namath declined any pain-killing injections for either hand. Like a safecracker, he needed his touch.

Jim Turner and George Blanda traded field goals late in the first half, and the Jets led, 13–10, as they went out to kill the clock on their last drive before the half. On the next-to-last play of the period, Namath passed incomplete for Sauer. But Lassiter was charging and he belted Namath to the ground just as he got rid of the ball. Joe was slow getting up, but it was fourth down coming up and time only for Curley Johnson's punt. Namath headed directly for the dressing room.

In the locker room, the Jets suddenly realized that Namath was acting strangely. He didn't know where he was! Had he been knocked silly by Lassiter's blow or had it been an accumulation of previous clouts by the Raiders? Nobody could be sure. Dr. Jim Nicholas and Jeff Snedeker led Namath off to a side room, where they ministered to him like seconds treating a dazed fighter who'd just been saved by the bell. Just before the team started getting ready to go back on the field, Dr. Nicholas warned Ewbank, "You may have to go with Parilli."

Ewbank told Parilli to be prepared, but Namath seemed to be okay when they moved out for the third period. The Jets received the kick-off and Namath lost his footing and stumbled for a four-yard loss when he took the snap on the very first play. But like a veteran fighter who can survive for many rounds on instinct and memory, Namath hung in. On the sidelines, Ewbank, Dr. Nicholas, and Parilli watched Namath's every move. Bad knees, bad hands, head throbbing, Namath refused to surrender.

The Raiders weren't giving up either. Lamonica moved his team out from dangerous territory and passed to Biletnikoff, who took the ball away from Gordon for a 37-yard gain to the Jet 46. Then he threw to Warren Wells, the split end who was supposed to be hurt all week, and the play carried for 40 yards and a first down at the Jet six. Jim Hudson, the man who had lost his head in Oakland, arose with all his fire and was in on three straight tackles as the Raiders were halted short at the one. Oakland had to settle for another field goal by Blanda and a 13–13 tie.

By now, Namath was beginning to shake the cobwebs. Connecting on three straight third-down plays (two passes and a Snell run), he moved the Jets from their 20 to the Raider 20. The last pass was a 20-yarder to Maynard. Atkinson was all over the Jet flanker, but Namath drilled it home. That's when Parilli knew he could relax. Namath was okay. Two more passes to Maynard missed, but then

Namath threw to tight end Pete Lammons, who just made it into the end zone for a touchdown with 58 seconds left in the third period. Turner's PAT made it 20–13, Jets.

Sample was back in the game as the contest turned into the final period, but Lamonica completed a 57-yard pass play over him to Biletnikoff for a first down at the Jet 11. But again the Jet defense braced as Larry Grantham rallied them with the reminder, "Don't lose your poise, don't lose your poise." After three plays the Raiders showed a net of minus one yard. Again they had been barred from a touchdown by gut defense and again they had to settle for a Blanda field goal. With less than 10 minutes to play, the Jets were still in front by 20–16 and now the clock was on their side.

The clock, however, is a fickle friend. On the first play after the Raider kickoff, Namath again turned to Maynard, but this time the battered Atkinson was ready. He smelled the sideline pattern and cut in front of Maynard for a brazen interception at the Jet 37. The speedy rookie ran it all the way to the five, where Namath helped with the tackle. Pete Banaszak punched left tackle on the next play for the touchdown. The Raiders for the first time were in front, 23–20, with 8:18 to go. The descending numbers flashing the time on the scoreboard seemed to be counting out the Jets' dream.

But the Jets wouldn't stay down for that count. "We'll get it back, we'll get it back," the offense promised as they went back on the field and Earl Christy returned the kickoff from three yards deep in the end zone to the Jet 32. On first down, Namath passed to George Sauer on the left for 10 yards. Then he sent Maynard off again down the sideline against the rookie Atkinson, and Don pulled in his pass for 52 yards to the Raider six. Maynard and Atkinson had battled stride for stride like thoroughbreds down the stretch and Maynard had to make a great over-the-head baseball catch against his pursuer.

The pass was Namath's game now, but he faked a hand-off to Matt Snell going into the line, pulled the ball back, and slipped slightly as he looked for a receiver. Bill Mathis was his primary target, but Mathis was covered. George Sauer was his secondary receiver, but Sauer was covered, too. Snell might have been a possible receiver, but Matt was busy blocking linebacker Gus Otto. As he moved around in the backfield, looking desperately for an open man, Namath saw Maynard cutting across the end zone. Maynard was only the third or fourth alternate receiver, but he never gave up on the play. Even though he knew the ball might never come to him, he gave Atkinson a 60-yard fake in the corner of the end zone and came driving across from the right. Drilling the ball almost sidearm, Namath whipped it to Maynard at knee level and the veteran flanker caught it falling and diving. Turner's PAT made the score 27–23. The Jets had been behind for all of 31 seconds.

Still, almost eight minutes remained to play. The Raiders had required only nine seconds to destroy the Jets last time they met. The New Yorkers couldn't even hold a lead for 65 seconds in that game. Cold as it was, nobody was leaving Shea Stadium now.

Two big plays after the kickoff and the Raiders had moved to a first down at the Jet 26, but they got no farther. On fourth down, Lamonica, looking for a receiver, was smothered by Verlon Biggs for a six-yard loss. Only five and a half minutes remained, but the Jets were still unable to kill the clock. They had to punt, and with three and a half minutes left, Oakland got another chance. Lamonica passed to Biletnikoff for 24 to the Raider 39. Then he threw to Wells for 37 more and the Jets were penalized for a personal foul on the tackle. First down, Oakland, on the Jet 24 with just over two minutes remaining.

Lamonica faded again to pass, but the monstrous figure of Verlon Biggs was fading with him and gaining. No receivers opened up, so Lamonica hurriedly lobbed a pass to Charlie Smith, his "safety valve," out in the right flat. It was a rushed pass. In fact, it wasn't a pass at all. It was thrown at a backward angle. It was a lateral. Smith, caught by surprise (he was a secondary receiver) seemed mesmerized as the ball fell uncaught. An incomplete pass, dead ball, he thought. But Ralph Baker, the unsung linebacker, knew what it was. It was a lateral, a free ball. He scooped it up and started to run. Earlier in the season, against Boston, one of the Patriots had picked up a loose lateral against the Jets and run it in for a touchdown. But this time the officials knew the rules. No runback, no touchdown, just the Jets' ball. That was enough.

The Jets killed almost a minute and that was enough, too. Johnson punted deep, and Oakland, looking for bombs, learned how little can be accomplished when that's your only weapon. As the seconds clicked off and frozen fans joined the countdown, Lamonica completed his last pass of the season to Hewitt Dixon. The Raider fullback struggled to get out of bounds to stop the clock for just one more chance, but he couldn't escape Jim Hudson. Hudson, such a key figure in the last two

Emotion—and possibly pain—etch Weeb Ewbank's features as players carry him from the field.

Oakland games, made the final tackle in the 27–23 victory. The Jets were champions of the AFL.

Fans and players swarmed onto the field and two rookies lifted Ewbank to their shoulders—six-foot-five Steve Thompson and six-foot-two Mike D'Amato, Ewbank teetered uncertainly as they wobbled him off the field and a little boy came along and exuberantly chinned himself on Ewbank's outstretched right leg. The stunt painfully wrenched Ewbank's right hip, and the tears he shed were not merely tears of joy. As newsmen crowded the dressing room, Ewbank was so excited he didn't even remember the score.

By its usual edict, always honored in the breach, the AFL prohibited champagne in the winning dressing room. But the celebratory nectar was soon pulled out of hiding. Ewbank was given the game ball by Sample and then he got a clothes-on shower from Gerry Philbin. Off to one side, Namath was telling reporters, "Lamonica is a better passer than Morrall," because the Colts had emerged that same afternoon as their Super Bowl opponent.

Ewbank's moves had worked out. Sample, though needing a reminder, had been where he was supposed to be in the final clutch minutes. Herman, the new tackle, had done his job on Lassiter. Rasmussen, the baby-faced guard, had grown up against Birdwell. They would all do it again, just that way, in the Super Bowl.

After the dressing room hoorah, the Jets went on to Joe Namath's restaurant, Bachelors III, for an impromptu celebration that roared on well into the morning.

On Monday night there was the official team victory dinner at Shea Stadium. Players' wives always tittered when Ewbank got up to speak. He usually ended up reminding them of his Tuesday Rule: "Whenever we have a game coming up, I tell my married players I want them to stay away from their wives after Tuesday and I tell my single players I just hope they don't get lucky," Weeb liked to say. This time he thanked all the wives for their help and sacrifice and gave them full credit for their part in the Jets' championship.

Then Joe Namath got up. Speaking for the bachelors as he prepared to shift his base of operations, on the field and off, to Miami, he offered grandly, "I just want to thank all the broads in New York."

Epilogue: Back to Broadway

For Johnny Sample it was a historical nose-tickling moment. The veteran cornerback, thirty-one years old and eleven years a professional football player, was taking the first drink of his life. Champagne, naturally, at the Jets' Super Bowl victory party, and he savored the taste that washed away all the years of bitterness. He figured there was no danger he'd turn into a regular drinker. There'd never be another moment like this.

One by one, the players came to the fore in the crowded, smoky, steamy room in the Galt Ocean Mile Hotel. And one by one they raised their voices over the hum from several hundred family members, friends, and boosters, all still half-hysterical with excitement, all telling each other now, "I knew it all the time."

"I've played on all three teams in New York—the Giants, the Titans, and the Jets," said Don Maynard, speaking for the old hands. "I'm the only one who can make the comparison. This is the greatest of them all!"

And the crowd cheered.

Walt Michaels pointed to his seventy-three-year-old mother, a tiny gray-haired lady, sitting proudly at a table. Once she had been named Pro Football Mother of the Year. "She's the only one here who's in the Hall of Fame," the Jet assistant coach said with a fond smile splitting his broad face. (He and his brother Lou of the Colts pooled their Super Bowl checks to give a full share to their mother.)

Dave Herman, the guard who had nullified Bubba Smith, applauded Joe Namath's inspirational pregame performance. "He told the truth. He said we would beat them and we did. If Joe told me right this minute there was a lion standing behind me . . . I'd jump."

Namath got the biggest cheer and spread credit among his teammates. "We didn't win on passing or running or defense. We beat

Baltimore in every phase of the game. If ever there was a world champion, this is it," Namath declared.

For Ewbank, with his wife, Lucy, beaming from the back of the room, this was the proudest of moments. When he won the AFL title, he became the first coach to win championships in both leagues. Now he was the first AFL coach to defeat the older league in the Super Bowl, and against the team that had once fired him. His eventual place in the Hall of Fame was secure.

"Some people say that the 1958 game against the Giants [sudden-death overtime for the NFL title] was the greatest ever played, but I'll take this one," Ewbank said emotionally. "You know, sometimes it's for the best getting kicked upstairs. Before the game today I ran into Carroll Rosenbloom [owner of the Colts]. He's got a house down here and he told me, 'Weeb, after the game we're having a party at my place. You remember where it is. I want you and Lucy to come on over.'

"Well, Lucy and I couldn't make it," Weeb continued. "We've got a party of our own . . . and I'd rather be here."

The crowd cheered and hooted again, and several miles down the

On the steps of New York's City Hall Mayor Lindsay presents official medallions to Jet captains Namath and Sample.

New York Department of Public Events (Bill Stahl)

beach road, a solitary policeman stood at the entrance to the Rosen-blooms' home. A huge tent had been set up, but the yard and the house were dark.

The next morning, the Jets split up. Many of the players, especially those from the South and Southwest, went directly home, some after resting a few more days in the Miami sunshine.

A contingent of eleven went on to Jacksonville, Florida, where they would play in the AFL All-Star game the following week.

The Jets had completely dominated voting by the coaches for the Eastern All-Star squad. Of New York's 24 starters (including kickers), 18 had been named to the first or second teams. Namath, Maynard, Philbin, Sauer, Biggs, Herman, Hill, and kicker Jim Turner received first-team honors. Snell, Boozer, Lammons, Talamini, Elliott, Baker, Atkinson, Grantham, Hudson, and Baird were chosen for the second team. Since no more than 11 members of any club could play in the game, the 8 starters were joined by only Atkinson, Boozer, and Elliott in Jacksonville. Atkinson, despite his injured shoulder, went ahead and played. This was his first All-Star game. The first is always the best.

These were just the beginning of honors that would roll in for the Jets, starting with Weeb Ewbank's designation as AFL Coach of the Year and recognition by the New York Chapter of the Pro Football Writers Association as the sport's Man of the Year.

Namath swept every poll: AFL Player of the Year, Hickok Pro Athlete of the Year, the George Halas Award as Most Courageous Player, Most Valuable Player in the Super Bowl and quarterback on every All-AFL and combined All-Pro team.

Jim Turner, George Sauer, and Gerry Philbin also were named on various All-Pro teams. In addition to Namath, Sauer, Philbin, Her-man, Hill, Jim Turner, Hudson, Schmitt, and Elliott, the guy everyone thought would be too small, were named to All-AFL teams. Gran-tham, Hudson, Sample, and Curley Johnson received second-team mention.

Only a handful of players, the coaching staff, and club president Phil Iselin were on the charter plane back to New York the morning after the Super Bowl. It was a pretty bleary-eyed crew, which couldn't be blamed for a minor oversight. Their Super Bowl trophy, a gleaming 21-inch sterling silver showpiece from Tiffany's worth $2,500, and the game ball, sentimentally priceless, had been left behind in the hotel vault. The valuable keepsakes were flown up later, the trophy occupying a first-class plane seat all its own.

The Jets were greeted at the airport by a tumultuous reception. Even though it was a schoolday, some 500 youngsters of various ages crowded the terminal, where a five-piece band helped whip up excitement. New York's Mayor John Lindsay was there and so were the president of the city council and other dignitaries trying to elbow into pictures with the city's newest heroes. WHAT UPSET? THE COLTS WERE OVERRATED, JUST AS THE NFL IS, one homemade sign proclaimed.

"When was the last time New York had anything like this?" Ewbank asked.

A week later the Jets were guests at a City Hall reception called by Mayor Lindsay. An enthusiastic crowd of 10,000, more than five times as many as had been on hand for the Apollo 8 astronauts a couple of weeks earlier, gave the Jets another riotous greeting. Namath struck the keynote. Pointing to his young teammates and the predominantly teen-age crowd, he noted, "We are the youth of this generation."

Namath and the Jet party then went uptown, where Joe received his sports car from *Sport Magazine* for being named MVP in the Super Bowl. When he was introduced, his teammates rose spontaneously to lead the standing ovation. What a change in four years!

After the presentation, Namath confided that this might very well be his "last hurrah." His parents had been after him to quit football before he was crippled. The doctor had just told him a further operation on his painful left knee would be more risky than helpful. A lot of promoters were buzzing around with big-money movie offers. Squealing teen-agers outside testified to his appeal.

"I'm very happy with my life the way it is now, but you've got to make it while you're on top and before you get destroyed," Namath said thoughtfully.

He pointed out that Jimmy Brown, the great Cleveland fullback, had quit pro football for a successful movie career while at the peak of his powers. "He got out while he was still healthy," Namath stressed.

Namath was scheduled to leave on a tour of military hospitals in the Far East the following week. When he returned, he would sort out the offers with the help and guidance of Sonny Werblin, no longer his boss but still his friend and adviser . . . and a good one to have in the entertainment jungle.

Everybody loves Joe.

A lot of decisions had to be made as the Jets brushed the confetti from their shoulders.

Namath came back from his trip and cleared away the froth and cigar smoke to take a good look at those movie offers. They were mostly smoke. Those he might accept would allow him to play football again. And being a football player wouldn't hurt his new chain of drive-in restaurants, Broadway Joe's, or the New York nightspot in which he owned an interest, Bachelors III. (Little did he know that even then pro commissioner Pete Rozelle's staff of former FBI agents was collecting evidence that the clientele attracted to his bar would be ruinous to his football career and, faced with a choice of selling out or being suspended, he would threaten to quit the game.)

Ewbank, sixty-one years old, had to decide whether to continue coaching. Nobody had enjoyed the frenzy of Super Bowl week more. He elected to return to the dual position of coach and general manager and signed his third three-year contract with the Jets. Sonny Werblin had told him when he came to the AFL, "This will be your last football job." It looked as if Sonny was right. Ewbank had found a home in the big city, and one of his most touching tributes came when he walked into Toots Shor's restaurant several days after the Super Bowl and the whole dining room in that hard-boiled sports guys' hangout rose to applaud.

With Ewbank remaining, it was time for his heir apparent, Clive Rush, to be moving on. Rush had been Weeb's top assistant from the day they all came to New York in 1963. He had developed into a sought-after head coaching prospect during the championship year and he accepted the vacant post at Boston. "I hope you don't get him," Namath had told Billy Sullivan, president of the Patriots. "We need him too much." Many close to the team had credited a closer relationship between Namath and Rush with the quarterback's 1968 improvement. Soon after Rush left, personnel director George Sauer, one of the last links to the Titan era, joined him in Boston as general manager.

The Jet owners were faced with a decision, too. Running the football team hadn't been as much fun as they had expected. Phil Iselin had assumed the president's job under protest. His heart remained at Monmouth Park, and he always seemed a little uncomfortable with the football crowd. It soon became known that the team was for sale. But the asking price was a discouraging $20,000,000.

Verlon Biggs had to make his mind up, too. But only 48 hours before the option clause on his contract expired and he became a free agent, he finally signed with the Jets. Ewbank's record of never having a man play out his option on him remained intact. (George Shaw, a quarterback, almost did it, but Weeb traded him to the Giants just in time.)

Retirement was on the mind of several players, but Billy Mathis, one of the originals who had been coaxed into playing the year before, was the only one who appeared to be that serious about it. Most of the older players seemed to reflect the feelings of Larry Grantham, another original, and Babe Parilli, at thirty-nine the oldest man on the team.

"You know I'm not quitting. I've got to be around on August the seventeenth," Grantham snapped when asked about possible retirement. On August 17 the Jets were playing their long-awaited exhibition game against the Giants. Grantham had been waiting for that game for ten years. As for Parilli, he knew he could last several more years in the rocking chair job of No. 2 quarterback and he knew that those years would be fun. The excitement of playing for a championship, the cheers of big crowds as contrasted to boos from a sullen handful in Boston, had rejuvenated him, too. "This is basically a young team," he pointed out. "We should be back there next year, too. This team will win a lot of championships."

For Ewbank, as winter turned into spring, the cycle was beginning again, the cycle that kept him young, that kept him and such as Paul Brown and Vince Lombardi, who had tried to quit, at coaching.

There were new coaches to hire, an exhibition schedule to be arranged, a college draft to be run, and free agents to be found and signed. "The draft, that's where we built this team," Rush said as he was preparing to leave for Boston.

As Ewbank scanned his list of top college players, he wondered: Would there be a Namath, a Sauer, a Biggs, a Boozer, an Elliott, a Philbin, or a Snell in this group? When people called him about a young man who had not been drafted, but wanted a chance to play pro football, he wondered if one of them would be a Hudson, a Schmitt, or a Beverly. Of 22 Super Bowl starters for the Jets, 17 had been signed to their first pro contracts by Ewbank. This is the way he built, brick by brick.

There was so little time this year. The Super Bowl victory meant the Jets would be starting their exhibition season early. As World Champions, they would play the College All-Stars in Chicago on August 1, the first AFL team ever to participate in the charity contest that officially opened the football season.

"I guess," one of the Jets muttered, "we'll be eighteen-point underdogs in that one, too."

Appendix: Records

New York Jets

1968 NEW YORK JETS

Front Row, Left to Right: TRAINER JEFF SNEDEKER, KARL HENKE, JIM RICHARDS, MIKE D'AMATO, HARVEY NAIRN, RANDY BEVERLY, BILL BAIRD, CORNELL GORDON, BILL RADEMACHER, GEORGE SAUER, HATCH ROSDAHL, ROBERT TAYLOR.

Second Row, LARRY GRANTHAM, BAKE TURNER, DON MAYNARD, BILL MATHIS, CURLEY JOHNSON, RALPH BAKER, EARL CHRISTY, MIKE STROMBERG, TOMMY BURNETT, PAUL CRANE, AL ATKINSON, JEFF RICHARDSON, JOE NAMATH, HEAD COACH WEEB EWBANK.

Third Row, COACH CLIVE RUSH, EQUIPMENT MANAGER BILL HAMPTON. COACH WALT MICHAELS, PETE LAMMONS, MARK SMOLINSKI, VERNON BIGGS, LEE WHITE, JIM TURNER, JIM HUDSON, JOHN SAMPLE, PAUL ROCHESTER, EMERSON BOOZER, MATT SNELL, TONY DiMIDIO, COACH JOE SPENCER, COACH BUDDY RYAN.

Fourth Row, CARL McADAMS, JOHN ELLIOTT, RAY HAYES, SAM WALTON, WINSTON HILL, JOHN SCHMITT, STEVE THOMPSON, RANDY RASMUSSEN, BOB TALAMINI, DAVE HERMAN, BABE PARILLI, GERRY PHILBIN.

Appendix

Records

ALL-TIME NEW YORK ROSTER 1960-68

PLAYER-POS.-SEASONS-COLLEGE

Abruzzese, Ray, DB, 1965-66, Alabama
Allard, Donald, QB, 1961, Boston Col.
Ames, David, HB, 1961, Richmond
Apple, James, HB, 1961, Upsala
Atkins, William, DB, 1962-63, Auburn
Atkinson, Al, LB, 1965-68, Villanova
Baird, William, DB, 1963-68,
  San Francisco St.
Baker, Lawrence, T, 1960, Bowling Green
Baker, Ralph, LB, 1964-68, Penn State
Barnes, Ernest, T, 1960, No. Caro. Col.
Bates, Theodore, LB, 1963, Oregon St.
Bell, Edward, DB, 1960, Pennsylvania
Beverly, Randy, DB, 1967-68
  Colorado State
Biggs, Verlon, DE, 1965-68, Jackson St.
Bobo, Hubert, LB, 1961-62, Ohio State
Bohling, Dewey, HB, 1960-61,
  Hardin-Simmons
Bookman, John, DB, 1961, Miami (Fla.)
Boozer, Emerson, HB, 1966-68
  Maryland State
Brannan, Solomon, DB, 1967,
  Morris Brown
Brooks, Robert, HB, 1961, Ohio U.
Browning, Charlie, HB, 1965,
  Washington
Budrewicz, Thomas, G, 1961, Brown
Burton, Leon, HB, 1960, Arizona State
Butler, Bob, OG, 1963, Kentucky
Callahan, Daniel, E, 1960, Akron
Campbell, Kenneth, E, 1960,
  West Chester State
Carson, Kern, HB, 1965, San Diego St.
Chlebek, Edward, QB, 1963,
  W. Michigan
Chomyszak, Steve, DT, 1966, Syracuse
Christy, Earl, HB, 1966-68,
  Maryland St.
Christy, Richard, HB, 1961-63,
  No. Carolina St.
Cockrell, Eugene, T, 1960-62,
  Hardin-Simmons
Cooke, Edward, DE, 1960-63, Maryland
Cooper, Thurlow, OE, 1960-62, Maine
Crane, Paul, LB, 1966-68, Alabama
Cummings, Ed, LB, 1964, Stanford

PLAYER-POS.-SEASONS-COLLEGE

D'Agostino, Frank, G, 1960, Auburn
D'Amato, Mike, DB, 1968, Hofstra
DeFelice, Nick, OT, 1965, So. Conn. St.
DeLuca, Sam, G, 1964-66, So. Carolina
Dockery, John, DB, 1968, Harvard
Dombrowski, Leon, G, 1960, Delaware
Donnahoo, Roger, DB, 1960, Mich. St.
Dorow, Albert, QB, 1960-61, Mich. St.
Dudek, Mitch, OG, 1966, Xavier
Dukes, Mike, LB, 1965, Clemson
Dupre, Charles, DB, 1960, Baylor
Elliott, John, DT, 1967-68, Texas
Ellis, Roger, C, 1960-63, Maine
Evans, Jim, E, 1964, Texas Western
Felt, Richard, DB, 1960-61,
  Brigham Young
Ficca, Daniel, G, 1963-66, So. Calif.
Fields, Jerry, LB, 1961-62, Ohio State
Flowers, Charles, FB, 1962, Mississippi
Flynn, Donald, HB, 1961, Houston
Fontes, Wayne, HB, 1962, Michigan St.
Fournet, Sidney, G, 1962-63, L.S.U.
Fowler, Bob, FB, 1962, Tennessee
Furey, James, DB, 1961, Kansas State
Glenn, Howard, G, 1960, Linfield
Gordon, Cornell, DB, 1965-68,
  NC A & T
Grantham, Lawrence, LB, 1960-68,
  Mississippi
Gray, Jim, DB, 1966, Toledo
Gray, Moses, T, 1961-62, Indiana
Green, John, QB, 1962-63, Chattanooga
Gregory, Kenneth, OE, 1963, Whittier
Grosscup, Clyde Lee, QB, 1962, Utah
Gucciardo, Pat, DB, 1966, Kent State
Guesman, Richard, DT, 1960-63,
  West Virginia
Hall, Galen, QB, 1963, Penn State
Harris, Jim, DT, 1965-67, Utah State
Hart, Dee, FB, 1960, Hardin-Simmons
Hayes, Ray, DT, 1968, Toledo
Haynes, Abner, HB, 1967,
  North Texas State
Haynes, Paul, HB, 1961-62,
  Louisiana Tech
Heeter, Eugene, OE, 1963-65,
  West Virginia

ALL-TIME NEW YORK ROSTER 1960-68

PLAYER–POS.–SEASONS–COLLEGE

Henke, Karl, DE, 1968, Tulsa
Herman, Dave, G, 1964–68,
Michigan St.
Herndon, Donald, DB, 1960, Tampa
Hill, Winston, OT, 1963–68,
Texas Southern
Holz, Gordy, DT, 1964, Minnesota
Hord, Ambrose Roy, G, 1963, Duke
Hudock, Michael, C, 1960–65,
Miami (Fla.)
Hudson, Jim, DB, 1965–68, Texas
Iacavazzi, Cosmo, FB, 1965, Princeton
Jacobs, Proverb, T, 1961–62, California
Jamieson, Richard, QB, 1960–61,
Bradley
Janerette, Charles, DT, 1963, Penn St.
Joe, William, FB, 1967–68, Villanova
Johnson, John Curley, HB, 1961–68,
Houston
Johnston, Mark, DB, 1964, Northwest'n
Julian, Frederick, DB, 1960, Michigan
Kaimer, Karl, OE, 1962, Boston Univ.
Katcik, Joseph, T, 1960, Notre Dame
Kenerson, John, G, 1962, Kentucky St.
King, Henry, DB, 1967, Utah State
Klotz, John, T, 1960–62, 63,
Penn Military
Kovac, Edward, HB, 1962, Cincinnati
Kroll, Alexander, C, 1962, Rutgers
Lamberti, Pasquale, HB, 1961,
Richmond
Lammons, Pete, TE, 1966–68, Texas
Lawson, Alphonzo, FL, 1964,
Delaware St.
Lewis, Sherman, DB, 1966, Mich. St.
Liske, Pete, QB–DB, 1964, Penn State
Look, Dean, QB, 1962, Michigan State
Mackey, Dee, OE, 1963–65, E. Texas St.
Marques, Robert, C, 1960, Boston Univ.
Martin, Blanche, HB, 1960, Mich. St.
Mathis, William, HB, 1960–68,
Clemson
Matlock, John, C, 1967, Miami (Fla.)
Maynard, Donald, FL, 1960–68,
Texas Western
McAdams, Carl, LB, 1967–68, Oklahoma
McAdams, Robert, DE, 1963–64,
No. Carolina Col.
McCusker, Jim, T, 1964, Pittsburgh
McDaniel, Wahoo, LB, 1964–65,
Oklahoma

PLAYER–POS.–SEASONS–COLLEGE

McMullan, John, G, 1960–62,
Notre Dame
Michaels, Walter, LB, 1963,
Washington & Lee
Mischak, Robert, G, 1960–62, Army
Morelli, Francis, T, 1962, Colgate
Mumley, Nicholas, E, 1960–62, Purdue
Namath, Joe, QB, 1965–68, Alabama
Neidert, John, LB, 1968, Louisville
O'Mahoney, Jim, LB, 1965–66,
Miami (Fla.)
O'Neil, Robert, G, 1961, Notre Dame
Pagliei, Joseph, FB, 1960, Clemson
Parilli, Babe, QB, 1968, Kentucky
Pashe, Bill, DB, 1964, Geo. Washington
Paulson, Dainard, DB, 1961–66,
Oregon State
Perkins, William, FB, 1963, Iowa
Perreault, Peter, OT, 1963–67,
Boston Univ.
Philbin, Gerry, DE, 1964–68, Buffalo
Plunkett, Sherman, OT, 1963–67,
Maryland State
Powell, Arthur, OE, 1960–62,
San Jose State
Price, James, LB, 1963, Auburn
Rademacher, Bill, DB, 1964–68,
Northern Michigan
Randall, Dennis, DT, 1967,
Oklahoma State
Rasmussen, Randy, OG, 1967–68,
Kearney State
Rechichar, Albert, FB, 1961, Tennessee
Reifsnyder, Robert, DE, 1960–61, Navy
Renn, Robert, DB, 1961, Florida State
Richards, Perry, OE, 1962, Detroit
Richardson, Jeff, OG, 1967–68,
Michigan State
Riley, Leon, DB, 1961–62, Detroit
Robinson, Jerry, OE, 1965, Grambling
Robinson, William, HB, 1960, Lincoln
Rochester, Paul, DT, 1963–68,
Michigan St.
Ross, David, E, 1960, Los Angeles St.
Rowley, Bob, LB, 1964, Virginia
Ryan, Joseph, E, 1960, Villanova
Saidock, Thomas, T, 1960–61,
Michigan State
Sample, John, DB, 1966–68, Maryland
St.
Sapienza, Americo, HB, 1960, Villanova

244

ALL-TIME NEW YORK ROSTER 1960–68

PLAYER–POS.–SEASONS–COLLEGE

Sauer, George, OE, 1965–68, Texas
Schmidt, Henry, DT, 1966, So. Calif.
Schmitt, John, C, 1964–68, Hofstra
Schwedes, Gerhard, FB, 1960, Syracuse
Schweickert, Bob, OE, 1965, 1967, VPI
Scrabis, Robert, QB, 1960–62, Penn St.
Seiler, Paul, OT, 1967, Notre Dame
Shockley, William, HB, 1960, 1962,
   West Chester State
Simkus, Arnie, DT, 1965, Michigan
Smith, Allen, HB, 1966, Findlay
Smolinski, Mark, FB, 1963–68,
   Wyoming
Snell, Matt, FB, 1964–68, Ohio State
Songin, Edward, QB, 1962, Boston Col.
Starks, Marshall, DB, 1963–64, Illinois
Stephens, Harold, QB, 1962,
   Hardin–Simmons
Stricker, Anthony, DB, 1963, Colorado
Stromberg, Mike, LB, 1968, Temple
Strugar, George, DT, 1962–63,
   Washington
Talamini, Bob, G, 1968, Kentucky
Taliaferro, Mike, QB, 1964–67, Illinois
Tharp, Thomas, DB, 1960, Alabama
Thompson, Steve, DE, 1968, Washington
Tiller, James, HB, 1962, Purdue
Torczon, LaVerne, DE, 1962–65,
   Nebraska

PLAYER–POS.–SEASONS–COLLEGE

Turner, Jim, K–QB, 1964–68,
   Utah State
Turner, Robert Bake, OE, 1963–68,
   Texas Tech
Turner, Vince, DB, 1964, Missouri
Walsh, Edward, T, 1961, Penn Military
Walton, Sam, OT, 1968, E. Texas State
Washington, Clyde, DB, 1963–65,
   Purdue
Waskiewicz, Jim, LB, 1966–67,
   Wichita St.
Watters, Robert, DE, 1962–64, Lincoln
Wegert, Theodore, HB, 1960 (None)
Werl, Bob, DE, 1966, Miami (Fla.)
West, David, DB, 1963, Central State
West, Melvin, HB, 1961–62, Missouri
West, Willie, DB, 1964–65, Oregon
White, Lee, RB, 1968, Weber State
Whitley, Hall, DB, 1960, Texas A & I
Wilder, Bert, DT, 1964–67,
   N. Caro. St.
Wood, Bill, DB, 1963, W. Va. Wesleyan
Wood, Richard, QB, 1963–64, Auburn
Wren, Lowe, DB, 1961, Missouri
Yearby, Bill, DT, 1966, Michigan
Yohn, John David, LB, 1963, Gettysburg
Youngelman, Sidney, DE, 1960–61,
   Alabama

Career Statistical Leaders

SCORING

PLAYER	TD's	PAT	FG	PTS.
Jim Turner, 1964–68	0	177	102	483
Don Maynard, 1960–68	78	1	0	470
Bill Mathis, 1960–68	41	6	0	252
Art Powell, 1960–62	27	0	0	162
Bill Shockley, 1960, 1962	2	76	22	154
Matt Snell, 1964–68	25	0	0	150
Emerson Boozer, 1966–68	24	0	0	144

PASSING

PLAYER	ATT.	COMP.	INT.	YDS.	TD's
Joe Namath, 1965–68	1682	841	87	12753	78
Al Dorow, 1960–61	834	398	56	5399	45
Dick Wood, 1963–64	708	328	43	4503	34
John Green, 1962–63	264	130	19	1761	10
Mike Taliaferro, 1964–67	243	98	15	1145	8

RUSHING

PLAYER	ATT.	YDS.	TD's
Matt Snell, 1964–68	802	3309	19
Bill Mathis, 1960–68	948	3267	33
Emerson Boozer, 1966–68	359	1338	20
Mark Smolinski, 1963–68	305	960	9
Dick Christy, 1961–63	221	803	6

RECEIVING

PLAYER	CAUGHT	YDS.	TD's
Don Maynard, 1960–68	499	9351	78
George Sauer, 1965–68	233	3710	16
Art Powell, 1960–62	204	3178	27
Bake Turner, 1963–68	180	2779	19
Matt Snell, 1964–68	169	1166	6
Bill Mathis, 1960–68	131	1592	8
Pete Lammons, 1966–68	128	1480	9

INTERCEPTIONS

PLAYER	NO.	YDS.	TD's
Bill Baird, 1963–68	29	347	2
Dainard Paulson, 1961–66	29	343	1
Larry Grantham, 1960–68	20	257	0
John Sample, 1966–68	17	173	2
Jim Hudson, 1965–68	12	173	2
Al Atkinson, 1965–68	12	133	0

ALL–TIME RESULTS 1960–68

1960				1961	
W–7, L–7				**W–7, L–7**	
27	BUFFALO	3	21	*BOSTON	20
24	Boston	28	31	*Buffalo	41
28	DENVER	24	35	DENVER	28
37	*DALLAS	35	37	BOSTON	30
21	*Houston	27	10	San Diego	25
17	*BUFFALO	13	10	*Denver	27
28	Houston	42	14	*OAKLAND	6
27	Oakland	28	13	*San Diego	48
7	Los Angeles	21	23	OAKLAND	12
21	*Boston	38	13	*Houston	49
41	DALLAS	35	21	BUFFALO	14
30	*DENVER	27	28	DALLAS	7
31	*OAKLAND	28	21	Houston	48
43	*Los Angeles	50	24	*Dallas	35
382		399	301		390

1962
W–5, L–9

28	*OAKLAND	17
14	*San Diego	40
17	*BUFFALO	6
10	Denver	32
14	Boston	43
17	*Houston	56
17	*Dallas	20
23	SAN DIEGO	3
31	OAKLAND	21
31	Dallas	52
46	*DENVER	45
17	*Boston	24
3	Buffalo	20
10	Houston	44
278		423

1963
W–5, L–8, T–1

14	*Boston	38
24	HOUSTON	17
10	OAKLAND	7
31	BOSTON	24
20	*San Diego	24
26	*Oakland	49
35	Denver (T)	35
7	San Diego	53
27	*Houston	31
14	*DENVER	9
17	KANSAS CITY	0
14	*Buffalo	45
10	Buffalo	19
0	*Kansas City	48
249		399

1964
W–5, L–8, T–1

30	DENVER	6
10	*Boston	26
17	San Diego (T)	17
35	OAKLAND	13
24	HOUSTON	21
24	*Buffalo	34
35	BOSTON	14
7	Buffalo	20
16	*Denver	20
26	*Oakland	35
27	KANSAS CITY	14
3	*San Diego	38
17	*Houston	33
7	*Kansas City	24
278		315

1965
W–5, L–8, T–1

21	*Houston	27
10	Kansas City	14
21	*Buffalo	33
13	*Denver	16
24	Oakland (T)	24
9	San Diego	34
45	DENVER	10
13	*KANSAS CITY	10
30	*BOSTON	20
41	HOUSTON	14
23	Boston	27
7	*San Diego	38
14	*Oakland	24
14	BUFFALO	12
285		303

1966
W–6, L–6, T–2

19	*MIAMI	14
52	HOUSTON	13
16	*DENVER	7
24	*Boston (T)	24
17	SAN DIEGO	16
0	*Houston	24
21	Oakland	24
23	Buffalo	33
3	*Buffalo	14
30	MIAMI	13
24	Kansas City	32
28	*Oakland (T)	28
27	*San Diego	42
38	BOSTON	28
322		312

1967
W–8, L–5, T–1

17	*Buffalo	20
38	*DENVER	24
29	MIAMI	7
27	OAKLAND	14
28	Houston (T)	28
33	*MIAMI	14
30	BOSTON	23
18	*Kansas City	42
20	BUFFALO	10
29	*BOSTON	24
24	Denver	33
7	Kansas City	21
29	*Oakland	38
42	*SAN DIEGO	31
371		329

1968
W–13, L–3

20	*KANSAS CITY	19
47	*BOSTON	31
35	*Buffalo	37
23	SAN DIEGO	20
13	Denver	21
20	*HOUSTON	14
48	BOSTON	14
25	BUFFALO	21
26	HOUSTON	7
32	*Oakland	43
34	*SAN DIEGO	15
35	MIAMI	17
27	CINCINNATI	14
31	*MIAMI	7
419		280

Championship game

27	OAKLAND	23

Super Bowl

16	*BALTIMORE	7

*Away games

All-Time Records
TEAM

Game

MOST POINTS:

52 vs. Houston, Sept. 18, 1966
Opponent: 56, Houston, Oct. 14, 1962

LEAST POINTS:

0 vs. Kansas City, Dec. 22, 1963, and vs. Houston, Oct. 16, 1966
Opponent: 0, Kansas City, Dec. 1, 1963

MOST YARDS RUSHING:

284 vs. Houston, Nov. 21, 1965
Opponent: 287, San Diego, Oct. 13, 1963

LEAST YARDS RUSHING:

27 vs. Buffalo, Dec. 8, 1962
Opponent: 28, Boston, Nov. 14, 1965

MOST YARDS PASSING:

415 vs. Miami, Oct. 1, 1967
Opponent: 413, Denver, Sept. 25, 1960

LEAST YARDS PASSING:

79 vs. Kansas City, Dec. 22, 1963
Opponent: 6, Denver, Nov. 15, 1964

MOST PASSES ATTEMPTED:
62 vs. Denver, Dec. 3, 1967
Opponent: 54, Denver, Sept. 24, 1961

MOST PASSES COMPLETED:
29 vs. Oakland, Dec. 11, 1960
Opponent: 28, Denver, Sept. 24, 1961

LEAST PASSES COMPLETED:
3 vs. Oakland, Oct. 10, 1964
Opponent: 3, Cincinnati, Dec. 8, 1968

MOST YARDS TOTAL OFFENSE:
528 (287 passing, 241 rushing) vs. Boston, Dec. 17, 1966
Opponent: 573, Houston, Dec. 10, 1961

MOST YARDS PUNTS RETURNED:
142 vs. Denver, Sept. 24, 1961
Opponent: 134, San Diego, Nov. 5, 1961

MOST YARDS KICKOFFS RETURNED:
257 vs. Los Angeles, Dec. 18, 1960
Opponent: 164, Dallas, Nov. 11, 1962

MOST INTERCEPTIONS MADE:
5 vs. Denver, Oct. 31, 1965; Boston, Oct. 27, 1968
Opponent: 6, Denver, Nov. 15, 1964; Houston, Oct. 15, 1967

MOST YARDS INTERCEPTIONS RETURNED:
113 vs. Oakland, Sept. 28, 1963
Opponent: 188, Dallas, Dec. 17, 1961

MOST YARDS PENALIZED:
145 vs. Oakland, Nov. 17, 1968
Opponent: 148, San Diego, Oct. 13, 1963

INDIVIDUAL

MOST POINTS:
Game: 19, Jim Turner vs. Buffalo, Nov. 3, 1968 (6 FG's, 1 PAT)
Season: 145, Jim Turner, 1968 (34 FG's, 43 PAT's)
Career: 483, Jim Turner, 1964-68 (102 FG's, 177 PAT's)

MOST TOUCHDOWNS:
Game: 3, Joe vs. Boston, Oct. 27, 1968; Boozer vs. Denver,
Sept. 24, 1967; vs. Miami, Oct. 1, 1967; Maynard vs. Denver,
Oct. 26, 1963; Art Powell vs. Denver, Dec. 4, 1960
Season: 14, Maynard, 1965; Powell, 1960
Career: 63, Maynard, 1960-67

MOST FIELD GOALS:

Game: 6, Jim Turner vs. Buffalo, Nov. 3, 1968
Season: 34, Jim Turner, 1968
Career: 102, Jim Turner, 1964-68

MOST EXTRA POINTS:

Game: 7, J. Turner vs. Houston, Sept. 18, 1966
Season: 47, Shockley, 1960
Career: 177, J. Turner, 1964-68

MOST RUSHING ATTEMPTS:

Game: 31, Matt Snell vs. Houston, Oct. 17, 1964
Season: 215, Snell, 1964
Career: 948, Bill Mathis, 1960-68

MOST YARDS RUSHING:

Game: 180, Snell vs. Houston, Oct. 17, 1964
Season: 948, Snell, 1964
Career: 3059, Mathis (874 rushes), 1960-67

MOST TOUCHDOWNS RUSHING:

Game: 3, Joe vs. Boston, Oct. 27, 1968; Boozer vs. Denver,
Sept. 24, 1967; vs. Miami, Oct. 1, 1967
Season: 10, Boozer, 1967
Career: 28, Mathis, 1960-67

MOST PASSES ATTEMPTED:

Game: 60, Joe Namath vs. Denver, Dec. 3, 1967
Season: 491, Namath, 1967
Career: 1682, Namath, 1965-68

MOST PASSES COMPLETED:

Game: 29, Al Dorow vs. Oakland, Dec. 11, 1960
Season: 258, Namath, 1967
Career: 841, Namath, 1965-68

MOST YARDS PASSING:

Game: 415, Namath vs. Miami, Oct. 1, 1967
*Season: 4,007, Namath, 1967
Career: 12,753, Namath, 1965-68

MOST TOUCHDOWN PASSES COMPLETED:

Game: 5, Namath vs. Houston, Sept. 18, 1966; John Green vs.
Denver, Nov. 22, 1962
Season: 26, Namath, 1967; Dorow, 1960
Career: 78, Namath, 1965-68

MOST PASSES HAD INTERCEPTED:

Game: 6, Namath vs. Houston, Oct. 15, 1967
Season: 30, Dorow, 1961
Career: 87, Namath, 1965-68

MOST PASSES CAUGHT:

Game: 12, Maynard vs. Oakland, Dec. 17, 1967; Powell vs. Denver, Oct. 22, 1961
Season: 75, George Sauer, 1967
Career: 499, Maynard, 1960–68

MOST YARDS RECEIVING:

Game: 228, Maynard vs. Oakland, Nov. 17, 1968
Season: 1,434, Maynard, 1967
*Career: 9,351, Maynard, 1960–68

MOST TOUCHDOWN PASSES CAUGHT:

Game: 3, Maynard vs. Denver, Oct. 26, 1963; vs. Miami, Dec. 1, 1968; Powell vs. Denver, Dec. 4, 1963
Season: 14, Maynard, 1965; Powell, 1960
Career: 68, Maynard, 1960–67

MOST KICKOFF RETURNS:

Game: 7, Dick Christy vs. Boston, Oct. 6, 1962
Season: 38, D. Christy, 1962
Career: 77, D. Christy, 1961–63

MOST YARDS KICKOFFS RETURNED:

Game: 169, E. Christy vs. Buffalo, Sept. 29, 1968
Season: 891, Leon Burton, 1960
*Career: 1769, D. Christy, 1961–63

MOST PUNTS RETURNED:

Game: 4, D. Christy vs. Denver, Nov. 17, 1963
Season: 25, Bill Baird, 1967
Career: 84, Baird, 1963–68

MOST YARDS PUNTS RETURNED:

*Game: 137, D. Christy vs. Denver, Sept. 24, 1961
Season: 383, D. Christy, 1961
Career: 766, Baird, 1963–68

MOST INTERCEPTIONS MADE:

Game: 3, Dainard Paulson vs. Oakland, Sept. 28, 1963
*Season: 12, Paulson, 1964
Career: 29, Paulson, 1961–66; Baird, 1963–68

MOST YARDS INTERCEPTIONS RETURNED:

Game: 90, Paulson vs. Oakland, Sept. 28, 1960
Season: 157, Paulson, 1964
Career: 347, Baird, 1963–68

PUNTING AVERAGE:

Season: Curley Johnson, 45.3, 1965

LONGEST PLAYS:

Run: 79, Bill Mathis vs. Houston, Nov. 21, 1965
Pass: 87, Joe Namath to Don Maynard vs. San Diego, Nov. 24, 1968

LONGEST PLAYS (Continued):

Punt Return: 93, Bill Baird vs. Houston, Nov. 10, 1963
Kickoff Return: 101, Leon Burton vs. Oakland, Oct. 28, 1960
*Field Goal Return: 97, Marshall Starks vs. Houston, Sept. 22, 1963
Interception Return: 83, Wayne Fontes vs. Houston, Dec. 15, 1962
Field Goal: 51, Dick Guesman vs. Oakland, Oct. 20, 1963
Punt: 73, Curley Johnson vs. Denver, Oct. 3, 1965

*AFL Record

New York First-Team All-League Choices

1960	Bob Mischak, G
1961	Bob Mischak, G Bill Mathis, FB
1962	Larry Grantham, LB
1963	none
1964	Larry Grantham, LB Dainard Paulson, S
1965	Curley Johnson, punter
1966	Sherman Plunkett, T
1967	George Sauer, Jr., SE Joe Namath, QB
1968	George Sauer, Jr., SE Dave Herman, G Joe Namath, QB Gerry Philbin, DE

THE SUPER BOWL

DATE __January 12, 1969__ DAY OF WEEK __Sunday__ STARTING TIME __3:05 p.m. EST__

__New York Jets__ VS. __Baltimore Colts__ AT __Miami, Florida__

WEATHER __Partly cloudy__ TEMPERATURE __73__ WIND AND DIRECTION __12 N__

OFFICIALS REFEREE __Tom Bell__ UMPIRE __Walt Parker__ LINE JUDGE __Cal Lepore__

LINESMAN __George Murphy__ BACK JUDGE __Jack Reader__ FIELD JUDGE __Joe Gonzales__

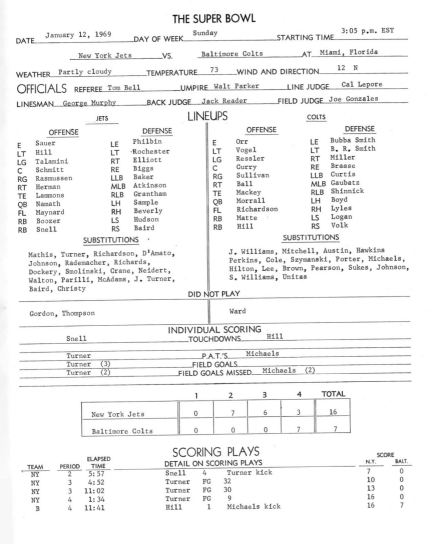

LINEUPS

JETS

	OFFENSE		DEFENSE
E	Sauer	LE	Philbin
LT	Hill	LT	Rochester
LG	Talamini	RT	Elliott
C	Schmitt	RE	Biggs
RG	Rasmussen	LLB	Baker
RT	Herman	MLB	Atkinson
TE	Lammons	RLB	Grantham
QB	Namath	LH	Sample
FL	Maynard	RH	Beverly
RB	Boozer	LS	Hudson
RB	Snell	RS	Baird

SUBSTITUTIONS

Mathis, Turner, Richardson, D'Amato,
Johnson, Rademacher, Richards,
Dockery, Smolinski, Crane, Neidert,
Walton, Parilli, McAdams, J. Turner,
Baird, Christy

COLTS

	OFFENSE		DEFENSE
E	Orr	LE	Bubba Smith
LT	Vogel	LT	B. R. Smith
LG	Ressler	RT	Miller
C	Curry	RE	Braase
RG	Sullivan	LLB	Curtis
RT	Ball	MLB	Gaubatz
TE	Mackey	RLB	Shinnick
QB	Morrall	LH	Boyd
FL	Richardson	RH	Lyles
RB	Matte	LS	Logan
RB	Hill	RS	Volk

SUBSTITUTIONS

J. Williams, Mitchell, Austin, Hawkins
Perkins, Cole, Szymanski, Porter, Michaels,
Hilton, Lee, Brown, Pearson, Sukes, Johnson,
S. Williams, Unitas

DID NOT PLAY

Gordon, Thompson | Ward

INDIVIDUAL SCORING

TOUCHDOWNS __Snell__ __Hill__

P.A.T.'S __Turner__ __Michaels__

FIELD GOALS __Turner (3)__

FIELD GOALS MISSED __Turner (2)__ __Michaels (2)__

	1	2	3	4	TOTAL
New York Jets	0	7	6	3	16
Baltimore Colts	0	0	0	7	7

SCORING PLAYS

TEAM	PERIOD	ELAPSED TIME	DETAIL ON SCORING PLAYS			SCORE N.Y.	BALT.
NY	2	5:57	Snell	4	Turner kick	7	0
NY	3	4:52	Turner	FG	32	10	0
NY	3	11:02	Turner	FG	30	13	0
NY	4	1:34	Turner	FG	9	16	0
B	4	11:41	Hill	1	Michaels kick	16	7

FINAL TEAM STATISTICS

	JETS	COLTS
TOTAL FIRST DOWNS	21	18
FIRST DOWNS RUSHING	10	7
FIRST DOWNS PASSING	10	9
FIRST DOWNS BY PENALTY	1	2
TOTAL OFFENSIVE YARDAGE	337	324
TOTAL NO. OFFENSIVE PLAYS (Inc. times thrown passing)	74	64
AVERAGE GAIN PER OFFENSIVE PLAY	4.5	5.1
NET RUSHING YARDAGE	142	143
TOTAL RUSHING PLAYS	43	23
AVERAGE GAIN PER RUSHING PLAY	3.3	6.2
NET PASSING YARDAGE	195	181
GROSS YARDS GAINED PASSING	206	181
TIMES THROWN AND YARDS LOST ATTEMPTING TO PASS	2—11	0—0
PASSES ATTEMPTED—COMPLETED—HAD INTERCEPTED .	29—17—0	41—17—4
AVERAGE GAIN PER PASS PLAY (Inc. times thrown passing)	6.4	4.4
PUNTS—NUMBER AND AVERAGE	4—38.8	3—44.3
HAD BLOCKED	0	0
FUMBLES—NUMBER AND LOST	1—1	1—1
PENALTIES—NUMBER AND YARDS	5—28	3—23
TOTAL RETURN YARDAGE	34	139
NO. AND YARDS PUNT RETURNS	1—0	4—34
NO. AND YARDS KICKOFF RETURNS	1—25	4—105
NO. AND YARDS INTERCEPTION RETURNS	4—9	0—0
NO. AND YARDS MISCELLANEOUS RETURNS (Fumbles and Field Goals)	0	0

FINAL INDIVIDUAL STATISTICS

JETS

RUSHING	ATT.	NET YARDS	AVG.	LONG GAIN	TD
Boozer	10	19	1.9	8	0
Snell	30	121	7.0	12	1
Mathis	3	2	0.7	1	0

PASSING	ATT.	COMP.	YARDS	TKD/YDS.	TD	LG.	Had Int.
Namath	28	17	206	2/11	0	39	0
Parilli	1	0	0	0/6	0	0	0

PASS RECEIVING	NO.	YARDS	LG.	TD
Snell	4	40	14	0
Lammons	2	13	11	0
Mathis	3	20	13	0
Sauer	8	133	39	0

INTERCEPTIONS	NO.	YARDS	LG.	TD
Beverly	2	0	0	0
Sample	1	0	0	0
Hudson	1	9	0	0

PUNTING	NO.	AVG.	LG.
C. Johnson	4	38.8	39

PUNT RETURNS	NO.	FC	YARDS	LG.	TD
Baird	1	1	0	0	0

KICKOFF RETURNS	NO.	YARDS	LG.	TD
Christy	1	25	25	0

COLTS

RUSHING	ATT.	NET YARDS	AVG.	LONG GAIN	TD
Morrall	2	-2	-1.0	0	0
Matte	11	116	10.5	58	0
Hill	9	29	3.2	12	1
Unitas	1	0	0.0	0	0

PASSING	ATT.	COMP.	YARDS	TKD/YDS.	TD	LG.	Had Int.
Morrall	17	6	71	0/6	0	30	3
Unitas	24	11	110	0/6	0	21	1

PASS RECEIVING	NO.	YARDS	LG.	TD
Mackey	3	35	19	0
Mitchell	1	15	15	0
Richardson	6	58	21	0
Matte	2	30	30	0
Hill	2	1	1	0
Orr	3	42	17	0

INTERCEPTIONS	NO.	YARDS	LG.	TD

PUNTING	NO.	AVG.	LG.
Lee	3	44.3	51

PUNT RETURNS	NO.	FC	YARDS	LG.	TD
Brown	4	0	34	21	0

KICKOFF RETURNS	NO.	YARDS	LG.	TD
Brown	2	46	25	0
Pearson	2	59	33	0

51